# Preface

Our book is intended to be used either as a supplementary text or as the principal text for beginning freshman English classes with students who need work in the basic grammatical structures of "standard" English. Particularly with the establishment of special and open admission policies in urban schools, many students matriculate unprepared to respond to the performance levels expected in most college courses involving writing. The students we are addressing, then, are those who traditionally are overlooked in freshman English texts and even in "remedial" texts, that is, those students whose spoken, or "community," dialects vary more widely from the written forms of standard English than do the dialects of other freshmen.

Our premise is that all dialects of English, American or otherwise, are equally valuable, equally effective modes of communication. We believe that the standard English dialect is linguistically no better nor worse than any other dialect of English, and that "standard" English is accepted as standard only for non-linguistic—historical, political, and sociological—reasons. Ideally, then, there should be no need to teach standard English at all, since speakers of various dialects of the same language can all communicate with one another if they want to. However, we do not live in an ideal society. Many students will find themselves at a disadvantage in a variety of situations, especially on the job market, if they do not have mastery of the standard dialect. While we believe in the students' right to their own language, we also believe in their right to choose to use the standard dialect. Our book is intended for students who have made this choice.

Our book aims at helping students to learn another dialect, much as we might help a student of modern languages to become bilingual. We have discovered in working with our own students that this can be done best by contrasting grammatical features of community dialects with grammatical features of the standard dialect. We believe our method not only produces competent writers of standard English, but also helps students to become sensitive to the creative possibilities inherent in the English language and to have a better understanding of "grammar" because they know the grammar of more than one dialect.

We wish to express our gratitude to our students, who encouraged us with their enthusiastic response to the book. We owe our thanks, as well, to the instructors who have tried our materials and have continued to use them, especially

Joan Brinich and Linda Michalowski. They, along with Donna Brook, offered suggestions and additional exercise materials.

Special thanks go to the scholars and instructors who read our book in manuscript and offered criticism, including Harold Allen, Max James, and Ernece Kelly. We are grateful for the support of the administrators at Wayne State University, in particular James Moore, who encouraged the use of our exercises in classes. Finally, we thank Florence Gefvert for her competent and patient typing of the manuscript.

Constance Gefvert
Richard Raspa
Amy Richards

# Contents

# INTRODUCTION

The title of our book, *Keys to American English*, echoes the title of the first book ever written about language in this country. In 1642, Roger Williams, a colonial missionary to the Narragansett Indians, wrote a book about their language called *A Key Into the Language of America*. He wrote the book to teach colonial Englishmen how to speak the Narragansett language, for he realized that America was a land that was to have a variety of cultures and languages. But he also wanted to teach the Indians the English language, so that there would be mutual cooperation between cultures.

While Roger Williams was dealing with two separate languages in his book (English and the Narragansett Indian language), our book deals with only one language—English—but with many varieties or dialects of English. Like Roger Williams, we realize that the language of America is extremely varied, but we also believe students need to have the chance to master the dialect (sometimes called standard English) that is used in schools and in business. Our purpose in writing this book, then, is to present a "key" or a basic introduction to the grammar of the standard dialect in relation to the grammar of other dialects of American English. Just as Roger Williams taught the Naragansett language by comparing it with English, we teach the standard American English dialect by comparing it with other dialects. But before we begin to do that, let's look at how the wide variety of American dialects came about and why one has come to be called standard.

The English language, like all languages, is made up of many different varieties of speech. There are as many different varieties of speech as there are people. Especially if you live in a city, you will have noticed that few of your friends speak exactly the same way you do. In fact, none of your friends or family speak exactly as you do. Language is like personality—it is unique to each individual. Each human being has a different manner of speaking just as each human being has a different personality.

There are many things that make your speech different from everyone else's: the way you pronounce words, the kinds of words you use, your tone of voice, even the way you form the past tense of a verb or make a noun plural. For instance, some people say the past tense of RUN is *ran*, but others say it is *run*. Some people say two *sheep* and others say two *sheeps*. Some people pronounce *tomato* so that the *mat* rhymes with *pot*, and others so that the *mat* rhymes with *fate*. All of these individual differences are what make language interesting.

While there are many differences between one person's speech and another's, there are also many similarities—if there weren't, we wouldn't be able to communicate. Any group of people who are joined together geographically or socially are likely to have many similarities in their speech. We call such a group a speech community and the combination of all the individual speech styles in that community we call a dialect. *Dialect* comes from the Greek roots *dia*, meaning "together" and *lect* meaning "speech." There are several ways in which individual speech styles can be grouped to form dialects.

## Geography

People share similarities in language when they live in the same geographical region. In America, for instance, Southerners share certain patterns of pronunciation. Northerners differ from Southerners in the way they pronounce certain words. For example, if a Southerner wants to say that his or her eggs are too *greasy* he or she pronounces the *s* like the *z* in *zoo*, while a Northerner pronounces the *s* like the *s* in *sun*.

Northern and Southern speech patterns can be broken down into finer geographical distinctions. For example, people from a place in Eastern New England like Boston often don't pronounce *r* when it occurs before a consonant or at the end of a word. *Park* is pronounced *pahk*, *car* is pronounced *cah*, and *far* is pronounced *fah*.

Vocabulary also varies from region to region. What a Northerner means by a *faucet*, a Southerner might call a *spigot* or a *spicket*. People from the Midland area of the United States (between North and South) have a different word for *cottage cheese* than those from either the North or South. In the North cottage cheese is sometimes called *dutch cheese* or *pot cheese*; in the Midland it can be called *smearcase*; and in the South it might be called *clabber cheese* or *curds*. Standardized marketing procedures, however, have produced a standard form—*cottage cheese*—that is used throughout the country along with the other forms that are now used, for the most part, in rural areas and among older people. *Soda* is a word that has different meanings in different parts of the country. If you ordered a soda in New York City, you would get a carbonated drink, but if you ordered a soda in Detroit, you would get a concoction made with ice cream.

There are grammatical differences, too, in different parts of the country. For example, a Northerner would be likely to say "I'm sick *to* my stomach," while a Southerner would more likely say "I'm sick *at* my stomach," and a person from the Midland might say "I'm sick *in* my stomach." Northerners often ask "Is it a long *way* to your house?" Midlanders, on the other hand, would ask "Is it a long *ways* to your house?" Either a Northerner or a Southerner would tell you he or she had two *pair* of shoes, but a Midlander would probably say he or she had two *pairs* of shoes.

All of these examples—in matters of pronunciation, vocabulary, and grammar—reflect regional dialects. They are, in other words, examples of geographical speech communities.

## Social Groups

Dialects also can be grouped along social lines. Pronunciation, vocabulary, and grammar can vary according to the social group you belong to, and that group is determined by many factors: age, economic level, education, ethnic background, and sometimes even sex. We often recognize people as members of our social group, or members of a different social group, by the language they use. For example, many people believe it sounds more educated to say the words *either* and *neither* like "*eye*ther" and "*neye*ther" instead of like "*ee*ther" and "*nee*ther." Therefore people who want to sound educated will be careful to choose the pronunciation they think has the greater social value.

Slang is an example of how vocabulary can have a social function. Slang terms are used in certain social groups, often in order to set that group apart and give it an identity of its own. Slang is often determined by age and sex. There are certain four-letter words, for example, that almost everyone knows, but that are more likely to be used by younger people than older ones, and by males more than females (though that distinction is rapidly disappearing). Other slang words are used more by teenagers and college students. For example "he plays some bad tunes on the piano" means to some people "he plays some good tunes."

There are grammatical differences, too, that set certain social groups apart from others. For example, people in one social group might say "I have went," while people in another group would get the same idea across by saying "I have gone." We are constantly changing from one social group to another. Many college students, for example, speak differently among their friends than they do at home or with their teachers. A student, in the social group made up of his or her friends, might say "I ain't got none of that." Later in the day in a different group—say history class—he or she would say "I don't have any of that."

The pronunciation, vocabulary, and grammar of each speech community allow communication within that group, and frequently across group lines. However, one dialect has become the standard used for formal speeches, radio and T.V., national relations, business letters, newspapers, college writing, and many other modes of communication where large numbers of people from different dialect groups come together. This standard dialect differs from other dialects mostly in grammar (that is, sentence structure and word endings). There is no single national standard for pronunciation and vocabulary, but there is for grammar, in both speech and writing. When we refer to the term "standard dialect" in this book therefore, we will be speaking about a grammatical standard. Why and how has this standard dialect developed?

To answer this question, we have to look at the origin of the various dialects of English. So far we have been talking about dialects as collections of individual speech styles grouped into speech communities. But we can look at them from the other point of view as well. A dialect is a subdivision of a language. For example, the English language can be broken down into many dialects and those dialects can be further broken down into individual speech styles. To find out why we have so many varieties of English in America, it is necessary to see where the American varieties of English came from.

## History of American English

Many people are surprised to discover that English was not the first (native) language in the British Isles, nor was it ever a single language. Until 1500 years ago, the only languages spoken in the British Isles were Celtic (the language of the ancestors of the Scots, Welsh, and Irish) and varieties of Latin, the language of Roman armies that had occupied the British Isles for so long. When the Roman armies were withdrawn from the British Isles, the native Celts were left vulnerable to attacks by various Germanic tribes wandering about on the European continent. About 450 A.D., several Germanic tribes invaded the British Isles, settled there, and took political control. The various dialects of their language became dominant over the earlier Celtic language. All these tribes spoke various Germanic dialects but none was exactly like the other. Each tribe settled in a different part of the British Isles, and therefore the people of each geographical area spoke a different dialect of the old Germanic language. After these tribes had been in the British Isles for several centuries, their dialects differed considerably from those of the Germanic tribes that had remained on the continent; they were no longer able to understand each other and therefore we say that they spoke different languages. When groups of people who originally spoke different dialects of the same language can no longer understand each other, their dialects have evolved into separate languages. Thus the various Germanic dialects that were spoken by tribes both on the continent and in the British Isles evolved into several languages, including what we today recognize as German, Dutch, Swedish, Norwegian, Danish, and English.

What we call the English language, then, was in the beginning a collection of Germanic dialects (called Old English, or Anglo-Saxon) spoken in different parts of the British Isles by different Germanic tribes, including the Jutes, the Saxons, and the Angles. (The word *English* comes from the name of one of those tribes—the Angles.) While one tribe was in political power, a literary culture developed there, and the dialect of that tribe had social prestige and was considered standard. The first center of culture and political strength was in the north of the British Isles. It shifted to the southwest and finally, by 1400, stabilized itself in the East Midland area, around London. The dialect of London eventually became standard, and after 1400, political and literary power remained centered there.

In the fifteenth and sixteenth centuries, when the American colonies were being settled by the British, they were settled by people from many geographical areas of Britain who spoke various dialects of English. That pattern of settlement partially explains why there are so many geographical variations in our language today. People who settled the New England area came largely from midland England, often from London, and so the dialect they spoke was different from that spoken by those who settled the (American) Midland and Southern colonies. But because the London dialect had had prestige in England, it came to be considered the prestige or standard dialect in the United States, and evolved into our present day standard dialect. Therefore, what we consider standard English today is really a historical accident. Most people today associate *ain't* with a certain social class or with lack of education. But if political power in England had not shifted from the southwest (where *ain't* was a common form) to the London area, *ain't* might have been considered standard today.

### Non-British Origins of American English

American English, however, is different today from the British dialects spoken by the first American settlers. There are two reasons for this: All languages constantly change, and when two groups of people who originally spoke the same dialect no longer have close contact with each other (like the British who stayed in London and those who emigrated to the North American colonies) the dialect of each group changes in different ways. So it is natural that after three hundred years the dialect spoken by present day Londoners would be different from the dialect spoken by their American counterparts. Second, there is an even more complex reason for the variety of American dialects and their differences from British English. The American people are not, of course, of purely British origin. The original British dialects spoken by the American colonists underwent radical changes as they were influenced by a large number of other languages spoken by native American Indians and by immigrants to the colonies (later to become the United States). The American language has been influenced in both vocabulary and pronunciation, and in some cases even in grammar, by the languages of all of these people: by American Indian languages like Cherokee, Seminole, and Naragansett (the language Roger Williams translated); by European languages like Dutch, French, German, and Spanish; and by various African-English creole languages spoken in the United States by African slaves and their descendants.

### The American Indian Heritage

Because the British (as well as the French, Spanish, and Portuguese) were more powerful than the American Indian tribes, the English language also became dominant over the languages of the Indians. But English has been greatly enriched by the vocabulary of some Indian languages. For example, many of our names for natural objects like trees and animals come from various Indian languages: *hickory, pecan, chipmunk, skunk, woodchuck, coyote*. There are innumerable other words that are of Indian origin: a political *caucus*; items of clothing like *moccasin* and *mackinaw*; and foods like *hominy, pone, succotash, tamale*. There are also hundreds of towns, cities, states, rivers, and lakes that have names of Indian origin.

### The European Heritage

Just as the languages spoken by the various tribes of American Indians were dominated by English, so were the various European languages spoken by immigrants to America. These languages, however, have left their mark on

English, especially in terms of vocabulary. American English has become richer because of the contributions of these languages.

From Spanish (especially Mexican Spanish) we have many words for animals and plants, like *mustang, alfalfa, marijuana*; words for buildings, like *plaza, patio, cafeteria*; words for food, like *chili, taco*; and many others.

From French we have some of our words dealing with money (*cent, dime*) and words for geographical description, like *bayou, rapids, prairie, levee, crevasse*. And there are many words dealing with food and the social act of eating, such as *à la mode, hors d'oeuvres, restaurant*.

Dutch too has given us words for food (*cookie, waffle, cruller, cole-slaw*) and many others, like *Santa Claus, sleigh, spook*.

German has given us more words for food than any other language. To mention just a few: *frankfurter, hamburger, noodle, pretzel, pumpernickel, sauerkraut*. We also owe many of our words dealing with social and educational activities to German, like *beer garden, pinochle, poker, seminar, semester, kindergarten*.

We could go on and on. This is just a small sampling of how much we owe to the people of many language backgrounds who settled in America. It is one of the things that makes American varieties of English different from British dialects (although some of these words have been borrowed by the British dialects). Our vast history of immigration and our contact with other nations has put American English in touch with an almost infinite variety of languages (many, like Chinese, outside the European borders).

### The African Heritage

What is often referred to today as Black English is of course a dialect of English, but most linguists agree that its origins are not purely British, but African as well. Its history goes back to the fifteenth century, before the slave trade opened on the west coast of Africa. Slave traders deliberately chose Africans from a variety of tribes to put together on one slave ship. In this way, their captors (the slave-traders) hoped to prevent mutiny on ship.

Human beings, however, are remarkably resourceful when it comes to language. In spite of the large number of different African languages spoken by the slaves, they inevitably found a way to communicate with each other and with their English captors. They did this by using a kind of emergency language or "pidgin" language that was a combination of English and African languages. It was probably first created by Africans trading with Europeans in the fifteenth century in order that English-speaking and African-speaking tradesmen could communicate with each other.

Many of the Africans who were forced into slavery learned this pidgin. In fact, some of the captured slaves communicated so well with each other that they managed to stage not just a mutiny but an escape, and jumped ship when the slave ships anchored temporarily at the islands off the eastern coast of the Carolinas and Georgia. The people who now inhabit these islands, and the coastal regions of South Carolina and Georgia, speak a language today that is very close to that pidgin spoken in the sixteenth century. It is referred to today as *Gullah* or *Gee-chee*. Gullah derives from a combination of English and West African languages. Hence, it is referred to as a creole language: a creole is a pidgin language that lasts longer than one generation, and becomes the native language of the descendants of the people who created the emergency or pidgin language.

Slaves who did not escape the ships and labored in the American colonies spoke at first the same pidgin as those who jumped ship. But their pidgin (which also became a creole since it was passed on to subsequent generations) was further influenced by English dialects spoken by the white families on the plantations where the slaves worked. As a result, the original creole became more and more like other dialects of English and less and less apparently like the African languages whose grammatical structure had formed the basis of the creoles. In the 350 years since the original slave immigration, this English-African creole has undergone a process of "decreolization," until today the dialect of English spoken by many blacks in the United States bears little apparent resemblance to Gullah, which it was originally so close to.

However, there are many aspects of English-African creole that do remain today in Black English. They are seldom recognized as such, however, because most people are unaware of the African origin of Black English, and they mistake African influences in Black English for what they think is the influence of southern white dialects of English. It is easy to show, however, that Black English is not merely a variety of southern English. For example, a common grammatical construction in Black English is "I be sick." It does not only mean, as people often assume, "I am sick;" rather it often may mean "I am always, or chronically, sick." Thus Black English can express easily some subtle differences in time that other English dialects have more difficulty doing; that particular expression goes back to the African-English creoles from which Black English has descended.

Not only have African languages influenced the grammar of our language, they have also, like European and American Indian languages, contributed a large number of words to the American language. Some of them are *tote, juke, jazz, zebra, ebony,* as well as many words for food: *banana, okra, cola, yam, gumbo, goober, turnip, parsnip,*

### Putting It All Together

As we have seen, the English language, especially American English, is a diverse language. It has many varieties, spoken by people in many different speech communities. And ultimately, the English language is as varied as the people who speak it. In fact, it is even more varied than the people who speak it, because as we have seen, each person changes his or her speech to fit the group he or she is in at the moment.

While each dialect is effective within the speech community the person belongs to, students whose dialects vary widely from the standard will be at a disadvantage in college courses and later in the business world. This book is an attempt to deal with the social realities of American life. We want to encourage you to master the written form of the standard dialect. (The spoken form, however, is outside the limitations of our book.) The important difference between this book and other books that teach the standard dialect is that we do not believe you should abandon the dialect you already speak. Instead, we suggest that you learn the standard dialect as a second dialect in addition to the one you already use. What are some of the reasons for this?

First, if all dialects of English are equally valid, then it is inappropriate to say "Stop speaking your dialect and learn this one instead." It would be as foolish to tell a French student "Stop speaking French and learn English instead." Obviously French and English are equally good languages—but they are used in different situations. Where people use French, the French language works well, and where people use English, the English language works well. If you travel a lot, you'd like to be able to switch back and forth from one language to another. Likewise, the standard dialect and other dialects are equally good systems of communication, but they have different functions. The standard dialect functions well in certain social and business contexts. Other dialects, spoken in various speech communities, function well in those communities. If you travel between the two communities you of course would like to be able to switch back and forth from one to another. That is precisely our goal in this book—to make it possible for you to use the standard dialect in appropriate situations, but to continue to use your everyday dialect in situations where it is called for.

We hasten to add, moreover, that it is much easier for a speaker of any dialect of English to learn the standard dialect than it is for a speaker of English to learn French. An Englishman and a Frenchman would have more difficulty talking to each other than would speakers of two different English dialects. The standard dialect of English and the other dialects of English have a lot in common; that's why speakers of different dialects of English can understand each other. In fact, there are many more similarities than differences in various English dialects, and so really the job of mastering the standard dialect is not as difficult as it sounds. This book does not try to cover every aspect of English grammar; that's not necessary, since all speakers of English know the basic grammar of English—otherwise they wouldn't be able to speak it. By "know" we don't mean necessarily being able to explain it, or to put labels like "subject" and "predicate" on parts of a sentence. We don't necessarily mean conscious knowledge, but rather unconscious knowledge. Let's use an example. No native speaker of English would say "I like ice cream strawberry." He or she would say "I like strawberry ice cream." Why is that? Because there is a rule of English grammar that says adjectives come before nouns. *Strawberry* in this case is an adjective and *ice cream* a noun—so *strawberry* goes before *ice cream*. The important point is that you put *strawberry* before *ice cream* unconsciously, or automatically. You don't need to know the labels "adjective" and "noun"—you know unconsciously, though, which is which. If you didn't, you could easily come up with sentences like "I like ice cream strawberry." (As a matter of fact, that's exactly what a Spanish student of English might do, since in Spanish, the rule is just the opposite—adjectives usually go after nouns instead of before them.)

The particular rule of English grammar that we've just been talking about is the same in all dialects of English. But there are other rules that are not the same in all dialects. The rules that are part of the grammar of your

8

own dialect you follow automatically without thinking about them. The only rules you have to learn are those that are not the same in your dialect and the standard dialect.

Let's look at another example. In some dialects of English (including Black English, Appalachian, and many others), the past tense of RUN is *run*. In the standard dialect, on the other hand, the past tense of RUN is *ran*. Hence in some community dialects (the term we will use for convenience, to indicate any dialect other than the standard) you would say "yesterday I *run* to school" but in the standard dialect you would say "yesterday I *ran* to school." Those are the features of the standard dialect, then, that we will concentrate on in this book—those features that differ from the community dialects. There is obviously no point in teaching you what you already know. Instead we have concentrated throughout the book on just those features that are different from the standard dialect, and have tried to give you lots of practice in using each of those features. But we have also tried to give you practice in recognizing the features of dialects other than the standard—so that you can become more at ease in switching back and forth from one dialect to another.

Here, then, is the general plan of the book. In each part we first present a single feature that differs in some community dialects from the standard dialect. Next we have a series of exercises that we call Recognition Drills; the purpose of these is to give you practice in recognizing which sentences are written in a community dialect and which in the standard dialect. Next we have exercises we call Pattern Practice that give you intensive drill in using the standard forms. Finally, we have Conversion Drills in which we ask you to convert, or translate, from the community dialects into the standard dialect.

One word of caution: while there are many different dialects of English in the United States, we don't try in this book to deal with each one individually—if we did that we would waste a lot of space and time because many features are similar in various dialects. But we are not implying that all community dialects are the same, for as we have seen they are not. Remember that a dialect is a collection of features (pronunciation, vocabulary, and grammar) shared by the members of a particular speech community. We are not concerned in this book with pronunciation, and very little with vocabulary—we are primarily concerned with grammar. Many community dialects share verb forms (like the past tense of RUN we looked at above). But there are also many differences among them. So we have organized the book not according to different dialects but according to grammatical features that vary from the standard dialect. It is likely that some of these features won't apply to you—because in some cases your dialect may be the same as the standard. If that's the case, you can breeze through that section and concentrate on the sections that do describe your dialect.

# PART I: VERBS

There are two kinds of verbs in English—main verbs and helping verbs. Main verbs are used in sentences either alone or together with helping verbs. Here are some examples of main verbs used alone (main verbs are in italics):

**EXAMPLES**

> I *walked* to school today.
> The book *is* on the table.
> My brother *has* five dollars.
> She *cries* a lot.

Here are some examples of main verbs used together with helping verbs (both helping verbs and main verbs are in italics):

**EXAMPLES**

> My sister *can sing* very well.
> He *is going* to work.
> The bus *had come* too early.
> He *might be coming* late to the party.

In this part we will first discuss main verbs used alone, and then main verbs used with helping verbs.

Verbs are either regular or irregular. Regular verbs are easy to recognize because they are always predictable. They use one method to show simple present time and one method to show simple past time. Irregular verbs are harder to recognize because they all have different ways of showing past time. We will first study regular verbs and, in later chapters, irregular verbs.

All verbs have a base form. The base form is the form the verb has before anything is added to it or anything is done to change it.

In the standard dialect, if you want to use a verb in present time (like "they *run* now"), you use a base form like RUN without changing it except when the verb follows *he, she, it,* or one singular noun. Then you add an *s.* Notice that you do not add an *s* to a verb that follows *I, you, we, they,* a plural noun, or a compound noun—that is, two nouns joined with *and.* (There is another verb form that is used to show present time. We will talk about it in Chapter 19.)

**EXAMPLES**              Standard Dialect

| **Singular** | **Plural** |
|---|---|
| I walk | we walk |
| you walk | you walk |
| he walk*s*, she walk*s*, | they walk, the boys walk, |
| it walk*s*, the boy walk*s* | my mother and father walk |

Occasionally you have to add *es* to the base form instead of just *s.* You do this whenever the base form of the verb ends in *ch, sh, s, z, x,* or *o.*

**EXAMPLES**              Standard Dialect

| **Singular** | **Plural** |
|---|---|
| I miss | we miss |
| you miss | you miss |
| he miss*es*, she miss*es*, | they miss, the ballplayers |
| the ballplayer miss*es* | miss |
| | |
| I fish | we fish |
| you fish | you fish |
| he fish*es*, she fish*es*, | they fish, all the |
| the boy fish*es* | fishermen fish |

When the base form ends in *y* following a consonant, you change the *y* to *i* and then add *es.* When the *y* follows a vowel, however, you simply add *s* to the base form.

EXAMPLES                    Standard Dialect

*Read*

**Singular**                              **Plural**

I cry                                     we cry
you cry                                   you cry
he cr*ies*, the baby cr*ies*              they cry, the children cry


I play                                    we play
you play                                  you play
he play*s*, the girl play*s*              they play, the children play


In some community dialects when you write about something happening in the present time, the *s* is not added to the base form when the subject is *he*, *she*, *it*, or one singular noun.

EXAMPLES                    Community Dialect

**Singular**                              **Plural**

I play                                    we play
you play                                  you play
he play, she play,                        they play, the children play
  it play, the girl play


In some community dialects, the *s* is added where it is not added in the standard dialect.

EXAMPLES                    Community Dialect

**Singular**                              **Plural**
I play*s*                                 we play*s*
you play*s*                               you play*s*
he, she, it play*s*                       they play*s*

Summary:   Regular Verbs in Present Time

| **Community Dialect** | **Standard Dialect** |
|---|---|
| I<br>you<br>we<br>they<br>the children<br>the boy and girl } plays | I<br>you<br>we<br>they<br>the children<br>the boy and girl } play |
| he<br>she<br>it<br>the child } play | he<br>she<br>it<br>the child } play*s* |

## Recognition Drill

Underline the regular verbs in present time in the following sentences. Then mark SD next to each sentence written in the standard dialect. The first three have been done for you

|          |                                  |
|----------|----------------------------------|
| _____   | 1. He <u>decide</u>.             |
| __SD__   | 2. I <u>had fallen</u> down.     |
| _____   | 3. The book <u>change</u> nothing. |
| _____   | 4. The dog play.                 |
| _____   | 5. The ball bounces.             |
| _____   | 6. David boast.                  |
| _____   | 7. Henrietta ask her father.     |
| _____   | 8. Bill ask his mother.          |
| _____   | 9. The fox barks.                |
| _____   | 10. The cat scratch.             |
| _____   | 11. The fire burn.               |
| _____   | 12. The boy resist.              |
| _____   | 13. The car travel.              |
| _____   | 14. Sally wish.                  |
| _____   | 15. My father deserve first prize. |
| _____   | 16. The preacher state a question. |
| _____   | 17. The tiger climb the fence.   |
| _____   | 18. He drop the dish.            |
| _____   | 19. The brake stop the train.    |
| _____   | 20. Aunt Rose visit me.          |
| _____   | 21. Leo avoid me.                |
| _____   | 22. Margaret act silly.          |

_____ 23. The veterans march down the street.

_____ 24. He ruins the game.

_____ 25. I misses you.

_____ 26. Tea stimulate me.

_____ 27. Sprinters breathe heavily.

_____ 28. The seeing eye dog guide Donna downtown.

_____ 29. She treat us mean.

_____ 30. You bakes good cakes.

_____ 31. We invade the kitchen whenever you bake cookies.

_____ 32. I love to go skating.

_____ 33. The airplane approach the airport at 5 P.M.

_____ 34. I prefer judo to karate.

_____ 35. Fred like boxing.

_____ 36. You asks too many questions.

_____ 37. Harvey believe in ghosts.

_____ 38. The kittens amuses the children.

_____ 39. Whenever Irma arrange a party, Isaac come.

_____ 40. Elm street and Maple avenue intersect near my house.

_____ 41. The smoke and flame disappear up the chimney.

_____ 42. They imagines noises.

_____ 43. We cough hard when we have colds.

_____ 44. You damage your lungs when you smoke.

_____ 45. The little boy and girl adjust to school well.

_____ 46. The months rolls around to summer again.

_____ 47. Drugs controls you.

OK. 48. Her mother and father sends her to school.

_____ 49. These books interests me.

_____ (50) Selma uses my bike too roughly.

_____ (51) I type well.

OK 52. We practice on our instruments every day.

_____ 53. You succeeds because you practice.

_____ 54. The dish drop.

OK 55. I measure my own pulse.

_____ 56. You and I unites against the enemy.

OK 57. My two little sisters search for my love letters.

_____ 58. I irons all my towels.

_____ 59. Little brother want bread.

_____ 60. We telephones her at lunch.

_____ 61. She rock the baby.

_____ 62. Nick raid the ice box every night.

_____ 63. The accident happen.

_____ 64. The vine cover the fence.

_____ 65. You pleases me.

OK 66. Teachers always pronounce my name wrong.

_____ 67. They always mispells mine.

_____ 68. We values our freedom.

OK 69. Ruby pleases me more and more as time goes on.

_____ (70.) I volunteer!

_____ 71. He wait for the train.

_____ 72. Uncle Sam want you for the Marines.

_____ (73.) We whistle together.

__OK__ 7̶4̶. The lawyer defends the client.

__OK__ 75. He earns money for college.

_____ 76. Barry maintain good grades.

__OK__ 77. My mother and father sacrifice for me.

_____ 78. He operate an IBM machine.

_____ (79.) Cigar smoke offends me.

_____ 80. John like football.

## Conversion Drill

Convert each sentence that you did not mark SD in the above exercise into the standard dialect in present time.

## Pattern Practice

Complete the following sentences by inserting the appropriate present form in the standard dialect of the verbs whose base is given in the margin. The first two have been done for you.

EXPECT | 1. Dorothy _expects_ a baby.

IMPRESS | 2. You _impress_ me with your fine talk.

WISH | 3. I _wish_ I had a Thunderbird.

FEEL | 4. I _feel_ cold today.

ATTEND | 5. Virginia _Attends_ the university.

CONTAIN | 6. This bottle _contains_ a fifth of London Dry Gin.

SUPPOSE | 7. I _suppose_ you think I am a flirt.

SCARE | 8. Lions _scare_ raccoons.

WORK | 9. My father _works_ at the Naval shipyard.

BORE | 10. English _Bores_ me.

TALK | 11. Amy _talks_ a lot.

s
ss
sh  } — es
ch
x

17

| | |
|---|---|
| LIKE | 12. All of us _like_ Baskin-Robbins ice cream. |
| SEEM | 13. Donald and Rachel _seem_ to be friendly people. |
| INTEREST | 14. What _interests_ you in your psychology class? |
| DISCUSS | 15. The ministers _discuss_ religion. |
| APPEAR | 16. Robins _appear_ in the spring. |
| WONDER | 17. I _wonder_ who's kissing her now. |
| MOVE | 18. Tom _moves_ fast. |
| INVOLVE | 19. The teacher _involves_ the students in discussions. |
| COMMUNICATE | 20. Inez and Tony _communicate_ well. |
| STOP | 21. I _stop_ when you call my name. |
| RELATE | 22. The doctor _relates_ well to his patients. |
| ENJOYS | 23. Anthony _enjoys_ Frankenstein movies. |
| WANT | 24. Wallace _wants_ to go back to Mexico. |
| COOK | 25. My father _cooks_ spaghetti every Thursday night. |
| AGREE | 26. How many people _agree_ with you? |
| URGE | 27. My counselor always _urges_ me to attend college. |
| DESIRE | 28. I strongly _desire_ hot tea. |
| LOVE | 29. Concetta _loves_ to listen to country-western tunes. |
| HATE | 30. I _hate_ to be late for work. |
| KILL | 31. He _kills_ for revenge. |
| ROB | 32. Robin Hood _robs_ the rich. |
| CRY | 33. Betty's baby _cries_ every morning at 3 A.M. |
| FRUSTRATE | 34. Carl _frustrates_ Linda Sue with his double talk. |
| FIX | 35. Mario _fixes_ Ann's broken fence. |

NEED          36. John and Sandra _____need_____ approval from their teacher.

WRESTLE       37. When Big Albert and Abdul _____wrestle_____, everyone goes to the arena.

WRECK         38. Abdul usually _____wrecks_____ Big Albert.

USE           39. I _____use_____ a stranglehold.

URGE          40. We _____urge_____ you to watch but not join in.

SEIZE         41. Abdul _____seizes_____ Big Albert by the hair and throws him.

SURPRISE      42. I _____surprise_____ my mother with a gift on her birthday.

SUSPECT       43. She never _____suspects_____ what the gift will be.

REFUSE        44. The young ladies always _____refuse_____ me.

PURSUE        45. I _____pursue_____ them with presents.

PERFORM       46. I _____perform_____ tasks for them.

OPPOSE        47. Their mothers _____oppose_____ me.

GUESS         48. I _____guess_____ that is why.

OCCUR         49. This accident _____occur_____ often.

INTEND        50. We _____intend_____ to tell him to buy some glue.

JUDGE         51. Josephine and Geraldine _____judge_____ all people by the way they dress.

INSURE        52. You _____insure_____ your health by eating a balanced diet.

INTEREST      53. That great big handsome man _____interests_____ me.

GRIEVE        54. We _____grieve_____ when one of our baby chicks dies.

ASK           55. My little girls _____ask_____ me embarrassing questions.

FULFILL       56. Lady Anna de Mère _____fulfills_____ her daily task of making nine beds.

SHOUT         57. Lord de Mère _____shouts_____ to the world that his wife is wonderful.

ANALYZE       58. My mother _____analizes_____ each new problem.

COUNT         59. We _____count_____ heads before bedtime.

*Do*

| | |
|---|---|
| ADJUST | 60. Cralia and Orion _Adjust_ their seat belts whenever they ride in the car. |
| ADVERTISE | 61. I _Advertise_ my mother's cooking. |
| PASS | 62. Miriam and Barbara Kay _pass_ every exam with an *A*. |
| SHOW | 63. You and she _show_ them how you do it. |
| AFFECT | 64. The weather _affects_ me strangely. |
| PRESENT | 65. She _presents_ her husband with a new baby each year. |
| ACCEPT | 66. Charmaine _accepts_ every present she gets. |
| DOZE | 67. We _Doze_ after dinner. |
| FAIL | 68. Sometimes the alarm clock _fails_ to ring. |
| YELL | 69. Mother _yells_ at him to wake up. |
| CRY | 70. You _Cry_ whenever you are hurt. |
| BOAST | 71. I _Boast_ about my children. |
| BLIND | 72. It _Blinds_ our eyes. |
| CONFUSE | 73. He _Confuses_ us with his knowledge of chemistry. |
| DEPART | 74. We _Depart_ for Florida on November 15. |
| STAY | 75. They _stay_ in Boston in the summer. |

## Conversion Exercise

*Do*

In the following sentences circle verbs ~~written in community dialects in~~ + rewrite them correctly in present ~~time.~~ tense

*EX*
1. The young lady hate her job as a waitress because she dislikes washing the dishes.
2. Her mother advise her to develop a new skill.
3. So she enroll in business school.
4. In school she learn how to type and to file.
5. She earn her diploma from this school.
6. She look for a job as a secretary and locate one at the college.
7. She type so well she earn a promotion.
8. College life seems interesting so she decide to register for a class in history.
9. The teacher encourage her to study hard.
10. Now she plan to be a history teacher.

Now rewrite these sentences in the standard dialect in present time. Use paragraph form.

_____

_____

_____

_____

_____

_____

_____

_____

_____

# REGULAR VERBS: PAST TIME

**2**

In the standard dialect, when you want to write about something that happened in the past, you add an *ed* to the base form of the regular verb.

EXAMPLES                    Standard Dialect

| **Singular** | **Plural** |
| --- | --- |
| I ask*ed* a question yesterday | we ask*ed* a question yesterday |
| you ask*ed* a question yesterday | you ask*ed* a question yesterday |
| he ask*ed*, she ask*ed*, the teacher ask*ed* a question yesterday | they ask*ed*, the students ask*ed* a question yesterday |

If the base form ends in *e*, then you add only a *d*.

Standard Dialect

| Singular | Plural |
|---|---|
| I bake*d* a cake last Sunday | we bake*d* a cake last Sunday |
| you bake*d* a cake last Sunday | you bake*d* a cake last Sunday |
| she bake*d*, my mother bak*ed* a cake last Sunday | they bake*d* a cake last Sunday |

With some base forms, you have to double the final consonant before adding the *ed*. Look at these examples:

| beg | be*gg*ed |
|---|---|
| permit | permi*tt*ed |

You double the final consonant when all three of the following occur:

1. when the word has only one syllable or when the last syllable is accented;
2. when the last syllable ends with a single consonant; and
3. when the vowel preceding that consonant is short. (Short vowels are those sounds in p*a*t, p*e*t, p*i*t, p*o*t, and p*u*t.)

EXAMPLES    Standard Dialect

| Present | Past |
|---|---|
| I beg him to go. | I be*gg*ed him to go. |
| He permi*t*s me to go. | He permi*tt*ed me to go. |

There is one other spelling change you sometimes have to make before adding the *ed*. If the base form ends in a consonant followed by *y*, you change the *y* to *i* before adding the *ed*.

EXAMPLES    Standard Dialect

| Present | Past |
|---|---|
| I tr*y* to be nice to him. | I tr*ied* to be nice to him. |
| We carr*y* the baby. | We carr*ied* the baby. |

In some community dialects, past time is shown by using the base form alone, and not by adding *ed*.

EXAMPLES    Community Dialect

| Singular | Plural |
|---|---|
| I bake a cake last Sunday | we bake a cake last Sunday |
| you bake a cake last Sunday | you bake a cake last Sunday |
| she bake a cake, my mother bake a cake last Sunday | they bake a cake, our mother bake a cake last Sunday |

## Summary: Past Time of Regular Verbs

| Community Dialect | Standard Dialect |
|---|---|
| I<br>you<br>he<br>she<br>it<br>my mother<br>we<br>you<br>they<br>our mothers } cook | I<br>you<br>he<br>she<br>it<br>my mother<br>we<br>you<br>they<br>our mothers } cook*ed* |

## Recognition Drill

The following are community and standard dialect sentences in past time. Underline the verbs. Then mark SD next to each sentence whose verb is in the standard dialect. The first three have been done for you.

_____  1. The farmer <u>reach</u> for the apple.

\_\_SD\_\_  2. The hogs <u>ruined</u> the garden.

_____  3. This morning the child <u>skin</u> his knee.

_____  4. Last night I climb the ladder.

_____  5. He always call me brother.

_____  6. We called him yesterday.

_____  7. I work hard all week.

_____  8. Last Saturday I fill the cookie jar.

_____  9. Last night George filled his stomach.

_____  10. Then he beg for more cookies.

_____  11. Yesterday the jury agree on the verdict.

_____  12. The other day my dad kill and skin a rabbit.

_____  13. He agreed with me then.

_____ 14. When I was little I like corn.

_____ 15. Last night I begged him to stop.

_____ 16. The boy always skip school.

_____ 17. The detective ask who rob the bank.

_____ 18. Until last week, I like him.

_____ 19. He supposed the thief escaped.

_____ 20. The old lady climbed the stairs.

_____ 21. She called him every day.

_____ 22. Last night the rain ruin the game.

_____ 23. Charles charm Charlene with his love poetry.

_____ 24. I believe you yesterday.

_____ 25. Last Saturday Mrs. Bell bleached her brown hair.

_____ 26. The lawyer question the value of John's testimony in court.

_____ 27. Everyone rave about Vincent's new Hush Puppies.

_____ 28. The police car worry the thief.

_____ 29. Joseph, the carpenter, hammer the nail into the wall.

_____ 30. The Red Cross appeal to all the people in the community for donations.

_____ 31. For three years Mattie correspond with her brother in Germany.

_____ 32. Bertha settle the fight between her mother and father.

_____ 33. Donald cried over the price of the lama coat.

_____ 34. Judy act crazy.

_____ 35. John volunteer for the Marine Corps.

_____ 36. Roberta compromise, and devote herself to the study of making money.

_____ 37. We surprise Linda for her birthday last Tuesday.

_____ 38. The preacher hover over us like an eagle.

_____ 39. I persevere to the end, maintain my course, and work for my bachelor of arts

degree from Columbia University.

_____ 40. I change my mind even though I try not to.

## Conversion Drill

Convert each sentence that you did not mark SD in the exercise above into the standard dialect in past time.

## Pattern Practice

Complete the following sentences by inserting the appropriate past form in the standard dialect of the verb whose base is given in the margin. The first two have been done for you.

EXPECT       1. I expected an *A* in my mathematics course.

IMPRESS      2. In the interview Tommy impressed the vice president.

WISH         3. Lily May _____ for a mink coat.

SKIN         4. I _____ my knee.

ATTEND       5. Forty people _____ the banquet.

CONTAIN      6. The little purple box _____ a $40,000 diamond ring.

SCARE        7. My German shepherd, Budweizer, _____ the poodle yesterday.

EXPLORE      8. The astronauts _____ the moon.

MIX          9. Last night Prentice _____ mustard and jelly in his sandwich.

CHANGE       10. I _____ the T.V. channel.

CELEBRATE    11. My grandparents _____ their fiftieth wedding anniversary.

WORK         12. I _____ at the Ford Motor Company for three years.

BORE         13. Harriet _____ everybody at the party.

TALK        14. We _____ to the mayor yesterday.

LIKE        15. I _____ everything about my old neighborhood.

SEEM        16. Martha _____ very nervous when I saw her last night.

INTEREST    17. Until last year folk dancing _____ me.

DISCUSS     18. We _____ our future job opportunities.

APPEAR      19. The ghost _____ in the attic.

WONDER      20. The children _____ which came first, the chicken or the egg.

SURPRISE    21. Chester _____ us all with his jokes.

WAIT        22. Pat _____ for Dick for three hours before she angrily left.

INTEND      23. They _____ to be good.

MOVE        24. Betty _____ to a new neighborhood.

SUGGEST     25. I _____ to Albert that we leave the party early.

INVOLVE     26. Josephine _____ Maria in the planning.

COMMUNICATE 27. The nurse _____ her sympathy to the patient.

STOP        28. The police _____ the robbery in progress.

RELATE      29. My aunt Pearl _____ the story of her childhood to me.

REGISTER    30. I _____ to vote.

REPRESENT   31. Councilman Fox _____ our voting district.

ENJOY       32. Our dog _____ barking at other dogs.

CHANGE      33. My brother _____ the baby's diapers.

WANT        34. I _____ to congratulate the winner of the fight.

WISH        35. Last weekend I _____ for sunshine.

COOK        36. We _____ eggs and bacon for breakfast.

AGREE       37. We all _____ that the best thing to do was to quit.

URGE    38. I _____ all the neighbors to join.

DESIRE    39. Juliet _____ Romeo.

HATE    40. I _____ to do it, but I had to.

## Conversion Exercise

The following are sentences written in past time. Circle verbs written in community dialects.

1. Last night Melvin and Gloria watch T.V.
2. They argue about what show to watch.
3. Melvin want to see the basketball game.
4. Gloria want to watch Mary Tyler Moore.
5. Since they were in Gloria's house, she insist on having her way.
6. Melvin beg Gloria and kiss her on the cheek.
7. "No!" she scream.
8. Gloria's mother enter the room, turn off the T.V. and announce the end of Melvin's visit.

Now rewrite these sentences in the standard dialect in present time. Use paragraph form.

_____

_____

_____

_____

_____

_____

_____

_____

_____

## Review Exercise

Examine the above picture. Write a paragraph telling what happened to this person to make him so sad.

# REGULAR VERBS: PRESENT AND PAST TIME

# 3

Remember that to form the present time of a regular verb in the standard dialect you leave the base form unchanged except when it follows *he, she, it,* or one singular noun. Then you add *s* or *es*. To form the past time of a regular verb you always add *d* or *ed,* no matter what the subject is.

Compare the past and present forms of the following verbs in the standard dialect.

EXAMPLES                    Standard Dialect

| **Present** | **Past** |
|---|---|
| I walk today | I walk*ed* yesterday |
| you walk today | you walk*ed* yesterday |
| she walk*s*, he walk*s*, it | he, she, it, the dog |
|    walk*s*, the dog walk*s* |    walk*ed* yesterday |
| we walk today | we walk*ed* yesterday |
| you walk today | you walk*ed* yesterday |
| they walk today | they walk*ed* yesterday |

## Review Exercise

In the following sentences supply the missing verb in the standard dialect in the time asked for.

WALK        (*Present*)   1. Every day I _____ to Johnnie's house.

START       (*Present*)   2. Johnnie _____ to complain about his wife.

WANT        (*Past*)      3. Yesterday he _____ to go to the fights.

INSIST      (*Past*)      4. But she _____ on his going shopping.

BORE        (*Present*)   5. He _____ me with his complaining.

PERSIST     (*Past*)      6. I _____ to the end.

HARDEN      (*Present*)   7. When I bake a cake the icing always _____ .

| | | |
|---|---|---|
| STIMULATE | (*Present*) | 8. Coffee_____ me. |
| RECEIVE | (*Past*) | 9. I_____ $305.49 for my birthday. |
| WARN | (*Past*) | 10. The principal_____ David to attend classes regularly. |
| MOVE | (*Past*) | 11. We_____ from St. Louis to Los Angeles. |
| TRAIN | (*Past*) | 12. The accountant_____ me in my new job. |
| INFLUENCE | (*Present*) | 13. Philosophy_____ all human behavior. |
| EXERCISE | (*Present*) | 14. She_____ for twenty minutes every day. |
| PERSUADE | (*Past*) | 15. Wes_____ Wanda to go to dinner with him. |
| CHARM | (*Present*) | 16. Milton_____ every woman he meets. |
| CAPTIVATE | (*Present*) | 17. Rosa_____ men with her vivacious personality. |
| FASCINATE | (*Present*) | 18. My piano playing_____ everyone who hears it. |
| ENTICE | (*Present*) | 19. French pastry always_____ me off my diet. |
| GREASE | (*Past*) | 20. Steve_____ the car yesterday. |
| BEWITCH | (*Present*) | 21. She_____ me with her smile. |
| FOLLOW | (*Present*) | 22. She_____ me wherever I go. |
| HUNT | (*Present*) | 23. Randy_____ deer in the autumn. |
| ENDEAVOR | (*Past*) | 24. Last year I_____ to be the best basketball player. |
| ABANDON | (*Past*) | 25. I_____ my 1957 Chevrolet in Muncie, Indiana. |
| WASH | (*Past*) | 26. Crazy Rosie_____ her clothes with Colgate Dental Cream. |
| DESIGN | (*Past*) | 27. Bill Blass_____ my red, white, and blue knit blazer. |
| PERFORM | (*Past*) | 28. Mrs. Pizza_____ Madame Butterfly at the opera. |
| DANCE | (*Past*) | 29. She_____ all night. |
| CHARGE | (*Past*) | 30. I_____ everything to my account. |

## Conversion Exercise

In the following sentences circle verbs written in past time in community dialects.

1. For years, I want to be a baseball player.
2. When I was young, I always collect baseball cards that I discover in bubble gum packages.
3. When I was about eleven, I join a Little League baseball team.
4. I work hard to become shortstop, and was successful.
5. We all play hard, and enter the state finals.
6. My parents, grandparents, and cousins travel a long way to watch me play in the finals.
7. Baseball interest them too.
8. We failed to win the finals.
9. The next day I decide to become a doctor.
10. I enter medical school last week.

Now rewrite these sentences in the standard dialect. Use paragraph form.

_____

_____

_____

_____

_____

_____

_____

_____

_____

# REGULAR AND IRREGULAR VERBS

# 4

In the standard dialect, regular verbs and irregular verbs are formed differently from each other in the past time. Instead of adding *ed* to the base, as you do for regular verbs, you either change the spelling of the base (DO/*did*, SEE/*saw*, COME/*came*, HAVE/*had*), or you leave the base alone (HIT/*hit*, BURST/*burst*).

Most irregular verbs are formed in the present time the same way as are regular verbs. Only two irregular verbs are formed differently in the present: BE and HAVE.

Compare the present and past forms of the following regular and irregular verbs in the standard dialect:

### Standard Dialect, Regular

| Base | Present | Past |
|------|---------|------|
| LOOK | I look | I look*ed* |
|      | he look*s* | he look*ed* |
| CRY | I cry | I cr*ied* |
|     | he cr*ies* | he cr*ied* |
| FIX | I fix | I fix*ed* |
|     | he fix*es* | he fix*ed* |

### Standard Dialect, Irregular

| Base | Present | Past |
|------|---------|------|
| DO | I do | I *did* |
|    | he do*es* | he *did* |
| SEE | I see | I *saw* |
|     | he see*s* | he *saw* |
| COME | I come | I *came* |
|      | he come*s* | he *came* |

Notice that the past time of regular verbs is formed by adding *ed* to the base, but the past time of irregular verbs is formed by changing the spelling of the base.

The next several chapters will give you practice in using irregular verbs. We will devote separate chapters to BE, HAVE, and DO because they are the most commonly used of the irregular verbs.

# IRREGULAR VERBS: BE IN PRESENT TIME

# 5

The verb BE is the most irregular of all verbs in the standard dialect. Both present and past time are formed differently than they are in regular verbs. Here are the standard dialect forms of BE in present time.

EXAMPLES                    Standard Dialect

| **Singular** | **Plural** |
|---|---|
| I *am* happy | we *are* happy |
| you *are* happy | you *are* happy |
| he *is* happy | they *are* happy |

Remember that with most verbs in the standard dialect, the present is always formed by using the base form alone except that you add *s* to the base form whenever the verb follows *he, she, it,* or one singular noun. With the verb BE, however, you almost never use the base form alone in the standard dialect.

In some community dialects, however, the base form BE is sometimes used for present time.

EXAMPLES                    Community Dialect

| **Singular** | **Plural** |
|---|---|
| I *be* happy | we *be* happy |
| you *be* happy | you *be* happy |
| he *be* happy | they *be* happy |

In some community dialects, the form *is* is used for present time.

EXAMPLES                    Community Dialect

| **Singular** | **Plural** |
|---|---|
| I *is* happy | we *is* happy |
| you *is* happy | you *is* happy |
| he *is* happy | they *is* happy |

In some community dialects, the verb BE is not used at all in present time.

EXAMPLES                    Community Dialect

**Singular**                                **Plural**
I happy                                      we happy
you happy                                    you happy
he happy                                     they happy

Summary:  *BE* in Present Time

| Community Dialect | Standard Dialect |
|---|---|
| I<br>you<br>we<br>he } be happy<br>she { is happy<br>it } happy<br>they<br>the child | I    *am* happy<br>you    *are* happy<br>he<br>she<br>it } *is* happy<br>the child<br>we<br>you } *are* happy<br>they |

## Recognition Drill

Underline the BE verbs in present time in the following sentences. (Some sentences in community dialects won't have a BE verb.) Then mark SD next to each sentence that is written in the standard dialect. The first three have been done for you.

_____  1. I <u>is</u> sad.

_____  2. He big.

\_\_SD\_\_  3. The dog <u>is</u> brown.

_____  4. The baseball players is here.

_____  5. We are brave men.

_____  6. Your face purple.

34

_____ 7. My dress is red.

_____ 8. They is big men.

_____ 9. I am sad.

_____ 10. He is bigger than his brother.

_____ 11. He be smaller.

_____ 12. Diane be beautiful.

_____ 13. Joe in college.

_____ 14. You is mean.

_____ 15. They are good cooks.

_____ 16. We is great pitchers.

_____ 17. I am angry.

_____ 18. You are kind.

_____ 19. My sister be at school.

_____ 20. He a doctor.

_____ 21. We be home.

_____ 22. They is at school.

_____ 23. Her baby fat.

_____ 24. My sister a social worker.

_____ 25. My brother is a lawyer.

_____ 26. He at the fights.

_____ 27. He is always the smallest one.

_____ 28. My father be at work.

_____ 29. My brother be sick.

_____ 30. The only reward of virtue is virtue.

## Conversion Drill

Convert each sentence that you did not mark SD in the above exercise into the standard dialect in present time.

## Pattern Practice

Complete the following sentences with the appropriate standard dialect form of BE in present time. The first two have been done for you.

1. I <u>am</u> a student at the community college.

2. My English teacher <u>is</u> hard on the class.

3. The students in the class_____ afraid of her.

4. We_____ afraid she will give us low grades.

5. You_____ lucky that she_____ not your teacher.

6. It_____ better.

7. I_____ sad today.

8. The judge_____ corrupt.

9. The council members_____ at a meeting this morning.

10. The American Dream_____ to get an education.

11. The curtains_____ beautiful.

12. Rubin_____ blond.

13. The dog_____ in the closet.

14. Jerry_____ in the kitchen.

15. Rosalind_____ in love with Romeo.

16. Danish pastry_____ good.

17. James_____ a fantastic football player.

18. Joshua_____ a fast talker.

19. Connie_____ a model student.

20. The class that I _____ in _____ interesting.

21. Gladys _____ the best student in the whole class.

22. The only thing that I disagree with _____ your conclusion.

23. Wilt the Stilt Chamberlain _____ the greatest basketball player in the history of that

   sport.

24. Robin Hood _____ my favorite hero.

25. Green _____ the color of money.


## Conversion Exercise

In the following sentences circle BE verbs written in community dialects
in present time, and circle spaces where the community dialects have no verb
but the standard dialect would have one.

1. There a crisis in American cities today.
2. Racial tension, drugs, pollution, and crime be the cause of this crisis.
3. For example, my two best friends, Betty Jane and Morris, be in the central city in a very
   tough area.
4. They stuck in an old apartment house and they is afraid to go out.
5. Betty Jane and Morris is very old people. They is seventy-seven years old and they afraid to
   go out and cash their Social Security checks.
6. It is sad. America be the land of opportunity. America be God's country, but some people
   be prisoners in their own houses.

Now rewrite these sentences in the standard dialect in present time. Use paragraph form.

_____

_____

_____

_____

_____

_____

_____

_____

_____

# IRREGULAR VERBS: *BE* IN PAST TIME

# 6

In the standard dialect, when you want to use BE in past time, use either of these two forms:

Use the form *were*
    with singular pronoun:     *you*
    with plural pronouns:     *we, you, they*
    with all plural nouns:     *the children, the men,* etc.
Use the form *was*
    with singular pronouns:     *I, he, she, it*
    with all singular nouns:     *the child, the man,* etc.

EXAMPLES                 Standard Dialect

| **Singular** | **Plural** |
| --- | --- |
| I *was* happy | we *were* happy |
| you *were* happy | you *were* happy |
| he, she, it *was* happy | they *were* happy |

In some community dialects, the form *were* is used instead of *was*, and the form *was* is used instead of *were*.

EXAMPLES                 Community Dialect

| **Singular** | **Plural** |
| --- | --- |
| I *were* happy | we *was* happy |
| you *was* happy | you *was* happy |
| he, she, it *were* happy | they *was* happy |

Summary:  *BE* in Past Time

| **Community Dialect** | **Standard Dialect** |
| --- | --- |
| I<br>he<br>she   } *were*<br>it<br>the book | I<br>he<br>she   } *was*<br>it<br>the book |
| we<br>you<br>they   } *was*<br>the books | we<br>you<br>they   } *were*<br>the books |

## Recognition Drill

Underline the BE verbs in past time in the following sentences. Then mark SD next to each sentence that is written in the standard dialect. The first three have been done for you.

_____ 1. <u>Was</u> you happy yesterday?

_____ 2. I <u>were</u> the only one in psychology class today.

__SD__ 3. I think she <u>was</u> a witch.

_____ 4. Her cats was all black.

_____ 5. He was bold.

_____ 6. We was bad.

_____ 7. They was an evil bunch.

_____ 8. Roses were in bloom last week.

_____ 9. The lions was in the zoo.

_____ 10. Baggy pants was "in" last year.

_____ 11. The deadline for applications was yesterday.

_____ 12. At ten o'clock it were too late.

_____ 13. Was your friends there?

_____ 14. Hate was the subject of the T.V. program.

_____ 15. Was you in school today?

_____ 16. The plot was easy to follow.

_____ 17. They was together.

_____ 18. It were an easy thing to say but it were a hard thing to do.

_____ 19. Pumpkins was in season in October.

_____ 20. Were Phil's friends at the party last night?

_____ 21. Was Constance and Georgia at the movies?

_____ 22. Was you at the employment agency on Friday?

_____ 23. Were you hoping to win first prize in the writing contest?

_____ 24. We was there.

_____ 25. That was here.

_____ 26. Was you there when Travis fell off the horse?

_____ 27. She was a showoff.

_____ 28. The preacher's friends were not my friends.

_____ 29. We was together for only ten minutes.

_____ 30. You was late for school.

_____ 31. Cecile was happy with her birthday gift.

_____ 32. We was pleased with our new house.

_____ 33. Elizabeth was the only woman at the conference.

_____ 34. Marsha were an animal doctor.

_____ 35. Was he a liberal?

_____ 36. Lily was a lady.

_____ 37. Dave was a religious person.

_____ 38. All of us was tall.

_____ 39. The coffee was stale.

_____ 40. The ribs was cold.

_____ 41. The movie was dull.

_____ 42. She were too fat.

_____ 43. I was on a diet.

_____ 44. Was you mad at the mayor for his speech?

_____ 45. Was all the men in your family bald?

_____ 46. Were you an only child?

_____ 47. Was your dog lost?

_____ 48. Tom were the last one to leave the dormitory.

_____ 49. Kathy were a nice girl.

_____ 50. You was Elaine's best friend.

## Conversion Drill

Convert each sentence that you did not mark SD in the above exercise into the standard dialect in past time.

## Pattern Practice

Complete the following sentences with the appropriate standard dialect form of BE in the past. The first two have been done for you.

1. <u>Were</u> you a good student?

2. I <u>was</u> not present at the time.

3. He _____ the only person at the show.

4. The best team _____ the Pistons.

5. _____ you in love with him?

6. She _____ the first lady mayor.

7. I _____ not the only person responsible.

8. The meat prices _____ too high.

9. The house _____ on fire.

10. I _____ afraid.

11. _____ they always your enemies?

12. They _____ together.

13. The vegetables _____ all a part of the life cycle.

14. _____ they in the same class?

15. They _____ at the supermarket yesterday.

16. The books _____ on sale yesterday.

17. Her boots _____ new.

18. Once upon a time Diahann _____ blond.

19. My dad _____ laid off.

20. The truck _____ his.

21. I _____ the only person who knew the answer.

22. Easter _____ a time of great joy for us.

23. The paper boy _____ late in delivering the paper yesterday.

24. We _____ encouraged to go to law school.

25. James _____ the most romantic person I ever knew.

26. Harvey and Peter _____ concerned about doing the right things when they _____ told.

27. Julie _____ a great teacher.

28. The turkey _____ good, but the sweet potatoes _____ too sweet.

29. The roses _____ in bloom last week.

30. My car _____ working all right until yesterday.

## Conversion Exercise

In the following sentences circle BE verbs written in community dialects in past time.

1. Once upon a time there was three witches.
2. They was bald and ugly.
3. Their names was Debby, Dewy, and Dawn.
4. Their magic words was "double, double, toil and trouble."
5. Macbeth were afraid of the witches.
6. They was prophets of the future.
7. He were nervous about his actions.
8. Macbeth were a murderer and he were afraid the witches knew.
9. Seeing the three witches saying their lines were frightening.
10. But it were more frightening when Macbeth saw the ghost of the man he murdered.

Now rewrite these sentences in the standard dialect in past time. Use paragraph form.

_____

_____

_____

_____

_____

_____

_____

_____

_____

# IRREGULAR VERBS:
# *HAVE* IN PRESENT TIME

# 7

In the standard dialect, when you want to use HAVE in the present time, use one of the following forms:

Use the form *have*

| with singular pronouns: | I, you |
| with all plural pronouns: | we, you, they |
| with all plural nouns: | the children, the men, etc. |

Use the form *has*

| with singular pronouns: | he, she, it |
| with all singular nouns: | the child, the man |

EXAMPLES                Standard Dialect

| **Singular** | **Plural** |
| I *have* a mustache | we *have* mustaches |
| you *have* a mustache | you *have* mustaches |
| he, she, it *has* a mustache | they *have* mustaches |

In some community dialects, when you use HAVE in the present time, the form *have* is used where the standard dialect uses *has*, and the form *has* is used where the standard dialect uses *have*.

EXAMPLES                Community Dialect

| **Singular** | **Plural** |
| I *has* a mustache | we *has* mustaches |
| you *has* a mustache | you *has* mustaches |
| he, she, it *have* a mustache | they *has* mustaches |

43

## Summary: *HAVE* in Present Time

| Community Dialect | Standard Dialect |
|---|---|
| I<br>you<br>we } has<br>they<br>the children | I<br>you<br>we } *have*<br>they<br>the children |
| he<br>she } have<br>it<br>the child | he<br>she } *has*<br>it<br>the child |

## Recognition Drill

Underline the HAVE verbs in present time in the following sentences. Then mark SD next to each sentence that is written in the standard dialect. The first three have been done for you.

__SD__  1. I <u>have</u> a dog.

_____  2. They <u>has</u> a hog.

_____  3. You <u>has</u> a hat.

_____  4. We have a cat.

_____  5. I have a date with Patricia.

_____  6. Dorothy have a date with me.

_____  7. Old Mother Hubbard have dog biscuits in the cupboard.

_____  8. We have a car.

_____  9. You has a bar.

_____ 10. He has a jar.

_____ 11. We have supper at six o'clock.

_____ 12. They have a new house.

_____ 13. You have a house.

_____ 14. He has a mouse.

_____ 15. You have a blouse.

_____ 16. Your weekly visit has a happy effect on us.

_____ 17. Curtis and I has lots of homework to do.

_____ 18. Lonnie has three girl friends.

_____ 19. We has a big job on our hands.

_____ 20. The word have seventeen different definitions.

_____ 21. We have special white uniforms to wear on the job.

_____ 22. He has too much money.

_____ 23. Lionel have blood all over him.

_____ 24. The A&P have a special sale on vegetables today.

_____ 25. Maynard have a new imported coat from Italy.

_____ 26. My mother has a new white fur jacket.

_____ 27. I have exciting plans for Easter.

_____ 28. The Easter Bunny also have exciting plans.

_____ 29. Our family always have a turkey with yams and sweet potatoes for Thanksgiving.

_____ 30. Mark Spitz have seven gold medals.

_____ 31. Phyllis and Cantrell has three baseball tickets.

_____ 32. Letetia have her own personalized greeting cards.

_____ 33. They has a new color television.

_____ 34. Sister Angela have a very devout religious congregation.

_____ 35. Father Kowalski has a large parish.

_____ 36. Maria and Benny have a Mardi Gras party.

_____ 37. We has another name for Mardi Gras: Fat Tuesday.

_____ 38. We have many religious celebrations during the holidays.

_____ 39. People have many needs.

_____ 40. We have the time and expertise for politics.

_____ 41. My sister have three children in her family.

_____ 42. I has a dream.

_____ 43. You have an opportunity.

_____ 44. They have fun.

_____ 45. They have new ice skates.

_____ 46. I have more friends than she have.

_____ 47. You has fewer friends than I has.

_____ 48. I have many plans for my education.

_____ 49. David have no plans for an education.

_____ 50. Delores have five sisters and three brothers.

## Conversion Drill

Convert each sentence that you did not mark SD in the above exercise into the standard dialect in present time.

## Pattern Practice

Complete the following sentences with the appropriate standard dialect form of HAVE in present time. The first two have been done for you.

1. He <u>has</u> a new suit.

2. The book <u>has</u> a high moral tone.

3. He _____ more than one sister.

4. Lonnie _____ thirteen dogs.

5. I _____ many things to do before tomorrow.

6. Leo Durocher _____ great pride in his baseball team.

7. He _____ a lot of team spirit.

8. My parents _____ a new house.

9. Ernestine _____ a picture of Johnny Mathis in her bedroom.

10. I _____ three cousins in Detroit.

11. We _____ two tickets to the all star game.

12. They _____ jobs.

13. My brothers _____ life insurance.

14. My folks _____ a bank account.

15. My friends _____ a lot of beer at parties.

16. Lolita _____ an old boyfriend.

17. Connie _____ the most fashionable clothes.

18. The Latin students _____ a party every Friday.

19. We _____ a church service at 10 A.M. on Sundays.

20. We _____ a friendly hour after the service.

21. My friends _____ ribs, enchiladas, and kielbasa at Saturday night parties all during July and August.

22. Harriet, Juanita, and Lisa _____ a pajama party every week.

23. I _____ a two-week vacation.

24. My grandfather _____ a farm in Arkansas.

25. Our garden _____ peas in it.

26. Our house _____ twelve rooms and a five-car garage.

27. My dream house _____ a yellow shag rug on the floor of all forty-three rooms, including three dining rooms, an elevator, and a bowling alley adjacent to an indoor pool.

28. You _____ more courses to take before you graduate.

29. The car _____ red seats.

30. Mary _____ the most beautiful pink ribbons in her hair.

31. Betty _____ a pool table in her basement.

32. My dog _____ worms.

33. My brother _____ the measles.

34. Carmella _____ more than seventy-two pairs of patent leather shoes.

35. Edward _____ a fine mind.

36. Marilyn and Caville _____ lunch together every Tuesday.

37. Bernice _____ a mind of her own.

38. The New York Sharks _____ a game with the Raiders this Friday night.

39. The Harlem Globetrotters _____ a great style.

40. We _____ a party to go to tonight.

41. Debbie _____ many silly friends.

42. Kathy and Kay _____ a great deal of work to do for the PTA.

43. Our refrigerator _____ problems.

44. My cousin _____ a little cottage on Lake Michigan.

45. San Francisco _____ many attractions for me.

46. She _____ a secret to tell you.

47. Bill always _____ his own way.

48. Connie sometimes _____ a temper that is uncontrollable.

49. Crazy Tony _____ plenty of money to give away.

50. I _____ a new joke to tell you.

## Conversion Exercise

In the following sentences circle HAVE verbs that are written in community dialects in present time.

Dear Ann Landers:

1. I hope you has an answer to my problem.
2. I has a job and I also go to school.
3. My mother have a job too.
4. My brother Otis have some of the housework to do, but I has most of it.

5. I has a strange schedule. First I has my job from midnight to 8 A.M. Next I go home and eat breakfast, and then I has the responsibility of getting my brothers and sisters ready for school.
6. I has a choice between getting myself or them to school on time.
7. They has their first class at 9:15 A.M.
8. I has my economics class at 9:10 A.M.
9. Every day at 9:15 I has the same excuse for my tardiness, and my teacher have a hard time believing my excuse.
10. I hope you has a suggestion on how to deal with my problem.

Now rewrite these sentences in present time in the standard dialect. Use paragraph form.

_____

_____

_____

_____

_____

_____

_____

_____

_____

# IRREGULAR VERBS: *HAVE* IN PAST TIME

# 8

In the standard dialect and in most community dialects, the past time of the verb HAVE is in all cases *had*.

EXAMPLES                    Standard Dialect

| Singular | Plural |
|---|---|
| I *had* | we *had* |
| you *had* | you *had* |
| he, she, it *had* | they *had* |

In some community dialects, the form *have* or *has* is used where the standard dialect uses *had* to express past time.

EXAMPLES                          Community Dialect

| **Singular** | **Plural** |
|---|---|
| last year I *have* (*has*) a Siamese cat | last year we *have* (*has*) a Siamese cat |
| last year you *have* (*has*) a Siamese cat | last year you *have* (*has*) a Siamese cat |
| last year he, she, it *have* (*has*) a Siamese cat | last year they *have* (*has*) a Siamese cat |

Summary:  *HAVE* in Past Time

| **Community Dialect** | **Standard Dialect** |
|---|---|
| I<br>you<br>we<br>they<br>he<br>she<br>it<br>the child<br>the children &rbrace; { *have* *has* | I<br>you<br>we<br>they<br>he<br>she<br>it<br>the child<br>the children &rbrace; *had* |

## Recognition Drill

Underline the HAVE verbs in past time in the following sentences. Then mark SD next to each sentence that is written in the standard dialect. The first three have been done for you.

_____ 1. Last week I <u>have</u> a car accident.

__SD__ 2. Last Sunday I <u>had</u> the folks to dinner.

_____ 3. Two years ago Philomena <u>have</u> a dog named Spot.

_____ 4. Three years ago Tom and Mabel had a baby boy.

_____ 5. Yesterday they have a baby girl.

_____ 6. Five hours ago he have an automobile accident.

_____ 7. Last year Melvin had a part-time job as a janitor while he had a full schedule of classes at the University of Michigan.

_____ 8. Last night I have a dream about being a baseball star for the Los Angeles Dodgers.

_____ 9. Roosevelt Grier had a successful career as a linebacker for the New York Giants.

_____ 10. Old MacDonald have a farm.

_____ 11. Noah had an ark.

_____ 12. He also have many animals.

_____ 13. Gregory have many plants.

_____ 14. Yesterday I have a cough.

_____ 15. As of Tuesday, Martha had $10,965 in the bank.

_____ 16. I had great admiration for Helen's honesty.

_____ 17. Cruelty have a human heart, and jealousy have a human face.

_____ 18. I has a bad memory for names.

_____ 19. After dinner, we have a conversation about wine and walnuts.

_____ 20. John have more faith in Julie than Julie have in John.

_____ 21. Patricia and Paul has an announcement to make.

_____ 22. Yesterday I have three suggestions to make.

_____ 23. Three years ago I have enough money in the bank to buy a Volvo.

_____ 24. Last night she have another chance to make up with James.

_____ 25. Claude have Thinas under control.

_____ 26. William Shakespeare have a vivid imagination.

_____ 27. The president have a family of four and a dog.

_____ 28. Selma have nothing more to give.

_____ 29. It had to be you, wonderful you.

_____ 30. As a matter of fact, I have something to tell you yesterday.

## Conversion Drill

Convert each sentence that you did not mark SD in the above exercises into the standard dialect in present time.

## Pattern Practice

Complete the following sentences with the appropriate standard dialect form of HAVE in past time. The first two have been done for you.

1. I <u>had</u> a dog named Bartholomew.

2. You <u>had</u> a garden full of roses last spring.

3. Last winter we _____ a lot of snow.

4. Yesterday my little brother _____ a new balloon.

5. Two weeks ago the whole family _____ the chicken pox.

6. A while ago the priest _____ services on Monday as well as on Sunday.

7. Before he moved to California, Uncle Benny _____ the largest model train set in the state of Maine.

8. For years, John _____ onions with his hot dogs.

9. After I drank the wine, I _____ a headache.

10. Before dessert, I _____ a fine steak.

11. Before he _____ his hair cut, Carlos looked like his sister.

12. Two years ago, my mother _____ twins.

13. For many years I _____ a good friend named Joe.

14. Madeline, our cat, _____ a litter of six kittens.

15. Ed _____ on his blue blazer and beautiful white pants the other day.

16. Last Sunday we _____ a meeting to discuss ways to raise funds for the party.

17. Four years ago, I _____ four cats and three dogs. Two years ago, I _____ only one cat and one dog.

18. Poor Richard _____ only one friend in all the world—his dog Cyril.

19. Amy _____ no desire to keep up a friendship with either Cyril or Richard.

20. Norma _____ one of the brightest minds at the university.

21. Our street _____ many decaying elm trees on it last year.

22. The astronauts _____ excellent health.

23. The girls at the office _____ a beautiful box of perfume for Tina.

24. Rachel _____ a great talent for playing the bugle.

25. Our poodle _____ a litter of three pups.

26. Arthur _____ a pleasant personality.

27. Leonard _____ a psychological problem.

28. The circus _____ many great attractions.

29. We _____ a great New Year's Eve party for all the orphans.

30. Until recently, I _____ the largest stamp collection in the state of Alaska.

31. We _____ meatloaf for supper last night.

## Conversion Exercise

In the following sentences circle HAVE verbs written in community dialects in past time.

1. Guess what kind of a party I have last week for my five-year-old nephew?
2. I have a kindergarten graduation party.
3. First we have the whole family over for supper.
4. We have popsicles for the children, popcorn, yo-yos, German chocolate cake, a huge honeyglazed ham, french-fried shrimp, and hot buttered corn bread.
5. We had a cake with Happy Graduation written on it.
6. We also have all the children's pets at the party.

Now rewrite these sentences in the standard dialect in past time. Use paragraph form.

_____

_____

_____

_____

_____

_____

_____

_____

_____

# IRREGULAR VERBS: *DO* IN PRESENT TIME

# 9

In the standard dialect, when you want to use DO in the present time, use either of the two following forms.

    Use the form *do*

| | |
|---|---|
| with singular pronouns: | I, you |
| with all plural pronouns: | we, you, they |
| with all plural nouns: | the children, the men, etc. |

    Use the form *does*

| | |
|---|---|
| with singular pronouns: | he, she, it |
| with singular nouns: | the child, the man, etc. |

EXAMPLES          Standard Dialect

| **Singular** | **Plural** |
|---|---|
| I *do* the laundry | we *do* the laundry |
| you *do* the laundry | you *do* the laundry |
| he, she, it *does* the laundry | they *do* the laundry |

In some community dialects, the form *do* is often used where the standard dialect uses *does*, and the form *does* is used where the standard dialect uses *do*.

EXAMPLES                          Community Dialect

**Singular**                                      **Plural**
I *does* the shopping                     we *does* the shopping
you *does* the shopping               you *does* the shopping
he, she, it *do*                              they *does* the shopping
    the shopping

Summary:   *DO* in Present Time

| Community Dialect | Standard Dialect |
|---|---|
| I<br>you<br>we<br>you<br>they<br>the children } *does* | I<br>you<br>we<br>you<br>they<br>the children } *do* |
| he<br>she<br>it<br>the child } *do* | he<br>she<br>it<br>the child } *does* |

## Recognition Drill

Underline the DO verbs in present time in the following sentences. Then mark SD beside each sentence that is written in the standard dialect. The first three have been done for you.

_____ 1. He <u>do</u> nothing.

__SD__ 2. What <u>do</u> we want?

__SD__ 3. She <u>does</u> the asking.

_____ 4. Thomas do the talking.

_____ 5. Who does the laundry in your house?

_____ 6. My brother and sisters do the cleaning.

_____ 7. We does most of our homework at night.

_____ 8. My mother do the driving.

_____ 9. You do well in school.

_____ 10. Lonnie does well in school.

_____ 11. We do our work singing.

_____ 12. Picasso do the painting.

_____ 13. My father does the house painting at our house.

_____ 14. Grandma do the polishing.

_____ 15. Aunt Stella do the embroidery.

_____ 16. Ajax Construction Company does the building.

_____ 17. The union do the hiring.

_____ 18. Who do the lead singing in your choir?

_____ 19. Olga do the baking.

_____ 20. My little brother does the sweeping.

_____ 21. The soldiers do the shooting.

_____ 22. You do something to me.

_____ 23. Mary Lou do more charity work for the hospital than anyone else in town.

_____ 24. Exercising one-half hour every night do a lot to keep me trim.

_____ 25. My doctor do a lot to build my self-confidence.

_____ 26. I do many things that I do not necessarily like.

_____ 27. My uncle Christopher does many things around the house to keep my aunt Jennifer happy.

_____ 28. Mr. Smith do an excellent job as the leader of the band.

_____ 29. Frank and Henry do most of the tap dancing.

_____ 30. Our lawyer, Carl Carlson III, do a lot of charity work.

## Conversion Drill

Convert each sentence that you did not mark SD in the above exercise into the standard dialect in present time.

## Pattern Practice

Complete the following sentences with the appropriate standard dialect form of DO in present time. The first two have been done for you.

1. He <u>does</u> the shopping.

2. You <u>do</u> the cooking.

3. Marybell _____ the testing.

4. My mother _____ the laundry.

5. Sheila _____ the scheduling.

6. The choir _____ the singing at my church on Sunday.

7. My father _____ the housework.

8. We all _____ the ironing at our house.

9. Who _____ the twist best?

10. Grandmom and Grandpop _____ the polka at every wedding.

11. Chico Gonzales _____ the pitching for the Detroit Tigers.

12. You _____ your homework better than anyone in the class.

13. He _____ a great deal of reading on his own.

14. Mrs. Richards _____ all the songwriting and music arranging for our band.

15. Thomas _____ his work quietly.

16. Anthony, however, _____ very little work loudly.

17. She _____ things to make herself appear more attractive.

18. Being a good student _____ the most to help me get into college.

19. I _____ the entertaining at my house.

20. The president _____ little for his self-image when he appears on T.V.

21. My aunt Rachel _____ the typing for the president of General Motors.

22. Your insults _____ nothing for my pride.

23. Ted's encouragement _____ a lot to strengthen my character.

24. She _____ everything for her family.

25. Most of the time, only one person _____ all of the work on a committee.

26. I _____ the best that I can in mathematics.

27. Senators and Congressmen _____ a lot of talking about improvements for people,

    but _____ little acting.

28. Taking vitamins _____ a lot to improve one's health.

29. I am the one who _____ the arrangements for the party.

30. Reading books _____ more to improve the quality of my thinking than anything else

    I _____ .


## Conversion Exercise

In the following sentences circle DO verbs written in community dialects in present time.

1. When April comes, our family do the spring housecleaning.
2. Mom do the wall-washing, while my two brothers and I does the dusting.
3. At the same time my father do the painting around the house.
4. My sisters does the cooking and cleaning up.
5. We all does the eating.
6. My younger brother do most of the talking during the dinner.
7. Then my oldest brother, Steve, do some singing and plays the guitar.
8. Working, eating, and singing together do a lot for our family spirit.

Now rewrite these sentences in the standard dialect in present time. Use paragraph form.

_____

_____

_____

_____

_____

_____

_____

_____

_____

# IRREGULAR VERBS: _DO_ IN PAST TIME

# 10

In the standard dialect, the past time of the verb DO is always _did_.

EXAMPLES                    Standard Dialect

**Singular**
I _did_ my homework
you _did_ your homework
he, she, it _did_
 the homework

**Plural**
we _did_ our homework
you _did_ your homework
they _did_ their homework

In some community dialects, the past form of DO is _done_.

EXAMPLES                    Community Dialect

**Singular**
I _done_ the dishes
you _done_ the dishes
he, she, it _done_ the dishes

**Plural**
we _done_ the dishes
you _done_ the dishes
they _done_ the dishes

## Summary: *DO* in Past Time

| Community Dialect | Standard Dialect |
|---|---|
| I<br>you<br>we<br>they<br>he<br>she<br>it<br>the child<br>the children } done | I<br>you<br>we<br>they<br>he<br>she<br>it<br>the child<br>the children } *did* |

## Recognition Drill

Underline the DO verbs in past time in the following sentences. Then mark SD next to each sentence that is written in the standard dialect. The first three have been done for you.

_____ 1. I <u>done</u> it.

__SD__ 2. You <u>did</u> your homework assignment.

_____ 3. They <u>done</u> everything in the proper order.

_____ 4. Debra did the washing.

_____ 5. The computer done the work of fifteen men.

_____ 6. Who done the cooking last night?

_____ 7. George Washington done more for our country than any other president.

_____ 8. Martha did the things that were expected of her.

_____ 9. The Pistons done the best job.

_____ 10. The jury done the fair thing.

_____ 11. Who did that?

_____ 12. The tornado done a lot of damage.

_____ 13. Yesterday I done the dishes.

_____ 14. Your grandmother done her sewing in the living room.

60

_____ 15. The boy scouts did their duty.

_____ 16. The farmer did the corn planting early this year.

_____ 17. Beavers done damage to the trees.

_____ 18. The owl did his hunting at night.

_____ 19. John did all the chores around your house.

_____ 20. The dentist done the drilling on my sensitive tooth.

_____ 21. I done most of my studying for the biology examination.

_____ 22. Under the circumstances Roy did the only thing possible.

_____ 23. My parents, sisters, and brothers done everything to help me attend college.

_____ 24. I done what I could to keep the relationship from falling apart.

_____ 25. She done nothing to better her condition.

_____ 26. My sister done all of the gossiping and none of the complimenting.

_____ 27. The fallen tree did $400 worth of damage to my 1975 Ford.

_____ 28. I done forty push-ups in twenty seconds.

_____ 29. My vacation done nothing to relax me.

_____ 30. Joining the Peace Corps and being sent to India done more to deepen my understanding of poverty than anything else I ever done.

## Conversion Drill

Convert each sentence that you did not mark SD in the above exercise into the standard dialect in past time.

## Pattern Practice

Complete the following sentences with the appropriate standard dialect form of DO in past time. The first two have been done for you.

1. Who <u>did</u> the work?

2. Years ago children always <u>did</u> what was expected of them.

3. The snowstorm _____ a great deal of damage to the farming community.

4. The FBI _____ an impressive study of drug dealers.

5. The Ford Motor Company _____ its recruiting for new employees.

6. Mark _____ well on his report card.

7. Which president _____ more than any other to advance the cause of civil and human rights?

8. The police _____ the best they could under the tight circumstances to save the man's life.

9. The chef _____ the cooking for 380 people in less than twenty-two minutes.

10. Last Tuesday the Chicago White Sox _____ the best they could in their final game.

11. Most of my neighbors _____ their duty by informing the police who the drug dealers were.

12. I _____ all of my assignments over the weekend.

13. Florence Nightingale _____ a lot for a lot of people.

14. Eating cookies and hot fudge sundaes _____ much to add fat to my already fat body.

15. Ten years of boxing and sixty-four fights _____ a lot of damage to Uncle Clarence's ears.

16. When my mother worked during the day, I _____ the laundry every day at 5 A.M.

17. Playing football every afternoon _____ wonders for my appetite when I was in high school.

18. Sigmund Freud _____ more for the advancement of psychology than any other man.

19. How can I be sure that I _____ everything I was supposed to do?

20. The University of Pennsylvania Glee Club _____ a lot of singing with the Philadelphia Orchestra a few years ago.

21. When I was a child I _____ what I was told to do.

22. In my younger days I _____ a lot of acting.

23. When my parrot died I _____ a lot of crying.

24. Thanks, you _____ what I asked you to do.

25. My great aunt _____ her own gardening for a long time.

26. Herbert _____ all his playing when he was young.

27. Thomas _____ the housework.

28. Arleen _____ her homework.

29. My rich cousin Egbert _____ the painting in all forty-seven rooms of his house.

30. I _____ the reading last night.

## Conversion Exercise

In the following sentences circle DO verbs written in community dialects in past time.

1. For years motorcycle gangs done more than anyone else to create the image of the rebel.
2. In the eyes of most citizens, motorcyclists never done anything right.
3. They done a lot of noisy riding in quiet neighborhoods at night.
4. They done nothing to improve their relations with the community.
5. Last year the City Council done away with motorcycle gangs by officially banning motorcycles in town.
6. Unfortunately some of the motorcyclists done no harm but they were banned along with the others.

Now rewrite these sentences in the standard dialect in past time. Use paragraph form.

_____

_____

_____

_____

_____

_____

_____

_____

_____

# REVIEW OF IRREGULAR VERBS: *BE, HAVE,* AND *DO*

**11**

When you want to write BE, HAVE, or DO in the standard dialect in present time, use the following forms:

### Standard Dialect

| **Singular** | **Plural** |
|---|---|
| I *am* | we *are* |
| you *are* | you *are* |
| he, she, it *is,* | they *are,* |
|    the book *is* |    the books *are* |
| | |
| I *have* | we *have* |
| you *have* | you *have* |
| he, she, it *has,* | they *have,* |
|    the boy *has* |    the boys *have* |
| | |
| I *do* | we *do* |
| you *do* | you *do* |
| he, she, it *does,* | they *do,* |
|    my friend *does* |    my friends *do* |

When you want to write BE, HAVE, or DO in the standard dialect in past time, use the following forms:

### Standard Dialect

| **Singular** | **Plural** |
|---|---|
| I *was* | we *were* |
| you *were* | you *were* |
| he, she, it *was,* | they *were,* |
|    the book *was* |    the books *were* |
| | |
| I *had* | we *had* |
| you *had* | you *had* |
| he, she, it *had,* | they *had,* |
|    the boy *had* |    the boys *had* |

| Singular | Plural |
|---|---|
| I *did* | we *did* |
| you *did* | you *did* |
| he, she, it *did* | they *did*, |
| my friend *did* | my friends *did* |

## Review Exercise

The following paragraph is written in standard dialect using the verbs BE, HAVE, and DO in present and past time. Circle those verbs:

A mother is a person who has the charge of bearing children. Most mothers are proud of their children, and do what is best for them. There are many kinds of mothers. There are old mothers and young mothers, single mothers and married mothers. In the past, most mothers did all the chores, such as cooking, sewing, washing, cleaning the house, keeping their husbands happy, tending the children, budgeting the money, to name only a few. In order for a mother to succeed in these things, she has to love what she does. However, today some mothers are ready to take on different responsibilities, such as working as a lawyer, a banker, a doctor, a nurse or dental technician, or executive secretary.

## Review Exercise

Using the appropriate standard dialect forms of BE, HAVE, and DO in present and past times, complete the following paragraph:

My mother _____ a good housekeeper. She _____ three children and she _____ a job as well. She _____ many things at home, such as cooking, washing, and cleaning. We also _____ much of the work. My younger sister _____ the laundry, while my older brother _____ responsible for shopping and dusting. My father also _____ some of the work. He _____ most of the heavy jobs, such as scrubbing, painting, and window washing.

# IRREGULAR VERBS: *HIT*, etc.

# 12

Remember the difference between regular and irregular verbs: regular verbs make the past by adding *ed* to the base form, while irregular verbs do not add *ed* to the base form. Irregular verbs either change the spelling of the base form, or they leave the base form alone. In this chapter we will study those irregular verbs that leave the base form alone. There are not many of them, and all of them end in the letter *t* or *d*.

They include:

| | | |
|---|---|---|
| BEAT | HIT | SET |
| BET | HURT | SLIT |
| BURST | LET | SPREAD |
| COST | PUT | |
| CUT | QUIT | |

The present time of these verbs is formed just like the present time of regular verbs—that is, you leave the base form alone except when the verb follows *he, she, it*, or one singular noun; then you add *s*.

EXAMPLES                    Standard Dialect

**Singular**
I *hit* the ball
you *hit* the ball
he, she, it, the batter
    *hits* the ball

**Plural**
we *hit* the ball
you *hit* the ball
they, the batters *hit*
    the ball

To form the past time of these verbs you don't add anything; you just leave the base form as it is.

EXAMPLES                    Standard Dialect

**Singular**
I *hit* the ball yesterday
you *hit* the ball yesterday
he, she, it, the batter *hit*
    the ball yesterday

**Plural**
we *hit* the ball yesterday
you *hit* the ball yesterday
they *hit* the ball yesterday

Some community dialects, however, add *ed* to these verbs (or double the final consonant and add *ed*), just as they do for regular verbs.

Community Dialect

**Singular**                                      **Plural**
I hitt*ed* the ball                      they hitt*ed* the ball

Summary:   Past Forms of *HIT*, etc.

| **Community Dialects** | **Standard Dialects** |
|---|---|
| I<br>you<br>we<br>they<br>he<br>she<br>it<br>the child<br>the children } *hitted* | I<br>you<br>we<br>they<br>he<br>she<br>it<br>the child<br>the children } *hit* |

## Recognition Drill

Underline the verbs in past time in the following sentences. Then mark SD next to each sentence that is written in the standard dialect. The first three have been done for you.

   **SD**    1. The balloon <u>burst</u> yesterday.

   **SD**    2. He <u>set</u> the pan on the stove an hour ago.

_____ 3. My brother <u>hitted</u> him.

_____ 4. Thomas let the dog out.

_____ 5. Mason cutted herself on the playground.

_____ 6. It hurt her.

_____ 7. When Mother put the bandage on, she burst out in tears.

_____ 8. The car costed too much.

_____ 9. The Tigers beated the Indians by a score of 3 to 2.

_____ 10. The St. Louis Cardinals beated the Oakland A's 6 to 2.

_____ 11. Yesterday I bet Tom that he would receive a scholarship.

_____ 12. When Joanna left, my dream of happiness bursted.

_____ 13. The color T.V. we bought cost too much.

_____ 14. I cut my finger playing the guitar.

_____ 15. Charles hurted the cat when he pulled his tail.

## Conversion Drill

Convert each sentence that you did not mark SD in the above exercise into the standard dialect in past time.

## Pattern Practice

Complete the following sentences with the appropriate standard dialect past form of the verb whose base form is given in the margin. The first two have been done for you.

HIT
1. Evel Knievel <u>hit</u> the accelerator.

BET
2. He <u>bet</u> none of the racing cars could pass him on the speedway.

LET
3. Fonstance _____ Flora know what she was thinking.

PUT
4. Last night the program sponsors _____ the Piston game on T.V.

CUT
5. Last night he _____ me off while I was still talking.

HIT
6. So I _____ him.

PUT/BURST
7. Last month Marsha _____ on weight and _____ the seams of her slacks.

SET
8. Marilyn _____ the tone of the meeting.

COST
9. The cars _____ $25,000 each because of all that custom equipment.

LET
10. He _____ it all hang out.

PUT
11. When she left, I _____ her out of my mind.

QUIT
12. I _____ the baseball team because I had choir practice at the same time.

BURST        13. I _____ out laughing after John told me he loved me.

SET/HIT      14. Harry _____ a new record when he _____ eighteen home runs in one game.

SPLIT        15. Tony and Orianel _____ up last night.

COST         16. My custom-made gray flannel suit _____ a lot of money.

SPREAD       17. Stanley _____ his talents over many areas.

BEAT         18. Stanford _____ Michigan in the Rose Bowl game.

LET          19. After she said no to me, I _____ her be by herself.

HURT         20. The shot of penicillin _____ me.


## Pattern Practice

Complete the following sentences with the appropriate standard dialect form of the verb in the margin, first in present and then in past time. The first two have been done for you.

COST    (*Present*)    1. A plane trip always <u>costs</u> a lot.

        (*Past*)       2. Last year the bus <u>cost</u> twenty cents.

HIT     (*Present*)    3. Hank Aaron _____ hard.

        (*Past*)       4. Yesterday the storm _____ hard.

HURT    (*Present*)    5. Today my head _____ .

        (*Past*)       6. Yesterday my stomach _____ .

BURST   (*Present*)    7. Soap bubbles always _____ .

        (*Past*)       8. At yesterday's game the football _____ .

PUT     (*Present*)    9. When my mother cleans, she _____ the papers away.

        (*Past*)       10. Last time she _____ them where I couldn't find them.

QUIT    (*Present*)    11. She _____ when she is tired.

        (*Past*)       12. She _____ early last night.

SPLIT    (*Present*)    13. Every day Sue _____ logs.

(*Past*)    14. Last Monday she _____ enough logs for the whole week.

LET    (*Present*)    15. I always _____ you get under my skin.

(*Past*)    16. Yesterday she _____ me have a piece of her mind.

CUT    (*Present*)    17. When I make stew I _____ the meat in small pieces.

(*Past*)    18. Last week he _____ down all the weeds.

HURT    (*Present*)    19. My head _____ when I think of Julia.

(*Past*)    20. For years my head _____ when I thought of Julia.

COST    (*Present*)    21. The trip to Ireland now _____ our family $4,528.19.

(*Past*)    22. Last Easter, lilies _____ only $5.00 each.

SPREAD    (*Present*)    23. I always _____ the payment of new clothes over three installments.

(*Past*)    24. Last year the flu _____ rapidly through the community.

HIT    (*Present*)    25. Barry _____ more home runs than any other player on our team.

(*Past*)    26. However, three years ago, Barry _____ fewer home runs than anybody.

LET    (*Present*)    27. Tommy always _____ the cat out of the bag.

(*Past*)    28. Yesterday I _____ Vera use my new Electra 225.

SET    (*Present*)    29. On Thanksgiving Verdell _____ the dinner table.

(*Past*)    30. Barbara _____ the world record for straight talking.

## Conversion Exercise

In the following sentences circle verbs written in community dialects in past time.

1. Lorenzo and Michelle setted the table for the club dinner.
2. Clarence cutted up the tomatoes for an elegant salad.
3. Darnell, Althera, Stanley, and Gina slitted the perch open.
4. Curtis putted the fish in the oven.
5. Donald beated the egg whites into a fluffy meringue for the lemon pie topping.

Now rewrite these sentences in the standard dialect in past time. Use paragraph form.

_____

_____

_____

_____

_____

_____

_____

_____

# OTHER IRREGULAR VERBS 13

So far we have studied the irregular verbs BE, HAVE, DO, and those like HIT. Let's summarize how these verbs are different from regular verbs:

1. BE and HAVE: The present is formed differently from regular verbs. The present of all the other irregular verbs is formed just like the present of regular verbs.
2. BE, HAVE, and DO: The past is formed by changing the spelling of the base form.
3. HIT and similar verbs: The past is formed by just leaving the base form alone.
4. All other irregular verbs: The past is formed by changing the spelling of the base form.

## Summary:   Present and Past Time

|  | **Present** | **Past** |
|---|---|---|
| Regular | Leave base form alone or add *s* (or *es*), depending on subject. | Add *ed* to base form. |
| Irregular: BE | Change base form to *am*, *are*, or *is*, depending on subject. | Change base form to *was* or *were*, depending on subject. |
| Irregular: HAVE | Leave base form alone or change to *has*, depending on subject. | Change spelling of base form to *had*. |
| Irregular: DO | Same as regular. | Change spelling of base form to *did*. |
| Irregular: HIT, etc. | Same as regular. | Leave base form as is. |
| All other irregular verbs | Same as regular. | Change spelling of base form. |

In this chapter we are going to study the past forms of other irregular verbs that we have not yet studied. Since these verbs are irregular, the past of each is formed in a slightly different way.

Compare the present and past forms of the following verbs in the standard dialect:

### Standard Dialect

**Present Time**
I *go* to school
you *go* to school
he, she *goes* to school

**Past Time**
I *went* to school
you *went* to school
they *went* to school

I *come* from Detroit
you *come* from Detroit
he, she, it *comes* from Detroit

I *came* from Detroit
you *came* from Detroit
they *came* from Detroit

In some community dialects of English, the past time is formed by adding *ed* as in regular verbs, or by using a different spelling change from the one the standard dialect uses. (Often the form used in the community dialect for the simple past is the one used in the standard dialect for the compound past forms, as discussed in Chapter 18.)

**EXAMPLES**　　Present Time, Standard Dialect

I *fly* to Minneapolis
she *falls* down
you *go* to school
we *drink* a lot of milk

Past Time, Standard Dialect

I *flew* to Minneapolis
she *fell* down
you *went* to school
we *drank* a lot of milk

Past Time, Community Dialect

I *flied* to Minneapolis
she *falled* down
you *gone* to school
we *drunk* a lot of milk

Summary:　Past Time of Irregular Verbs

| Community Dialect | Standard Dialect |
|---|---|
| the birds { flied / flown | the birds　　*flew* |

Here is a list of the present and past forms of some of the most common verbs in the standard dialect. Since each one is different, the only way to learn them is to memorize them, or to keep the list handy so you can refer to it whenever you're not sure.

Standard Dialect

| Present | Past | Present | Past |
|---|---|---|---|
| *arise(s)* | *arose* | *choose(s)* | *chose* |
| *awake(s)* | *awoke* | *come(s)* | *came* |
| *bear(s)* | *bore* | *creep(s)* | *crept* |
| *become(s)* | *became* | *deal(s)* | *dealt* |
| *begin(s)* | *began* | *dig(s)* | *dug* |
| *bite(s)* | *bit* | *dive(s)* | *dove* |
| *bleed(s)* | *bled* | *draw(s)* | *drew* |
| *blow(s)* | *blew* | *drink(s)* | *drank* |
| *break(s)* | *broke* | *drive(s)* | *drove* |
| *bring(s)* | *brought* | *eat(s)* | *ate* |
| *buy(s)* | *bought* | *fall(s)* | *fell* |
| *build(s)* | *built* | *feed(s)* | *fed* |
| *catch(es)* | *caught* | *feel(s)* | *felt* |

73

| Present | Past | Present | Past |
|---------|------|---------|------|
| *fight*(s) | *fought* | *shrink*(s) | *shrank* |
| *find*(s) | *found* | *sing*(s) | *sang* |
| *fling*(s) | *flung* | *sink*(s) | *sank* |
| *fly* (*flies*) | *flew* | *sit*(s) | *sat* |
| *forget*(s) | *forgot* | *slay*(s) | *slew* |
| *forgive*(s) | *forgave* | *sleep*(s) | *slept* |
| *freeze*(s) | *froze* | *slide*(s) | *slid* |
| *get*(s) | *got* | *speak*(s) | *spoke* |
| *give*(s) | *gave* | *spend*(s) | *spent* |
| *go*(es) | *went* | *spin*(s) | *spun* |
| *grind*(s) | *ground* | *spring*(s) | *sprang* |
| *grow*(s) | *grew* | *stand*(s) | *stood* |
| *hang*(s) | *hung* | *steal*(s) | *stole* |
| *hear*(s) | *heard* | *stick*(s) | *stuck* |
| *hide*(s) | *hid* | *sting*(s) | *stung* |
| *hold*(s) | *held* | *stink*(s) | *stunk* |
| *keep*(s) | *kept* | *stride*(s) | *strode* |
| *kneel*(s) | *knelt* | *strike*(s) | *struck* |
| *know*(s) | *knew* | *string*(s) | *strung* |
| *lay*(s) | *laid* | *strive*(s) | *strove* |
| *lead*(s) | *led* | *swear*(s) | *swore* |
| *leave*(s) | *left* | *swell*(s) | *swelled* |
| *lend*(s) | *lent* | *sweep*(s) | *swept* |
| *lie*(s) | *lay* | *swim*(s) | *swam* |
| *lie*(s) | *lied* | *swing*(s) | *swung* |
| *light*(s) | *lit* | *take*(s) | *took* |
| *lose*(s) | *lost* | *teach*(es) | *taught* |
| *make*(s) | *made* | *tear*(s) | *tore* |
| *meet*(s) | *met* | *tell*(s) | *told* |
| *mow*(s) | *mowed* | *think*(s) | *thought* |
| *pay*(s) | *paid* | *throw*(s) | *threw* |
| *ride*(s) | *rode* | *wake*(s) | *woke* |
| *ring*(s) | *rang* | *wear*(s) | *wore* |
| *rise*(s) | *rose* | *weave*(s) | *wove* |
| *run*(s) | *ran* | *weep*(s) | *wept* |
| *say*(s) | *said* | *win*(s) | *won* |
| *see*(s) | *saw* | *wind*(s) | *wound* |
| *sell*(s) | *sold* | *wring*(s) | *wrung* |
| *shake*(s) | *shook* | *write*(s) | *wrote* |
| *shine*(s) | *shone* (*shined*) | | |
| *shoot*(s) | *shot* | | |

# Review of Present Time

## Recognition Drill

Underline irregular verbs in present time in the following sentences. Then mark SD to each sentence that is written in the standard dialect. The first three have been done for you.

  **SD**   1. Doctor, every night my nose <u>bleeds</u>.

_____ 2. Every time I <u>blows</u> my nose, it <u>bleed</u>.

  **SD**   3. I <u>break</u> a blood vessel.

_____ 4. My dog bring me the evening newspaper.

_____ 5. John buy his imported Italian sweaters downtown.

_____ 6. Tiny catch cold every winter.

_____ 7. We chooses a new captain for our baseball team every season.

_____ 8. Esther come to English class every day.

_____ 9. When she come late, she creep into the room.

_____ 10. Ruth deals with her personal problems well.

_____ 11. Our dog, Prince, dig up old bones for breakfast.

_____ 12. My little brother, Alvin, draw pictures of dragons that draw wagons.

_____ 13. Carmella drinks wine with her hamburgers.

_____ 14. The ice-cream man drives down our street every night during the summer.

_____ 15. On Thanksgiving, all our relatives eats together.

_____ 16. Christmas falls on Monday this year.

_____ 17. I feeds my little kitten eight glasses of milk a day.

_____ 18. The kitten feel sick.

_____ 19. My little brother fight a lot at school.

_____ 20. George finds money all the time.

_____ 21. Flies fly faster than fleas flee.

_____ 22. Every Monday morning before work I forget what day of the week it is.

_____ 23. Waiting for the reindeer, Santa Claus freezes.

_____ 24. I get mad when people forgets my birthday.

_____ 25. Doris Day gives me a thrill; Frankenstein gives me a chill.

_____ 26. Janice and David go to the Englebert Humperdink concert.

_____ 27. The butcher grind horse meat for hamburgers, because of today's high prices.

_____ 28. Mrs. Hornsby grows geraniums.

_____ 29. Mr. Warner hangs light bulbs, tinsel, and balls on the Christmas tree.

_____ 30. I hear music when there's no one there.

_____ 31. Mother hide the birthday gifts in the closet.

_____ 32. Aunt Dorothy holds my hand.

_____ 33. He keep his temper during the long argument.

_____ 34. The priest kneel to pray.

_____ 35. I knows the answer to the math problem.

## Conversion Drill

Convert each sentence that you did not mark SD in the above exercise into the standard dialect in present time.

## Pattern Practice

Complete the following sentences with the appropriate standard dialect present forms of the irregular verbs whose base forms are given in the margin. The first two have been done for you.

LAY      1. George <u>lays</u> his new Bavarian hat on the table.

LEAD      2. Thomas <u>leads</u> the high school marching band.

LEAVE      3. Every day we _____ for work at 8 A.M.

LEND 4. Cleopatra _____ her earrings to Mark Antony.

LIE 5. She _____ often to her boyfriend.

LIGHT 6. Robert never _____ his pipe in the wind.

LOSE 7. Josephine _____ her boyfriend.

MAKE 8. My mother _____ delicious strawberry shortcake.

MEAN 9. She _____ well.

MEET 10. The lawyer _____ his clients in the bar.

PAY 11. We _____ too many taxes to Uncle Sam.

RIDE 12. On Sunday we _____ around in my cousin Lonnie's silver Rolls Royce.

RING 13. The alarm clock _____ too soon.

RISE 14. Gentlemen _____ when ladies walk into the room.

RUN 15. Ladies _____ when gentlemen appear.

SAY 16. They _____ that falling in love is wonderful.

SEE 17. The astronauts _____ the earth from the skylab.

SELL 18. Victor Lim _____ the best chop suey.

SEND 19. I _____ messages of love by carrier pigeon to my girlfriend.

SHAKE 20. I _____ all over when I have to give a speech.

SHINE 21. The moon _____ on my old Kentucky home.

SHOOT 22. A group of businessmen from Chicago _____ elephants in India.

KNOW 23. We _____ that the theater showed the film at 6, 8, and 10 P.M. on Saturday.

SHRINK 24. Wool sweaters _____ in the rain.

SING 25. The choir always _____ "Onward Christian Soldiers."

SINK 26. I usually _____ when I swim.

SIT 27. Aunt Sophronia _____ on the bridge and fishes and smokes a pipe.

SLEEP 28. I _____ in order to count sheep.

SLIDE    29. My car _____ on ice.

SPEAK    30. The judge _____ sternly.

SPEND    31. I _____ all my money on records and clothes.

SPRING    32. Rabbits _____ sprightly.

STAND    33. My English teacher always _____ when he lectures.

STEAL    34. Betty always _____ my boyfriends.

STICK    35. The stamp _____ to the letter.

STING    36. Bees _____ .

STRIKE    37. Casey _____ out in the third inning.

STRING    38. Indians _____ beads.

STRIVE    39. Most immigrants _____ hard for success in America.

SWEAR    40. I _____ on the Bible I am telling the truth.

SWEEP    41. My sister _____ up after her fourteen cats have breakfast.

FREEZE    42. My hands _____ in damp weather.

SWIM    43. Porpoises _____ gracefully.

SWING    44. Willie Mays never _____ at low pitches.

TAKE    45. It _____ too much time to drive to work.

TEACH    46. My cousin _____ high school in Los Angeles.

TEAR    47. Double-knit trousers _____ easily.

TELL    48. My girlfriend _____ her mother everything.

THINK    49. I _____ life is beautiful.

THROW    50. He _____ the ball faster than anyone on the team.

WAKE    51. Aunt Sarah _____ us at six every morning.

WEAR    52. I _____ a flower in my hair.

WEEP    53. Jean _____ for her lost sheep.

WIN     54. The baseball team _____.

WIND    55. The road _____ around a fantastic mountain.

RING    56. The school bell _____.

WRITE   57. My mother _____ to my Uncle Bill who is in Germany.

GIVE    58. Jean _____ all her love to Jack.

GET     59. We _____ up every day at 6 A.M.

GO      60. Michael _____ to work every day after school.


## Irregular Verbs in Past Time

### Recognition Drill

Underline the irregular verbs in past time in the following sentences.
Then mark SD next to each sentence that is written in the standard dialect.
The first three have been done for you.

_____ 1. Yesterday the sun <u>arise</u>.

_____ 2. The other day the dog <u>bite</u> me.

__SD__ 3. Last Monday school <u>began</u>.

_____ 4. My brother bring us gifts from Germany last year.

_____ 5. Last summer the hurricane blow down the whole town of Peru, Indiana.

_____ 6. The hurricane breaked the windows of downtown department stores and or-

dinary houses.

_____ 7. Philip bought his girlfriend a $25,000 mink coat.

_____ 8. When I was ten I catch the measles from my cousin's cat.

_____ 9. In 1972 our football team choose a homecoming queen and king.

_____ 10. For years, I believed that Santa Claus come on Christmas Eve.

_____ 11. I believe that he creep up the stairs.

_____ 12. He leave things under the tree.

_____ 13. They dig the foundation for the house.

_____ 14. Last Monday I drink 7-Up.

_____ 15. Last Tuesday I drinked Coke.

_____ 16. Last Wednesday I drank my Uncle Joe's special root beer.

_____ 17. Last summer I drive my car to Detroit.

_____ 18. While I was there I fell in love with Carmen.

_____ 19. She drove me crazy.

_____ 20. All summer she fed me fish.

_____ 21. She catched it in the Detroit river.

_____ 22. I finally feel like a fish.

_____ 23. We fought about the fish dinners and I went back to St. Louis.

_____ 24. Marisa dug the dirt out of the corners.

_____ 25. She lend her broom to Louis.

_____ 26. He telled her to fly on it.

_____ 27. Clarence gave a Halloween party for Dagmar last week.

_____ 28. He maked caramel apples.

_____ 29. The guests come in costumes.

_____ 30. I seen a real witch hiding behind the tree.

_____ 31. I heard a ghost crying.

_____ 32. I feeled a shiver down my spine.

_____ 33. I felt a cold hand touch my arm.

_____ 34. Someone sticked pins in my leg.

_____ 35. All of the guests spoke of their scary experiences.

_____ 36. Clarence and Dagmar freezed in their tracks.

_____ 37. But the rest of the guests ran into the house.

_____ 38. They drank the cider and ate the caramel apples.

_____ 39. Then they tell their host and hostess that they lie to them.

_____ 40. The guests went out and bought cider and doughnuts for Dagmar and Clarence.

_____ 41. Everyone eat together, then, and play games.

_____ 42. I knowed your name was Premus.

_____ 43. Jack's beanstalk grew very high.

_____ 44. He breaked his arm jumping off the roof.

_____ 45. I brought the doctor in my car.

_____ 46. We both catched the measles.

_____ 47. The teacher chose the best person.

_____ 48. Yesterday he came with me.

_____ 49. Last night you drank all the milk.

_____ 50. Richard fallen on his face.

_____ 51. Yesterday we set on the park bench for three hours.

_____ 52. My poor dog run away.

_____ 53. Last Sunday I rang the church bell.

_____ 54. The ship sank in the Delaware River.

_____ 55. He gone to the store.

_____ 56. She striked me when I yelled at her.

_____ 57. He swam across the Nile River.

_____ 58. Marjorie teached me how to swim.

_____ 59. Willie Mays stole forty-one bases last year.

_____ 60. The movie begun before I got to the theater.

_____ 61. We knew she would be late.

_____ 62. She growed very quickly.

_____ 63. The vase broke in a thousand pieces.

_____ 64. Sally brang us some salami.

_____ 65. The lion caught the rabbit.

_____ 66. Harriet choosed a different boy for each dance.

_____ 67. Tom come to my house last night.

_____ 68. She drunk all my Coke.

_____ 69. Jack fell down.

_____ 70. Three cats sat on a fence.

_____ 71. He ran out of the room in a hurry.

_____ 72. Alphonse, the paper boy, rung the bell.

_____ 73. Helen sunk a thousand ships.

_____ 74. We went to the baseball game yesterday.

_____ 75. He swam fifty yards in fifty seconds.

_____ 76. Micky Mantle struck out only three times in his life.

_____ 77. My brother taught me everything I know about grammar.

_____ 78. Oliver Twist stealed thirteen purses in one afternoon.

_____ 79. We began to pick strawberries in March.

_____ 80. I catched a cold from you.

## Conversion Drill

Convert each sentence that you did not mark SD in the above exercise into the standard dialect in past time.

## Pattern Practice

Complete the following sentences with the appropriate standard dialect past forms of the irregular verbs in the margin. The first two have been done for you.

WRITE

1. Many years ago Zane Grey <u>wrote</u> wild west stories.

WRING

2. Daisy <u>wrung</u> water out of her bathing suit.

WIND

3. We _____ the kite string.

WIN

4. MSU _____ their third game in a row.

WEEP

5. All the co-eds at U of M _____

WEAVE

6. The marching band _____ the figure eight.

WEAR

7. The majorettes _____ yellow and blue skirts.

WAKE

8. The roar of the crowds _____ the babies in the hospital.

THROW

9. He _____ the ball wild.

THINK

10. We all _____ he had better control than he has.

TELL

11. Butch Cassidy _____ a lie.

TEACH

12. A stiff jail sentence _____ him never to tell a lie.

TAKE

13. Cassidy _____ the jewels from the lady's purse.

SWING

14. The cowboy _____ the lariat.

SWEEP

15. He _____ the girl off her feet.

SWEAR

16. She _____ she would never speak to him again.

BECOME

17. But eventually she _____ his wife.

STRING

18. Big Joe _____ his guitar.

STRIKE

19. The old goldminer _____ pay dirt.

STRIDE/MEET

20. He _____ into town to tell about his luck but he _____ a skunk.

STINK

21. He _____ from the skunk's attack.

STING

22. In addition a bee _____ him.

| | |
|---|---|
| STICK | 23. He _____ in the quicksand. |
| STEAL | 24. Someone _____ his grub. |
| STAND | 25. A mountain lion _____ in his path. |
| SPRING | 26. It _____ at him and knocked him over the cliff. |
| SPIN/FORGET | 27. He _____ into town where he _____ all his troubles. |
| SPEND | 28. He _____ all his money. |
| SPEAK | 29. Everyone _____ cheerfully to him. |
| EAT | 30. He _____ all he wanted. |
| COME | 31. The girls _____ around to say hello. |
| SLIDE | 32. The old-timer _____ into bed exhausted. |
| SLEEP | 33. He _____ thirty-six hours straight. |
| SLAY | 34. He dreamed he _____ the mountain lion. |
| AWAKE/SAY | 35. When he _____, he _____ his prayers. |
| KNEEL | 36. He _____ down and promised some of his money to his church. |
| KEEP | 37. He _____ his promise. |
| COME | 38. After that no lions or skunks _____ near him again. |
| GO | 39. He _____ back to the mountains. |
| GET/FIND | 40. After three more years, he _____ lucky again and _____ a gold nugget the size of a lemon. |
| KNOW/SAID | 41. Thomas _____ Priscilla for three years before he _____ good morning to her. |
| GROW | 42. Marcella _____ three inches last year. |
| BEGIN | 43. I _____ to play the piano when I was eighty-three years old. |
| SWIM | 44. Ten ducks _____ across the Atlantic ocean. |
| SEE | 45. I _____ Alvert for three hours last Sunday. |

| | |
|---|---|
| DRINK | 46. Clyde _____ too much Coke. |
| RUN | 47. Montgomery _____ faster than anyone on the team except Philomena. |
| KNOW | 48. They _____ they won the game before it was finished. |
| GO | 49. Alva _____ to New York for the weekend. |
| STEAL | 50. Some thugs _____ my aunt's 1973 Thunderbird. |
| STRIKE | 51. A pick-up truck _____ my VW from behind. |
| BECOME | 52. I _____ a different person when I married Sue. |
| CATCH | 53. I _____ on to his practical joke after he played it on me. |
| DRAW | 54. For many years Erma _____ a cartoon strip for the local paper. |
| FALL | 55. The leaves _____ early this year. |
| FLING | 56. Judith _____ herself at Joseph, but he rejected her. |
| FORGET | 57. I _____ what I was supposed to get at the store. |
| SINK | 58. The ship _____ in the Pacific ocean. |
| FORGIVE | 59. I never _____ Violet for forgetting my birthday. |
| SEE | 60. My mother _____ all there was to see. |

## Conversion Exercise

In the following sentences circle verbs written in community dialects in past time.

1. I begun my trip to Chicago on Friday night.
2. My whole family gone with me.
3. We taken the Greyhound Bus as far as the depot in the loop, and then we rided the city bus to our hotel.
4. After we got settled, we ride to Maxwell Street where all the outdoor fruit stands are.
5. We chosen apples and plums, and took them back to the hotel, along with some bagels and cheese that we bought at a delicatessen.
6. We spoken to the doorman about places to visit.
7. He tell us to go to Buckingham Fountain, the Field Museum, and the Art Institute.
8. After a weary day of seeing all these great attractions, we rided the elevator to the top of the Prudential Building, where we seen all the places we gone that day.
9. Then we taken the bus back to the hotel, where we fall into bed to rest up for the next day of sightseeing.

Now rewrite these sentences in the standard dialect in past time. Use paragraph form.

_____

_____

_____

_____

_____

_____

_____

_____

_____

## Review Exercise

Write a composition in the past time using as many of the following verbs as possible in the standard dialect. (Verbs not included on this list may also be used.) Use paragraph form. Start with the sentence below.

| | | | |
|---|---|---|---|
| BECOME | SAY | SWEAR | BLOW |
| BEGIN | TEAR | EAT | WRITE |
| COME | BITE | STEAL | FORGIVE |
| RING | RUN | TAKE | FORGET |
| GIVE | KEEP | FREEZE | |

Geraldine _became_ the first postwoman on route 44.

_____

_____

_____

_____

_____

_____

_____

# COMPOUND VERBS: DISTANT AND RECENT PAST

**14**

In preceding chapters, we saw how to form the simple present and the simple past of regular and irregular verbs. The simple past, as we have seen, is formed in one of the following ways:

1. For regular verbs, by adding *ed* to the base form.

**EXAMPLES**                    Standard Dialect

Yesterday I *talked* to the president of the United States.
On Tuesday my dog *died*.

2. For some irregular verbs, by changing the spelling of the base form.

**EXAMPLES**                    Standard Dialect

Believe it or not, last Sunday a penguin *sat* outside my door
    and sang "The Battle Hymn of the Republic."
Two days ago I *ate* Mexican food for the first time.

3. For other irregular verbs, by not changing the base form at all.

**EXAMPLES**                    Standard Dialect

I *shut* the door hard after I *put* the cat out for the night.

The simple past, as above, is only one way of showing past time. Another way is to use compound past forms. The compound past is formed by using a helping verb and a main verb.

**EXAMPLES**              Standard Dialect

I *have sung* that song many times.
He *had finished* his homework early.
The leaves *had fallen* off the trees before the first snow fell.

Compound verbs show past action in two different ways. One of these ways shows the recent and the other shows the distant past.

The recent past describes an action that began in the past and continues into the present, or that occurred in the recent past.

Standard Dialect

> I *have gone* to college for one year.
> That movie *has been* on for over a week.
> I *have cut* the grass.

The distant past describes several actions that began and ended in the past.

EXAMPLES                    Standard Dialect

> I *had eaten* dinner before he came.
> They *had seen* the flying saucer.

The following dialogue will illustrate the difference between *have* in the recent past and *had* in the distant past.

### Dick and Jane and the Broken Heart

DICK  Darling, when should we get married?
JANE  I *had* decided to marry you.
DICK  You mean you *have* decided to marry me.
JANE  No, I *had* decided to marry you but I *have* changed my mind.
DICK  Why?
JANE  Because I *have* found someone else.
DICK  (Sob) I wish I *had* never seen you!

# COMPOUND VERBS: RECENT PAST OF REGULAR VERBS

# 15

In the standard dialect, the recent past of regular verbs is made by using the appropriate present form of the helping verb HAVE (*have* or *has*) and adding *ed* to the base form of the verb.

EXAMPLES                    Standard Dialect

*I've walked*

| Singular | Plural |
|---|---|
| I *have* walk*ed* | we *have* walk*ed* |
| you *have* walk*ed* | you *have* walk*ed* |
| he, she, it *has* walk*ed* | they *have* walk*ed* |

When you use HAVE as a helping verb, you use the same rules to form it as you do when you use HAVE as a main verb.

Use the form *have*

|  |  |
| --- | --- |
| with singular pronouns: | I, you |
| with all plural pronouns: | we, you, they |
| with all plural nouns: | the children, the men, etc. |

EXAMPLES            Standard Dialect

I *have* ask*ed* all my friends to the party.
The children *have* finish*ed* the candy.

Use the form *has*

|  |  |
| --- | --- |
| with singular pronouns: | he, she, it |
| with all singular nouns: | the child, the man, etc. |

EXAMPLES            Standard Dialect

He *has* walk*ed* to school since his car broke down.
The child *has* play*ed*.
The man *has* call*ed* his wife.

In some community dialects, the recent past of the regular verb is formed by using simply the base form of the verb and/or by using one of the community dialect forms of HAVE as we showed in Chapter 7.

EXAMPLES            Community Dialect

We *have* walk.
The child *have* played.
The man *have* call his wife.

In other community dialects *done* is used as the helping verb instead of *have* or *has*.

EXAMPLES            Community Dialect

He *done* finish(ed) his breakfast.
They *done* ask(ed) him a big favor.

To convert a community dialect into the standard dialect, use the appropriate form of the helping verb HAVE, and add *ed* to the base form of the verb.

## EXAMPLES

| Community Dialect | Standard Dialect |
|---|---|

He $\left\{\begin{array}{c} done \\ have \end{array}\right\}$ open the door.     He *has* open*ed* the door.

My mother $\left\{\begin{array}{c} done \\ have \end{array}\right\}$ skin     My mother *has* skinn*ed*

    the peach.                the peach.

The student $\left\{\begin{array}{c} done \\ have \end{array}\right\}$ finish     The student *has* finish*ed*

    the test.                the test.

### Summary:  Regular Verbs in the Recent Past

| Community Dialect | Standard Dialect |
|---|---|
| I<br>you<br>we } has walk(ed)<br>they<br>the children<br><br>I<br>you<br>we } have walk<br>they<br>the children | I<br>you<br>we } *have* walk*ed*<br>they<br>the children |
| he<br>she } have walk(ed)<br>it<br>the child<br><br>he<br>she } has walk<br>it<br>the children | he<br>she } *has* walk*ed*<br>it<br>the child |

## Recognition Drill

Underline the compound verbs in the recent past in the following sentences. Then mark SD next to each sentence that is written in the standard dialect. The first three have been done for you.

__SD__ 1. I <u>have smelled</u>.

_____ 2. You <u>has walked</u>.

_____ 3. We <u>have talk</u>.

_____ 4. He have chopped.

_____ 5. They have rowed.

_____ 6. She have baked.

_____ 7. I have touch.

_____ 8. It have bark.

_____ 9. How long have he smoked?

_____ 10. The band has already play the song.

_____ 11. Have you learned the verbs yet?

_____ 12. Have you call the doctor for an appointment?

_____ 13. He have work hard all day.

_____ 14. The police have suspected the people who live in apartment 1-A.

_____ 15. The event you spoke about has occurred.

_____ 16. We have already dance for four hours.

_____ 17. He have applied for the job.

_____ 18. Have you finish your assignment yet?

_____ 19. We have covered the baby with a blanket.

_____ 20. The teachers have dismiss the class.

_____ 21. When have it happen?

_____22. My brother has asked me two questions.

_____23. I have wanted that watch for three years.

_____24. I have not opened all the bottles of pop yet.

_____25. Have you ever skinned a tomato?

_____26. He have believed in Santa Claus for three years.

_____27. They have watch me on T.V.

_____28. We have ruin the soup.

_____29. The explorer has reach the top of the mountain.

_____30. The criminals have turn themselves in.

_____31. On every April Fools' Day my younger brother has dress up the dog in a red and

blue clown costume.

_____32. Have you ever judged a beauty contest?

_____33. Elsa have experience much suffering in her life.

_____34. Peter have play many tricks on Halloween.

_____35. I have look after my father's welfare for ten years.

_____36. The Air Force have defend our country against air missile attacks.

_____37. Vivian have wonder all these years about the birds and the bees.

_____38. Janet have betray her friends more than once.

_____39. The rangers has brand the cows with the sign of the ranch.

_____40. William and Mary has always observe the Sabbath.

## Conversion Drill

Convert each sentence that you did not mark SD in the above exercise
into the recent past of the standard dialect.

## Pattern Practice

Complete the following sentences by inserting the appropriate forms of HAVE and WALK to form the recent past. The first two have been done for you.

1. You <u>have</u> <u>walked</u> to the movies.

2. My brother <u>has</u> <u>walked</u> to school.

3. The three of us _____ _____ to school.

4. My mother _____ _____ to the store.

5. _____ you ever _____ to school?

6. They _____ _____ quickly down the street.

7. I _____ _____ to the zoo.

8. _____ he _____ to school?

9. Your father _____ always _____ to work.

10. The children _____ sometimes _____ to school.


Complete the following sentences by inserting the appropriate forms of HAVE and ASK to form the recent past.

1. I _____ _____ for a glass of water.

2. _____ he ever _____ a question in class?

3. You _____ never _____ me about my goals in life.

4. She _____ _____ her neighbors about the block club.

5. _____ you _____ the salesman about the prices?

6. The children _____ always _____ me to tell them a story.

7. Sabina and Nadine _____ _____ the policeman for directions.

8. We _____ _____ Dr. Bowman to speak at our annual banquet.

9. Florence and Ramona _____ _____ the king for permission to attend the concert.

10. _____ you _____ the instructor to postpone the examination?

11. He _____ always _____ silly questions in class.

12. The teacher _____ _____ Germaine about her assignment.

13. She _____ _____ her supervisor about her vacation.

14. The Spanish teacher _____ _____ the questions in Spanish.

15. I _____ _____ her very personal questions.

Complete the following sentences by inserting the appropriate forms of
HAVE with TALK, FIX, or PICK to form the recent past.

1. The teacher _____ _____ more than five hours on this subject.

2. Carmen, the mechanic, _____ always _____ my 1972 Chrysler.

3. My mother _____ never _____ up after me.

4. Our whole neighborhood _____ _____ to our Congressman about crime on our

   block.

5. The jeweler _____ _____ my gold watch again.

6. Bernard, the spoiled child, _____ sometimes _____ at his food for hours.

7. Evelyn _____ never _____ before 400 people before.

8. Mother _____ _____ dinner for all the poor people again.

9. The local street gang _____ always _____ fights with me.

10. Ruth _____ _____ with her doctor about her problem.

11. Irene _____ _____ things up between Harold and Maud.

12. For three years I _____ _____ apples in Michigan.

13. Aggressive people _____ always _____ the longest and loudest.

14. My father _____ _____ up and painted our kitchen.

15. You _____ always _____ the ripest fruit.

16. I _____ _____ with my brother about his refusal to go to school.

17. Gertrude and Claudius _____ _____ many television sets in their time.

18. I _____ _____ up students every Saturday to take them on a trip somewhere.

19. They _____ _____ and _____ but never acted.

20. My father _____ _____ pizza and beer every Saturday night for the past twenty-seven years.

21. I _____ _____ the boldest suit to wear to the prom.

22. Lydia _____ always _____ like an expert though we all know she is not one.

23. The plumber _____ finally _____ the leaky faucet.

24. Fred _____ _____ to the supervisor at the factory and _____ _____ up things between business and labor.

25. Al, the handyman, _____ always _____ things for the elderly in our community.

26. We _____ _____ the Rose Bowl Queen for this year; it's Bertha.

27. We _____ _____ to Bertha about what she is to wear and how she is to act.

28. Bertha _____ _____ herself up to look beautiful.

29. She _____ _____ a fine looking escort to take her to the Rose Bowl dance after the football game.

30. Bertha _____ _____ a whole lot about winning.

## Conversion Exercise

In the following sentences circle the recent past verbs written in community dialects.

1. Lana have call Clementine on the telephone.
2. They have exchange greetings.
3. They have talk to each other on the phone every Tuesday at 9:35 A.M. since they have start to work for IBM.
4. They has mostly discuss business matters pertaining to the office.
5. This time, however, Lana have open the conversation on a personal note.
6. Lana have ask Clementine if she have remember the tricks they has play on Dr. Evans, the company dentist, three Tuesdays in a row.
7. Clementine have blush each time she have stop to think and laugh about the tricks.
8. "I have wonder what Dr. Evans have suppose each time he pick up the phone on Tuesday and have listen to this soft, delicate, velvety voice on the other end that have first breathe, then sigh, then laugh, then cry, then whimper, then simper, then whisper: 'Oh Doctor, I

have finally reach you. I has live too long without you.' After saying that, the voice have pause and wish the doctor happy birthday."

9. Both Clementine and Lana have enjoy reminiscing.

Now rewrite these sentences using the recent past in the standard dialect. Use paragraph form.

_____

_____

_____

_____

_____

_____

_____

_____

_____

_____

_____

# COMPOUND VERBS: DISTANT PAST OF REGULAR VERBS

# 16

In the standard dialect, the distant past of regular verbs is made by using the past form of the helping verb HAVE (*had*), and adding *ed* (or *d*) to the base form of the main verb.

EXAMPLES                    Standard Dialect

**Singular**                        **Plural**
I *had* looked                      we *had* looked
you *had* looked                    you *had* looked
he, she, it *had* looked            they *had* looked

In some community dialects, the distant past is formed by using the base form of the main verb alone without adding *ed*.

## EXAMPLES

| Community Dialect | Standard Dialect |
|---|---|
| I *had look* for the book before he came | I *had* look*ed* |
| they *had ask* me what time it was | they *had* ask*ed* |

To convert a community dialect into the standard dialect, add an *ed* to the base form of the main verb.

### Summary:   Distant Past of Regular Verbs

| Community Dialect | Standard Dialect |
|---|---|
| I<br>we<br>you } had ask<br>he<br>they | I<br>we<br>you } *had* as*ked*<br>he<br>they |

## Recognition Drill

Underline the compound verbs in the distant past in the following sentences. Then mark SD beside each sentence written in the standard dialect. The first three have been done for you.

_____ 1. Dwight <u>had finish</u> his golf game before the rain began.

__SD__ 2. Martinez <u>had opened</u> the new store just before Christmas.

_____ 3. The bus <u>had complete</u> its run on time.

_____ 4. Joe had demolish his new Honda.

_____ 5. Mike had promised to repair it for Joe.

_____ 6. Before the farmer had milked the cow, she kicked over the pail.

_____ 7. After the farmer had milk the cow, she kicked over the pail.

_____ 8. By that time the farmer had kicked the cow.

_____ 9. In a few days Mike had repaired the Honda.

_____ 10. Since Joe had reward Mike by letting him ride the bike, Mike took Maria for a ride.

_____ 11. After they had pass the new store and the golf course, they came to the farm where the farmer had kick the cow.

_____ 12. The farmer had frightened the cow so much that she ran across the road.

_____ 13. Before Mike and Maria saw her coming, she had crash into the motorcycle.

_____ 14. Now Mike had ruined Joe's bike, had knocked the cow down, and had scraped his knees.

_____ 15. After he had fix the bike for the second time, he returned it to Joe.

_____ 16. By this time Maria had start to date Martinez and he had employ her in his store.

_____ 17. Mike had returned the repaired bike and had decided to forget Maria.

_____ 18. Until recently, the United States had monopolized the automotive industry.

_____ 19. The fortune teller had communicate the future to my aunt.

_____ 20. The puppy had amuse my three little cousins.

_____ 21. Thomas had always laugh at Geraldine until she became a doctor.

_____ 22. Miles Davis had practice the trumpet thirteen hours a day when he was young in order to become a great musician.

_____ 23. Molly had accompany Martin on the flute.

_____ 24. Alfreda had want to go to New York until she found out how expensive it was.

_____ 25. I asked for brandy with my peaches until I became allergic to brandy.

_____ 26. Victor had never like Vera because she was a smart alec.

_____ 27. I had love Susan until she left me to marry Archie.

_____ 28. As a child, I had always bother my aunt and uncle for gifts.

_____ 29. When I was young, boy scouts had always help old ladies to cross the street.

_____ 30. When I lived near the zoo, the bellowing elephants had sound like a foghorn.

## Conversion Drill

Convert each sentence that you did not mark SD in the above exercise into the standard dialect.

## Pattern Practice

Complete the following sentences with the appropriate standard dialect form of the distant past of regular verbs. The first two have been done for you.

CALL            1. She <u>had</u> <u>called</u> the plumber before the flood was bad.

EXPECT       2. They <u>had</u> <u>expected</u> to find buried treasure in their basement.

HELP           3. The new drug_____ _____8,000 people with colds.

PAINT         4. The new artist_____ _____his greatest works on tea bags.

SUFFER       5. She_____ _____from shingles all her life.

ORDER        6. The grocer_____ _____more Onion Delights.

FOLD           7. Mary_____ _____all the diapers by dawn.

LAUGH        8. The Eskimo_____ _____at the refrigerator salesman.

WANT          9. He_____ _____to kidnap a general.

PURCHASE   10. He_____ _____a one-way ticket to Tibet.

SURPRISE    11. Joan_____ _____her husband and his girl friend.

CLEAN        12. She_____ _____the stove for the first time in ten years.

HOPE           13. John_____ _____to break his arm before the test.

SMOKE        14. Paul_____ _____an exploding cigar by mistake.

WONDER     15. Carl_____ _____if Marge was a real blond.

WALK          16. They_____ _____across the desert for a six-pack.

START        17. He_____ _____to raise tulips.

OPEN          18. She_____ _____her mouth to yell "timber!"

KILL           19. The Indians_____ _____all the cowboys by the middle of the movie.

WASH      20. She _____ _____ her face with lemon juice to bleach all her freckles.

FIGURE      21. I _____ _____ Darell would not show up at the party.

BRIGHTEN      22. The moon _____ _____ the snowy street.

TWINKLE      23. The stars _____ _____ in the heavens when Tilly met Tyrone.

PRESENT      24. The president _____ _____ his latest plan for dealing with the energy crisis.

OPEN      25. Dora _____ _____ her present before Christmas day.

FOLD      26. I _____ _____ the letter twice before I mailed it.

PARDON      27. The king _____ _____ all the political prisoners.

INVEST      28. My mother _____ _____ her money in savings bonds.

SURROUND      29. The enemy _____ _____ us and we surrendered.

DISCOVER      30. Columbus _____ _____ America in 1492.

SUPPOSE      31. Veronica _____ _____ that Claud was an honest man.

LIVE      32. If John Kennedy _____ _____ until today, what kind of world would we have?

LOVE      33. If she _____ not _____ you, she would not have cried when you left.

SUPPORT      34. I _____ _____ the Republican Party in 1972.

COVER      35. Myrtle _____ _____ her mailbox with flowers.

SOUND      36. All of the pianos _____ _____ exactly the same to me.

MEASURE      37. I _____ _____ out four cups of sugar in order to make the cake.

PROMISE      38. We _____ _____ to take the children for a drive into the country.

CONTINUE      39. If I _____ only _____ school, I would not be where I am today.

PASS      40. We _____ _____ the French examination.

PRODUCE      41. The United States _____ _____ more wheat than any other country.

REPEAT      42. The teacher _____ _____ the assignment fourteen times.

COUNT      43. Romola_____ _____the number of people at the Ray Charles' concert.

FOLLOW      44. The swallows_____ _____the baseball team to spring training.

REALIZE      45. I_____ not_____that you loved me so much.

DETERMINE      46. The military commanders_____ _____to end the war.

DEFINE      47. I_____ not_____for myself the meaning of marriage.

COLLECT      48. The preacher_____ _____all the donations except mine.

FINISH      49. I_____ not_____my homework on time.

DANCE      50. Grace Kelly_____ _____all night with a prince.

## Conversion Exercise

In the following sentence, circle the simple past and distant past verbs written in community dialects.

1. Last Friday, I had fix pizza for my family.
2. I had mix green and red peppers, hot and sweet tomatoes, anchovies, radishes, Italian sausage, and mushrooms.
3. After I had stir all the ingredients in one big bowl, I drop them spoon by spoon onto the pizza.
4. When I had bake the pizza for forty-five minutes, and had remove it from the oven, I call my family.
5. At first they suppose that I had purchase the pizza from the store because it was so good, but later I convince them that I had prepare it myself.

Now rewrite these sentences using the simple and distant past in the standard dialect. Use paragraph form.

_____

_____

_____

_____

_____

_____

_____

_____

# COMPOUND VERBS: RECENT PAST OF IRREGULAR VERBS

In the standard dialect, the recent past of irregular verbs is formed differently from the recent past of regular verbs. Remember that in Chapter 15 we said that you make the recent past by doing two things:

1. Put the appropriate present form of the helping verb HAVE (*has* or *have*) in front of the main verb.
2. Add *ed* to the base of the main verb.

Step one is the same for the irregular verbs, but step two is different. To form the recent past of irregular verbs, you do the following:

1. Put the appropriate present form of the helping verb HAVE (*has* or *have*) in front of the main verb.
2. Use the compound past form of the main verb.

Remember that irregular verbs change the spelling of the base form in the past. Most irregular verbs have compound past forms different from their simple past forms. Since they are irregular, you simply have to memorize them, and keep the following chart handy to refer back to.

The following chart expands the one in Chapter 13. It includes the compound past forms as well as the present and simple past forms of some of the most common irregular verbs.

| Standard Dialect Present | Standard Dialect Simple Past | Standard Dialect Compound Past |
|---|---|---|
| *arise(s)* | *arose* | *arisen* |
| *awake(s)* | *awoke* | *awaked* |
| *bear(s)* | *bore* | *borne* |
| *become(s)* | *became* | *become* |
| *begin(s)* | *began* | *begun* |
| *bite(s)* | *bit* | *bitten* |
| *bleed(s)* | *bled* | *bled* |
| *blow(s)* | *blew* | *blown* |
| *break(s)* | *broke* | *broken* |
| *bring(s)* | *brought* | *brought* |
| *buy(s)* | *bought* | *bought* |
| *build(s)* | *built* | *built* |
| *catch(es)* | *caught* | *caught* |
| *choose(s)* | *chose* | *chosen* |

| Standard Dialect Present | Standard Dialect Simple Past | Standard Dialect Compound Past |
|---|---|---|
| come(s) | came | come |
| creep(s) | crept | crept |
| deal(s) | dealt | dealt |
| dig(s) | dug | dug |
| dive(s) | dived | dove (or dived) |
| draw(s) | drew | drawn |
| drink(s) | drank | drunk |
| drive(s) | drove | driven |
| eat(s) | ate | eaten |
| fall(s) | fell | fallen |
| feed(s) | fed | fed |
| feel(s) | felt | felt |
| fight(s) | fought | fought |
| find(s) | found | found |
| fling(s) | flung | flung |
| fly(flies) | flew | flown |
| forget(s) | forgot | forgotten |
| forgive(s) | forgave | forgiven |
| freeze(s) | froze | frozen |
| get(s) | got | got (or gotten) |
| give(s) | gave | given |
| go(es) | went | gone |
| grind(s) | ground | ground |
| grow(s) | grew | grown |
| hang(s) | hung | hung |
| hear(s) | heard | heard |
| hide(s) | hid | hidden |
| hold(s) | held | held |
| keep(s) | kept | kept |
| kneel(s) | knelt | knelt |
| know(s) | knew | known |
| lay(s) | laid | laid |
| lead(s) | led | led |
| leave(s) | left | left |
| lend(s) | lent | lent |
| lie(s) | lay | lain |
| lies(s) | lied | lied |
| light(s) | lit (or lighted) | lit (or lighted) |
| lose(s) | lost | lost |
| make(s) | made | made |
| meet(s) | met | met |
| mow(s) | mowed | mown |
| pay(s) | paid | paid |
| ride(s) | rode | ridden |
| ring(s) | rang | rung |
| rise(s) | rose | risen |

| Standard Dialect Present | Standard Dialect Simple Past | Standard Dialect Compound Past |
|---|---|---|
| run(s) | ran | run |
| say(s) | said | said |
| see(s) | saw | seen |
| sell(s) | sold | sold |
| shake(s) | shook | shaken |
| shine(s) | shone (or shined) | shone |
| shoot(s) | shot | shot |
| shrink(s) | shrank | shrunk |
| sing(s) | sang | sung |
| sink(s) | sank | sunk |
| sit(s) | sat | sat |
| slay(s) | slew | slain |
| sleep(s) | slept | slept |
| slide(s) | slid | slid |
| speak(s) | spoke | spoken |
| spend(s) | spent | spent |
| spin(s) | spun | spun |
| spring(s) | sprang | sprung |
| stand(s) | stood | stood |
| steal(s) | stole | stolen |
| stick(s) | stuck | stuck |
| sting(s) | stung | stung |
| stink(s) | stank | stunk |
| stride(s) | strode | stridden |
| strike(s) | struck | struck |
| string(s) | strung | strung |
| strive(s) | strove | striven |
| swear(s) | swore | sworn |
| sweep(s) | swept | swept |
| swell(s) | swelled | swollen |
| swim(s) | swam | swum |
| swing(s) | swang | swung |
| take(s) | took | taken |
| teach(es) | taught | taught |
| tear(s) | tore | torn |
| tell(s) | told | told |
| think(s) | thought | thought |
| throw(s) | threw | thrown |
| wake(s) | woke | waked |
| wear(s) | wore | worn |
| weave(s) | wove | woven |
| weep(s) | wept | wept |
| win(s) | won | won |
| wind(s) | wound | wound |
| wring(s) | wrang | wrung |
| write(s) | wrote | written |

In addition to these verbs, we should also look at the compound past forms of the other irregular verbs we have studied: BE, HAVE, DO, and verbs like HIT. (Notice that just as the HIT-type verbs do not change their base form for the simple past, neither do they for the compound past.)

## Standard Dialect

| Present | Simple Past | Compound Past |
|---------|-------------|---------------|
| *am, are, is* | *was, were* | *been* |
| *have, has* | *had* | *had* |
| *do, does* | *did* | *done* |
| *hit(s)* | *hit* | *hit* |

Community dialects can differ from the standard dialect in several ways:

1. Some community dialects use a different form for the compound past —sometimes it is the form that the standard dialect uses for the **simple** past.

## EXAMPLES

| Community Dialect | Standard Dialect |
|-------------------|------------------|
| I have *swam* | I have *swum* |
| he has *went* | he has *gone* |

2. Some community dialects use a different form of the helping verb HAVE.

## EXAMPLES

| Community Dialect | Standard Dialect |
|-------------------|------------------|
| I *has* swum (swam) | I *have* swum |
| he *have* gone (went) | he *has* gone |

3. Some community dialects use *done* as a helping verb instead of *have* or *has*.

## EXAMPLES

| Community Dialect | Standard Dialect |
|-------------------|------------------|
| I *done* swum (swam) | I *have* swum |
| he *done* gone (went) | he *has* gone |

To convert community dialect forms of the recent past into the standard dialect, use the appropriate form of the helping verb HAVE (either *have* or *has*) and the appropriate compound past form of the main verb (see list above).

## Summary: Recent Past of Irregular Verbs

| Community Dialect | | Standard Dialect |
|---|---|---|
| I<br>we<br>you<br>they } { has done } { swum swam | | I<br>we<br>you<br>they } *have swum* |
| he<br>she<br>it } { have done } { swum swam | | he<br>she<br>it } *has swum* |

## Recognition Drill

Underline the compound verbs in the recent past in the following sentences. Then mark SD next to each sentence that is written in the standard dialect. The first three have been done for you.

_____ 1. The sun <u>done arose</u> at 6 A.M. today.

__SD__ 2. Uncle George <u>has come</u> to visit us.

_____ 3. Uncle George <u>have told</u> us many stories.

_____ 4. Uncle George have seen several unidentified flying objects.

_____ 5. Several times ghosts have sprung out of the bedroom closet, according to Uncle

George.

_____ 6. Already the factory whistle at the Ford Motor Company has blown.

_____ 7. Seventeen pumpkins have grew in our backyard.

_____ 8. Stella has always worn her best imported cashmere sweater to church.

_____ 9. Mother and Father have begun to have more children.

_____ 10. Bill have broke more dishes than anyone else.

_____ 11. General Motors has built a new car factory in Indiana.

_____ 12. Caesar Chavez have led the boycott against lettuce.

_____ 13. Little Anthony has sung, "Why have fools fallen in love?"

_____ 14. The sun have arose at 6 A.M. today.

_____ 15. Uncle George done come to visit us.

_____ 16. Uncle George has told us many stories.

_____ 17. Uncle George has seen several unidentified flying objects.

_____ 18. Several times ghosts has sprung out of the bedroom closet, according to Uncle George.

_____ 19. Already the factory whistle at the Ford Motor Company have blown.

_____ 20. Seventeen pumpkins done growed in our backyard.

_____ 21. Stella always have wore her best imported cashmere sweater to church.

_____ 22. Mother and Father done began to have more children.

_____ 23. Bill has broken more dishes than anyone else.

_____ 24. General Motors have build a new car factory in Indiana.

_____ 25. Caesar Chavez has led the boycott against lettuce.

_____ 26. Little Anthony done sung, "Why have fools fell in love?"

_____ 27. The sun has arisen at 6 A.M. today.

_____ 28. Uncle George have came to visit us.

_____ 29. Uncle George done told us many stories.

_____ 30. Uncle George done seen several unidentified flying objects.

_____ 31. Several times ghosts done sprang out of the bedroom closet, according to Uncle George.

_____ 32. Already the factory whistle done blown at the Ford Motor Company.

_____ 33. Seventeen pumpkins have grown in our backyard.

_____ 34. Stella always done wore her best imported cashmere sweater to church.

_____ 35. Mother and Father has began to have more children.

_____36. Bill done broken more dishes than anyone else.

_____37. General Motors done built a new car factory in Indiana.

_____38. Caesar Chavez done led the boycott against lettuce.

_____39. Little Anthony have sang, "Why done fools fell in love?"

_____40. Uncle George done saw several unidentified flying objects.

_____41. Seventeen pumpkins have growed in our backyard.

_____42. Ben Franklin have say, "A penny a day keeps the doctor away."

_____43. Agnes done came a long way from St. Louis.

_____44. I have lost my hope in the future.

_____45. Sonny have run the 50-yard dash in seven seconds.

_____46. We have got to use our imagination to keep on going.

_____47. The principal have say all there is to say about education.

_____48. Ben Franklin done say, "A penny a day keeps the doctor away."

_____49. Agnes have came a long way from St. Louis.

_____50. I done lost my hope in the future.

_____51. Sonny done ran the 50-yard dash in seven seconds.

_____52. We done got to use our imagination to keep on going.

_____53. The principal done say all there is to say about education.

_____54. Ben Franklin has said, "A penny a day keeps the doctor away."

_____55. Agnes has come a long way from St. Louis.

_____56. I has lost my hope in the future.

_____57. Sonny has run the 50-yard dash in seven seconds.

_____58. We has got to use our imagination to keep on going.

_____59. The principal has said all there is to say about education.

_____60. Ben Franklin have said, "A penny a day keeps the doctor away."

## Conversion Drill

Convert each sentence that you did not mark SD in the above exercise into the standard dialect.

## Pattern Practice

Insert the appropriate standard dialect form of the recent past in the following sentences (a form of HAVE plus the compound past form of the verb in the margin). The first two have been done for you.

DRINK       1. The cows <u>have</u> <u>drunk</u> all the bear's water.

SINK       2. The bridge over troubled waters <u>has</u> <u>sunk</u>.

DRAW       3. Since June my cousin Albert _____ _____ 437 valentine cards.

SWIM       4. Thirty-two Americans, eleven Australians, and thirty-three Armenians _____ _____ the English Channel.

FLY       5. I _____ _____ in your beautiful balloon.

TEAR       6. The girl in red _____ _____ her dress.

FORGET       7. I _____ _____ to send my cousin a birthday card.

FORGIVE       8. Crystal _____ never _____ Ted for that insulting remark.

FREEZE/BREAK       9. Believe it or not, the milk _____ _____ and _____ _____ the bottle.

GET       10. I _____ _____ more optimistic about my writing.

GIVE       11. My boyfriend, Wesley, _____ _____ me a rabbit for Easter.

SHAKE       12. An earthquake _____ _____ San Francisco.

SPEAK       13. Sinclair _____ _____ to us about the New Year's Eve party.

STEAL       14. You _____ _____ my heart away.

TAKE       15. It _____ _____ me fifteen hours to tip-toe through the tulips.

WRITE       16. Audrey _____ _____ three "Dear John" letters to Tom, Dick, and Harry.

110

FALL        17. Why _____ the fool _____ in love?

SLEEP       18. I _____ always _____ through my psychology lectures.

SPEAK       19. Ralph Nader _____ _____ on our campus today.

SPEND       20. Coleman _____ _____ all his life in New York except for two years in the

            Navy.

SPIN        21. The wolf spider _____ _____ her web.

SPRING      22. The water pipe _____ _____ a bad leak.

STAND       23. For years I _____ _____ for life, liberty, and the pursuit of happiness.

STING       24. Hoards of mosquitoes _____ _____ me.

STRIVE      25. I _____ _____ to get good grades.

SWEAR       26. Gerald _____ _____ to be true to Erma.

SWEEP       27. Handsome Harry _____ _____ Alicia off her feet.

SWELL       28. My jaw _____ _____ from the toothache.

TAKE        29. I _____ _____ the subway uptown for years.

THINK       30. Heather _____ _____ of the solution to the problem.

BRING       31. We _____ _____ you this brand new fertilizer for your garden.

CHOOSE      32. King Richard III _____ _____ to sell his soul to the devil.

DRIVE       33. You _____ _____ me insane with your promises of love.

EAT         34. The praying mantis _____ _____ the spider.

FIGHT       35. The Baltimore Orioles _____ _____ their way to the pennant.

FIND        36. Dean _____ _____ that he cannot get along without Cinderella.

KNOW        37. I _____ always _____ that you are an honest man.

WEAVE       38. The Navaho Indians _____ _____ beautiful rugs.

LEAVE       39. I _____ _____ my heart in San Francisco.

SING

40. I _____ often _____ my favorite songs on the street where you live.

THROW

41. Robin Roberts _____ _____ more strike-outs than any other pitcher for the Phillies.

BECOME

42. The ugly duckling _____ _____ a handsome man.

BEGIN

43. Matthew _____ _____ to tell the time.

BITE

44. I _____ _____ into the apple that contained a worm.

BLOW

45. The strong wind _____ _____ our ship off course.

BEAR

46. LaDonna _____ _____ thirteen children.

COME

47. "You _____ _____ at last," cried Herbert.

CREEP

48. The lizard _____ _____ into my log cabin.

DRAW

49. I _____ never _____ anyone as beautiful as you.

DRINK

50. Tough Tony _____ always _____ every night until 2 A.M.

SPEAK

51. The prophet _____ _____ to her believers.

GO

52. My dog, Sherman, _____ _____ away from home.

GIVE

53. The engagement ring that Harvey _____ _____ to Geneva belongs to Harvey's mother, but Harvey's mother doesn't know Harvey _____ _____ the ring away.

SWIM

54. Lucy and Verna _____ _____ the English Channel three times.

RUN

55. At 8 A.M. I _____ often _____ after the bus that takes me to work.

SAY

56. I _____ _____ what I wish to say.

WRITE

57. Olivia _____ not _____ to me in eight weeks.

FALL

58. The needles _____ _____ off the spruce trees in Cleveland.

TAKE

59. I _____ _____ too little care of this.

SEE

60. You _____ _____ the best of times and the worst of times.

# COMPOUND VERBS: DISTANT PAST OF IRREGULAR VERBS

# 18

In the standard dialect, the distant past of irregular verbs is made by using the past form of the helping verb HAVE (*had*), together with the appropriate compound past form of the main verb. (See Chapter 17 for a list of common irregular verbs.)

EXAMPLES          Standard Dialect

I *had fought*
you *had known*
the authors *had written*

In some community dialects, the distant past, like the recent past, uses a different form of the compound past for the main verb.

EXAMPLES

Community Dialect        Standard Dialect

My nephew *had growed* taller    My nephew *had grown*.
since I saw him last.

She *had chose* him for her      She *had chosen* him.
partner.

To convert a community dialect form into the standard dialect choose the appropriate compound past form of the irregular main verb.

Summary:  Distant Past of Irregular Verbs

| Community Dialect | Standard Dialect |
|---|---|
| I<br>we<br>you  } had losed<br>he<br>they | I<br>we<br>you  } *had lost*<br>he<br>they |

## Recognition Drill

Underline the compound verbs in the distant past in the following sentences. Then mark SD next to each sentence that is written in the standard dialect. The first three have been done for you.

_____ 1. My pet sea lion <u>had swimmed</u> the entire length of the swimming pool.

__SD__ 2. I <u>had fallen</u> down.

_____ 3. Uncle George <u>had losted</u> his false teeth.

_____ 4. He said he had ate corn on the cob without them.

_____ 5. He said he had drank three glasses of red wine.

_____ 6. Later he had feeled pains in his stomach.

_____ 7. By the time three weeks had passed, my little brother Carvell had find the false teeth in the back seat of Uncle George's 1975 green Buick.

_____ 8. The teeth had catched on the chartreuse velvet upholstery.

_____ 9. Before he had leaved for home in St. Louis, he had put them back in his mouth.

_____ 10. He had fighted for what he believed in.

_____ 11. My mother had forget to tell me to pick up a jar of snails for dinner.

_____ 12. Edwin had forgiven Mattie for breaking up the romance with Leotus.

_____ 13. Rosita had gotten an unexpected surprise on her wedding day: her Aunt Theresa had flown in from Texas.

_____ 14. Aunt Theresa had bringed Pedro with her; he had growed six inches.

_____ 15. Rosita and her new husband, Rocco, had hanged the wedding pictures over the mantelpiece.

_____ 16. My pet sea lion had swam the entire length of the swimming pool.

_____ 17. I had felled down.

_____ 18. Uncle George had lost his false teeth.

_____ 19. He said he had eaten corn on the cob without them.

_____ 20. He said he had drunk three glasses of red wine.

_____ 21. Later he had felt pains in his stomach.

_____ 22. By the time three weeks had pass, my little brother Carvell had founded the false teeth in the back seat of Uncle George's 1975 green Buick.

_____ 23. The teeth had caught on the chartreuse velvet upholstery.

_____ 24. Before he had left for home in St. Louis, he had put them back in his mouth.

_____ 25. He had fought for what he believed in.

_____ 26. My mother had forgot to tell me to pick up a jar of snails for dinner.

_____ 27. Rosita had gotten an unexpected surprise on her wedding day: her Aunt Theresa had flowed in from Texas.

_____ 28. Aunt Theresa had brought Pedro with her; he had grown six inches.

_____ 29. Rosita and her new husband, Rocco, had hung the wedding pictures over the mantelpiece.

_____ 30. My pet sea lion had swum the entire length of the swimming pool.

_____ 31. I had fallen down.

_____ 32. Uncle George had lose his false teeth.

_____ 33. He said he had eat corn on the cob without them.

_____ 34. He said he had drink three glasses of red wine.

_____ 35. Later he had feel pains in his stomach.

_____ 36. By the time three weeks had passed, my little brother Carvell had found the false teeth in the back seat of Uncle George's 1975 green Buick.

_____ 37. The teeth had catch on the chartreuse velvet upholstery.

_____ 38. My mother had forgotten to tell me to pick up a jar of snails for dinner.

_____ 39. I had fell down.

_____ 40. If only I had seen you before I had seen Bernice, I would have fallen in love with

you.

## Conversion Drill

Convert each sentence that you did not mark SD in the above exercise into the standard dialect in distant past time.

## Pattern Practice

Insert the appropriate standard dialect form of the distant past in the following sentences. The first two have been done for you.

BEGIN      1. Billy Joe <u>had</u> <u>begun</u> to tell me the story of her life.

BREAK      2. "Love Story" <u>had</u> <u>broken</u> her heart.

BRING      3. Ed _____ _____ up unpleasant memories.

BUILD      4. We _____ _____ a whole life together.

BURST      5. Eric the Beast _____ _____ all the balloons at the office party.

CATCH      6. Herman _____ _____ fleas from his Doberman pinscher.

CHOOSE      7. At the dance, Barbara _____ _____ not to dance with Ken.

COME      8. The telephone bill _____ _____ when she couldn't pay for it.

DIG      9. After the blast they _____ _____ their way out of the coal mine.

DRAW      10. I _____ _____ her to me like a magnet.

DRINK      11. My pet bear Smokey _____ _____ all the beer.

DRIVE      12. We _____ _____ the teacher mad.

EAT      13. The nutritionist scolded Rhonda because she _____ _____ nothing but

pretzels and potato chips while she was pregnant.

FALL      14. Steve _____ _____ in love with girls with big feet.

FEEL      15. Steve _____ always _____ at home with girls with big feet.

FIND/STEAL 16. By the time I_____ _____my one true love, Benjamin_____

_____ her.

FLY 17. Cecile_____ _____the 747 supersonic jet to Indonesia.

GIVE 18. The nurse_____ _____Peter a pill.

GO 19. I_____ _____to South America to visit my aunt.

GET 20. Leneen_____ _____sick.

HOLD 21. Pam_____ _____Nora's baby while she went grocery shopping.

KNOW 22. Ronald_____ _____all along that Delia would leave him.

LEAVE 23. Why_____Emily_____Edgar at Edwina's?

MAKE 24. Last Sunday Trixie_____ _____hot buttered pop corn and chocolate

cake for breakfast.

RIDE 25. The Lone Ranger and Hopalong Cassidy_____ _____white horses.

RUN 26. Our star halfback_____ _____eighty yards before she was tackled.

SAY 27. Jean_____ _____evil things.

SEE 28. I_____ _____ the film three times.

SEEK 29. Einstein_____ _____the answer to the difficult mathematics problem.

SELL 30. Aaron_____ _____his red raccoon overcoat that had kept him warm for

many years.

SHINE 31. Our Christmas tree lights_____ _____ in the window.

SHOW 32. I_____ _____him the way.

SING 33. My three sisters_____ _____at the concert in Atlanta.

SIT 34. By the time the concert was over we_____ _____through three hours.

SLEEP 35. Some of the audience_____ _____through three hours.

SPEAK 36. Nobody_____ _____to Darla during the whole dance.

STING 37. The bee_____ _____Della.

STICK  38. Thurston's car_____ _____ in the mud.

SWEAR  39. He_____ _____ not to drive in the rain.

TAKE  40. It_____ _____ Omar a long time to learn English.

TEACH  41. I_____ _____ my rabbit how to type.

TEAR  42. Monroe_____ _____ a hole in his sweater during the football game.

TELL  43. Terence_____ _____ Tammy too many tall tales.

THINK  44. Thelma_____ _____ that Thurgood would no longer be part of her life.

AWAKE  45. Bridget_____ _____ to thoughts of love.

WEAR  46. Delores_____ _____ the same dress to the prom that Ivy_____

_____

WIN  47. Ohio State_____ _____ the game.

WRITE  48. Oscar_____ _____ Dido a letter.

BLEED  49. My foot_____ _____ for three days.

BREAK  50. The movers_____ _____ all the new imported china.

CHOOSE  51. My sister_____ _____ to become a doctor.

CAUGHT  52. In northern Minnesota I_____ _____ three bass, two white fish, and seven crabs.

DIG  53. The steam shovels_____ _____ the basement for a new skyscraper.

DRIVE  54. Last year I_____ _____ 4,000 miles through New England.

FEED  55. I_____ _____ the chickens some creamed cottage cheese.

FLY  56. In my dream I_____ _____ to the moon.

HOLD  57. Terrell_____ _____ up my part of the agreement.

KNOW  58. I_____ _____ Cindy, my bridesmaid, for three years.

SPEAK  59. Last year the Lord_____ _____ to Lucille.

STEAL 60. Roscoe _____ _____ more bases in his career than any other player.

STRIKE 61. I _____ _____ my name from the list of active club members.

TEACH 62. My teachers _____ _____ me everything I knew about philosophy.

WEAR 63. Last year I _____ _____ out my Levi trousers.

WRITE 64. Before 1590 Shakespeare _____ _____ two plays.

MEAN 65. Augusta _____ not _____ to be so insulting in the store.

MEET 66. Murray _____ _____ his wife at the supermarket near the frozen foods.

SAY 67. Yesterday she _____ _____ many complimentary things to me.

SHAKE 68. My father _____ _____ all the rugs in the house.

SINK 69. One of the Pacific Islands _____ _____ during the earthquake.

FALL 70. While reaching for her glass of milk and peanut butter cookies, Carol's

mother _____ _____ off the couch.

FIGHT 71. All the boys on the block _____ _____ in the war in Viet-Nam.

FORGET 72. I _____ _____ how beautiful your sister, Dellie, was.

FREEZE 73. My aunt _____ _____ six dozen cans of orange juice to last through the

winter.

BECAME 74. I _____ _____ bored in my old job doing the same thing again and again.

BECOME/BEAT 75. It _____ _____ quite apparent that I was no longer in love after I _____

_____ her at ping pong twenty-seven times.

EAT 76. My pet chameleon _____ _____ so little that he died.

COME 77. Robert and Ronald _____ _____ 6,000 miles to visit us.

GO 78. They _____ already _____ when we got there.

SEE 79. I _____ _____ Velveeta before she went to Trinidad.

GIVE 80. I _____ _____ you my heart and you have made me jealous.

119

## Conversion Exercise

In the following sentences circle verbs in the distant past written in community dialects.

1. At first, we thought Albert had catched some kind of disease.
2. He had creeped into the kitchen looking like he had drank too much.
3. Then, he had bit my sister, had broke a lamp, and had flied out of the room before we knew what was happening.
4. He had shook us all by his sudden strange behavior.
5. I had saw him act a little crazy before, but nothing like this.
6. After I had catched him in the dining room, and had saw how he had tore up the curtains, I knew we needed help.
7. By the time we got to Dr. Wilson's office, Albert had fell into a sound sleep.
8. In the car he had sinked down on the seat and had lied quietly and, by the time I carried him into the office, he was out cold.
9. After he had went over Albert for a minute, Dr. Jones made a one-word diagnosis.
10. It was only when the doctor had speaked that magic word that I understood what had happened.
11. Albert had took catnip.

Now rewrite these sentences using the distant past in the standard dialect. Use paragraph form.

_____

_____

_____

_____

_____

_____

_____

_____

_____

_____

_____

_____

_____

_____

## Review Exercise

In the last two chapters we have studied the distant and recent past of irregular verbs. Underline these verb forms in the following sentences. Identify which sentences contain distant past or recent past forms by placing DP or RP next to each sentence. The first two have been done for you.

<u> RP </u> 1. I <u>have been</u> a student at the university for four years.

<u> DP </u> 2. I <u>had been</u> a student at the university for four years.

_____ 3. I had taken engineering courses before I transferred to nursing.

_____ 4. I have taken engineering courses.

_____ 5. Thomas had bought Gillette After-shave Lotion for three years.

_____ 6. Thomas has bought Gillette After-shave Lotion for three years.

_____ 7. Percy and Amelia have brought mozzarella cheese for the pizza.

_____ 8. Percy and Amelia had brought mozzarella cheese for the pizza.

_____ 9. Sylvester had thought hard about the problem.

_____ 10. Sylvester has thought hard about the problem.

_____ 11. Spencer had wept about life.

_____ 12. Spencer has wept about life.

_____ 13. Claudette had knelt to pray.

_____ 14. Claudette has knelt to pray.

_____ 15. The cat had slept on my bed.

_____ 16. The cat has slept on my bed.

_____ 17. Willard had drunk alone in a saloon for many years.

_____ 18. Willard has drunk alone in a saloon for many years.

_____ 19. The cow had won a blue ribbon at the fair.

_____ 20. The cow has won blue ribbons at the fair.

_____ 21. Although I had seen the movie before, I enjoyed seeing it again.

_____ 22. Since I had never gone to Europe, I went on a tour to the Canary Islands.

_____ 23. I forgot that I had forgiven her.

_____ 24. I know that Jesus Christ has come to save the world.

_____ 25. I saw your mother's brother before your mother's brother had seen me.

_____ 26. If I had known that you were there, I would not have left until I finished my

beer.

_____ 27. I have known you since we were both in second grade.

_____ 28. Basil had spoken to the president of RCA about my chances for employment in

their sales' division.

_____ 29. I have often sung songs while taking a shower or bath.

_____ 30. I had never written a letter to my grandfather.

_____ 31. The sun had risen at 8:02 yesterday.

_____ 32. It has taken me three years to understand how to operate a camera.

_____ 33. Cornell has never shrunk from responsibility.

_____ 34. Ike and Tina Turner have sung at the music hall.

_____ 35. We had not eaten dinner before seeing the show last night.

_____ 36. I have forgotten what your sister's last name is.

_____ 37. Elizabeth has fallen in love with Timothy.

_____ 38. Musicians have given the world soul.

_____ 39. I have eaten alone downtown many times.

_____ 40. I had lost my brand new Parker green and white jotter pen at the library.

# COMPOUND VERBS: PRESENT PROGRESSIVE

# 19

In the next few chapters we will be studying another type of compound verb —the progressive. A progressive verb can be used to show an ongoing action or state, either in the past or the present.

EXAMPLES                              Standard Dialect

       I *am singing* in the college choir. (Present Progressive)
       Last year I *was singing* in the
          college choir.         (Past Progressive)

The present progressive sometimes is used for future time, especially when there is a time word or phrase included in the sentence.

EXAMPLES                              Standard Dialect

       Tomorrow I *am starting* a new job.
       Next week they *are going* to Florida.

In the standard dialect, you form the present progressive in the following way:

1. Use the present forms of the helping verb BE (I *am*; you *are*; he, she, it *is*; we *are*; you *are*; they *are*).
2. Add *ing* to the base of the main verb (walk*ing*, sing*ing*, read*ing*, etc).

EXAMPLES                              Standard Dialect

| **Singular** | **Plural** |
|---|---|
| I *am* walk*ing* | we *are* walk*ing* |
| you *are* walk*ing* | you *are* walk*ing* |
| he, she, it *is* walk*ing* | they *are* walk*ing* |

With a few verbs you have to double the final consonant before adding *ing*. You do this whenever the verb ends in a single consonant preceded by a single vowel, except when the consonant is *l*, *r*, or *w*.

EXAMPLES                          Standard Dialect

|          |            |
|----------|------------|
| plan     | pla*nn*ing |
| hit      | hi*tt*ing  |
| swim     | swi*mm*ing |

but:

|          |             |
|----------|-------------|
| show     | sho*w*ing   |
| answer   | answe*r*ing |
| travel   | trave*l*ing |

When the base form of the verb ends in *e*, you drop the *e* and add *ing*.

EXAMPLES                          Standard Dialect

|          |           |
|----------|-----------|
| skat*e*  | skat*ing* |
| tak*e*   | tak*ing*  |
| dat*e*   | dat*ing*  |

In some community dialects, the present progressive form of the verb is made in several different ways:

1. By using BE without change in places where the standard dialect uses other forms of BE.

EXAMPLES

| Community Dialect | Standard Dialect |
|-------------------|------------------|
| I *be* going      | I *am* going     |
| he *be* going     | he *is* going    |
| they *be* going   | they *are* going |

2. By using the *ing* form of the main verb and by using *is* where the standard dialect used the various irregular forms of BE.

EXAMPLES

| Community Dialect  | Standard Dialect    |
|--------------------|---------------------|
| I *is* runn*ing*   | I *am* runn*ing*    |
| he *is* runn*ing*  | he *is* runn*ing*   |
| they *is* runn*ing*| they *are* runn*ing*|

3. By using simply the *ing* form of the main verb without using any form of BE.

EXAMPLES

| Community Dialect | Standard Dialect |
|-------------------|------------------|
| I *going*         | I *am* going     |
| he *going*        | he *is* going    |
| they *going*      | they *are* going |

4. By using the base form or an *ed* form of the main verb where the standard dialect uses the *ing* form.

EXAMPLES

| Community Dialect | Standard Dialect |
|---|---|
| I is *walk* to school tomorrow | I am walk*ing* to school tomorrow |
| they is walk*ed* to school tomorrow | they are walk*ing* to school tomorrow |

### Summary:   Present Progressive

| Community Dialect | Standard Dialect |
|---|---|
| I you we they he she it the child the children } be walking | I *am walking* |
| I you we they he she it the child the children } is { walking walk walked | you we they the children } *are walking* |
| I you we they he she it the child the children } walking | he she it the child } *is walking* |

125

## Recognition Drill

Underline the compound verbs in the present progressive in the following sentences. Then mark SD next to each sentence written in the standard dialect. The first three have been done for you.

_____ 1. I <u>be dating</u> boys.

_____ 2. I <u>crying</u>.

__SD__ 3. I <u>am going</u> to the movies tonight.

_____ 4. I am eating an orange.

_____ 5. They are running home.

_____ 6. Seymour is cooking chicken.

_____ 7. Stan, Marshall, and Lottie is eating fried chicken.

_____ 8. They also eating salad.

_____ 9. They are getting some Alka Seltzer.

_____ 10. I is speeding down the boulevard.

_____ 11. The cop chasing me.

_____ 12. He is flashing his big blue lights.

_____ 13. He asking for my driver's license.

_____ 14. I is having trouble finding it.

_____ 15. We being ethical.

_____ 16. She be getting paid well for that job.

_____ 17. Bruno is barking all night.

_____ 18. I be singing in the church choir.

_____ 19. I dreaming of a love affair with my doctor.

_____ 20. I am having trouble with my car. What a lemon!

_____ 21. Detroit is having a lot of snow lately.

_____ 22. Joe is going on a diet every Monday, and every Friday he is going off the diet.

_____ 23. Joe is losing weight.

_____ 24. Fay always having a party.

_____ 25. The baby is crying all night.

_____ 26. His daddy changing his diaper, while his mother sleeping.

_____ 27. Fou-Fou is outgrowing his name.

_____ 28. Fou-Fou getting too big.

_____ 29. Now we are calling Fou-Fou by his right name.

_____ 30. Now we be calling him Frank.

_____ 31. She is always stuttering when she has to talk in class.

_____ 32. I be going to the university.

_____ 33. I am taking English 130.

_____ 34. I am going to the library to take out books for my history term paper.

_____ 35. James be going to work every day.

_____ 36. I be sick every Tuesday.

_____ 37. My brothers are both hoping to become doctors.

_____ 38. We are planning a vacation in Europe.

_____ 39. Melanie's baby be crying all the time, especially at night.

_____ 40. My father is always fixing something around the house.

_____ 41. The dogs are barking at the mailman.

_____ 42. Philip George is ask for more money.

_____ 43. The dentist is demanding his money.

_____ 44. We all is need more money.

_____ 45. Edgar Allen Poe is attempted to frighten us in his stories.

_____ 46. What is really scared me is my exam on Edgar Allen Poe.

_____ 47. I am studying hard for my exam.

_____ 48. I am try not to fall on my face.

_____ 49. George is going to discuss the success of freshmen in his class.

_____ 50. Hank is trying to cross the bridge during high water.

_____ 51. What is our hound dog looking for under that tree?

_____ 52. The way he is dig he must smell a rabbit.

_____ 53. The secretary is stapling together the report.

_____ 54. The boss is sended it to Washington.

_____ 55. The fisherman is catch mostly perch.

## Conversion Drill

Convert each sentence that you did not mark SD in the above exercise into the standard dialect, using the present progressive.

## Pattern Practice

Complete the following sentences to make them present progressive in the standard dialect. Insert the appropriate form of the helping verb BE and the *ing* form of the main verb (whose base is given in the margin beside each sentence). The first two have been done for you.

RUN   1. He <u>is</u> <u>running</u>.

GO   2. I <u>am</u> <u>going</u> to WSU.

STUDY  3. My brother _____ _____ medicine.

WORK  4. He _____ _____ at Ford Motor Company.

EAT   5. He _____ _____ cherry pie.

GO   6. They _____ _____ to shop tomorrow.

DO   7. They _____ _____ the Mexican hat dance.

SWIM      8. They _____ _____ in the meet on Saturday.

STUDY      9. They _____ _____ psychology together.

CRAM      10. I _____ _____ for the test tomorrow.

BUY      11. I _____ _____ a new Buick.

GET      12. I _____ _____ ready for a party this afternoon.

MAKE      13. I _____ _____ a cake.

PLAN      14. We _____ _____ to have about seventy-five people.

SERVE      15. We _____ _____ cake and coffee.

FORM      16. Our Y.M.C.A. _____ _____ a swimming team.

HOPE      17. We _____ _____ to beat the crocodile.

COME      18. The moving men _____ _____ today.

MOVE      19. We _____ _____ to a new neighborhood.

LOOK      20. I _____ _____ forward to it.

CLIMB      21. Fourteen squirrels _____ _____ the tree.

STARE      22. Fifteen beavers _____ _____ at them from the other tree.

THROW      23. One squirrel _____ _____ an apple at a beaver in the other tree.

HOPE      24. The squirrel _____ _____ to start a courtship with the beaver.

PLAN      25. We _____ _____ to give them all new apples.

EXPECT      26. I _____ _____ you to be on time.

NOTICE      27. We _____ _____ more and more men with very long hair.

ATTEND      28. Marcus _____ _____ the University of Notre Dame.

EXAMINE      29. The doctor _____ _____ the patient for measles.

ANSWER      30. I _____ _____ all of Hazel's telephone messages.

## Conversion Exercise

In the following sentences circle present progressive verbs written in community dialects:

1. I planning to buy a new car.
2. I looking for a Jaguar XKE.
3. My father be trying to tell me I cannot afford it.
4. My brother already buying a Cadillac Eldorado.
5. My father be objecting because it going to cost too much.
6. But I be work at a factory and I saving all my money.
7. My father be complain that I is paying too much in back debts, and I is buying too much on credit.
8. But I trying to convince my father otherwise.
9. We is having a man-to-man talk about it tonight and I hoping to win the argument.

Now rewrite these sentences using the present progressive in the standard dialect. Use paragraph form.

_____

_____

_____

_____

_____

_____

_____

_____

_____

_____

_____

_____

# COMPOUND VERBS: PAST PROGRESSIVE

**20**

In the standard dialect, you form the past progressive like the present progressive, except that you use the past forms of the helping verb BE instead of the present forms.

EXAMPLES                           Standard Dialect

| Singular | Plural |
|----------|--------|
| yesterday I *was* work*ing* in the garden | we *were* work*ing* |
| yesterday you *were* work*ing* in the garden | you *were* work*ing* |
| yesterday he, she, it *was* work*ing* in the garden | they *were* work*ing* |

In some community dialects, the past progressive uses the forms for BE that we described in Chapter 6.

EXAMPLES

| Community Dialect | Standard Dialect |
|-------------------|------------------|
| I *were* work*ing* | I *was* work*ing* |
| you *was* work*ing* | you *were* work*ing* |

Some community dialects use the base form or an *ed* form of the main verb where the standard dialect uses the *ing* form.

EXAMPLES

| Community Dialect | Standard Dialect |
|-------------------|------------------|
| I *were* (*was*) work | I *was* work*ing* |
| they *were* (*was*) work*ed* | they *were* work*ing* |

## Summary: Past Progressive

| Community Dialect | Standard Dialect |
|---|---|
| I you we they he she it the child the children } { were was } { walking walk walked | I he she it the child } *was* walk*ing*<br><br>we you they the children } *were* walk*ing* |

## Recognition Drill

Underline compound verbs in the past progressive in the following sentences. Then mark SD next to each sentence written in the standard dialect. The first three have been done for you.

<u>SD</u>   1. I <u>was</u> <u>going</u> to the store when I saw Bill.

_____  2. I <u>were</u> <u>beginning</u> my music lesson when the phone rang.

_____  3. We <u>was</u> <u>driving</u> our new Buick Electra.

_____  4. Armand were repairing the T.V.

_____  5. Boyd were crying.

_____  6. George was boiling potatoes.

_____  7. The university was enrolling students in a special project program.

_____  8. The U.C.L.A. basketball team was dominating the N.C.A.A. finals.

_____  9. Spiro and Frank was behaving like strangers.

_____  10. The A & P was selling lamb chops for nine dollars a pound.

_____  11. The prisoners of war was returning.

_____  12. The war in Indochina were still going on after the truce.

_____ 13. At Passover Aunt Rachel was coming for a visit.

_____ 14. The mayor announced that American cities was decaying.

_____ 15. Hugh was announcing a change in admission policies.

_____ 16. Our football team were shaping up for the title game.

_____ 17. Hector was proposing a meaningful relationship.

_____ 18. Jennifer and Jasper were buying a 158-year-old house.

_____ 19. I was laughing at the performing seals in the aquarium.

_____ 20. The Boston Bruins was flying the airplane to Boston.

_____ 21. All day yesterday the geese flying.

_____ 22. All last week the coach was pick the men for the team.

_____ 23. The altar boys were lighted the candles.

_____ 24. The people were come to hear the new minister.

_____ 25. The circus performing all last week.

_____ 26. The car was go ninety miles per hour.

_____ 27. The police were chasing it at speeds up to ninety miles per hour.

_____ 28. The engineers were rebuilding the town after the earthquake.

_____ 29. During his whole lifetime, the doctor curing sick people.

_____ 30. He was treating poor people for free.

_____ 31. He was also give them free medicine.

_____ 32. The girls were spend too much on cigarettes.

_____ 33. They were smoking a pack a day.

_____ 34. I felt I was suffocate when I was in the room where they were smoking.

_____ 35. The gas station attendant was overcharging me.

_____ 36. Last fall many students preparing to study law.

_____ 37. They were practicing writing.

_____ 38. They were study law cases.

_____ 39. Day after day she was attempted to cook for a family of eleven.

_____ 40. While the children were crying and fighting, she was peeling potatoes.

_____ 41. At this time last spring the tulips blooming.

_____ 42. The robins were flying into our neighborhood.

_____ 43. The pigeons were nesting on our roofs and in our trees.

_____ 44. They bothering me with their noise all day yesterday.

_____ 45. Last semester while he taking eight subjects, he flunking four.

_____ 46. He was trying to take too many subjects at once.

_____ 47. The neighborhood association was complaining that the factory was emitting fly

ash.

_____ 48. Yesterday she was laugh; today she is cry.

_____ 49. When he was working in the factory, he was bored with his job.

_____ 50. Last Saturday night Lavoreen and Louis living it up at the club.

## Conversion Drill

Convert each sentence that you did not mark SD in the above exercise into the standard dialect using the past progressive.

## Pattern Practice

Complete the following sentences to make them past progressive in the standard dialect. Insert the appropriate form of the helping verb BE and the _ing_ form of the main verb (whose base is given in the margin beside each sentence). The first two have been done for you.

RUST        1. Our car  <u>was</u> <u>rusting</u>.

SWIM        2. The boys  <u>were</u> <u>swimming</u>.

COOK        3. My mother _____  _____ .

EAT  4. The whole family _____ _____ pizza.

PET  5. Barth _____ _____ his dog, Bartholomew.

FORM  6. Manuel and Marvin _____ _____ a rock and roll band.

PUT  7. Debra and Mary Jane _____ _____ on a play.

DO  8. Myrtle _____ _____ exercises at 7 A.M.

PREPARE  9. Sharon _____ _____ a tuna fish supper.

DRINK  10. I _____ _____ a Coke.

TALK  11. You _____ _____ to Maria.

STAND  12. Paul _____ _____ on his head and getting lots of laughs.

REPAIR  13. The man _____ _____ Alva's glasses.

DANCE  14. Ed and Diane _____ _____ together.

REPAIR  15. Tom's father _____ _____ the broken radio.

GET  16. We _____ _____ together with all the people in the neighborhood until May.

OFFEND  17. Stephen _____ _____ all the guests with his jokes.

RELEASE  18. Larry's little brother _____ _____ all the chickens from the barnyard.

CARRY  19. We _____ _____ our camping equipment all through northern California.

BREAK  20. Stanley and Randolph _____ _____ all track records for the 440-yard run.

## Conversion Exercise

In the following sentences circle past progressive verbs written in community dialects.

1. Mario were playing the saxophone in a rhythm and blues band.
2. His girlfriend, Ann, were listen.
3. All the people in the hall was dancing, and even the lead singer, Larry, were having a good time.
4. After about four hours, people was discover that Mario and Ann were cool.
5. People was shouting: "Come on, Mario, dig it, let the good times roll."
6. Mario were smiling and Ann were grinning, and Larry were grooving.
7. Everybody were having such a beautiful time.
8. But Mario and Ann and Larry was growing tired.

Now rewrite these sentences using the past progressive in the standard dialect. Use paragraph form.

_____

_____

_____

_____

_____

_____

_____

_____

_____

_____

# OTHER HELPING VERBS (MODALS) 21

There are nine helping verbs in English that are unusual because their form never changes. They are always used together with the base form of the main verb. These nine helping verbs, called modals, are CAN, WILL, SHALL, MAY, COULD, WOULD, SHOULD, MIGHT, MUST.

Here are some examples of sentences in which these modal helping verbs are used with the base form of the main verb.

EXAMPLES                    Standard Dialect

I *can do* that assignment easily.
I *will help* you fix the engine tomorrow.
We *will finish* this chapter tomorrow.
I *could go* to the party if I had a new dress.
If I were you, I *would buy* that ring.
He *should go* to the doctor about his sore throat.

Yes, you *may buy* the book. (Note: in most community dialects, and even in the standard dialect when used in casual conversation, it is much more common to use *can buy* than *may buy*.)

He *might come* to class today.

You *must tell* me the truth.

Notice that these nine verbs have properties that distinguish them from all other verbs:

1. They only have one form, the base form. They do not add an *s* in the third person singular, and they have no past and present forms.
2. They all can express future time of some sort.
   a. WILL and SHALL both express an intention to do something in the future (though *shall* is rare in American dialects).

EXAMPLES                    Standard Dialect

Tomorrow I *shall go* to the store.

Tomorrow my brother *will come* home for a visit.

   b. MIGHT and sometimes MAY express the possibility of something happening in the future.

EXAMPLES                    Standard Dialect

Tomorrow I *might bake* an apple pie.

He *may want* that last piece of pizza.

   c. MAY, and often CAN, express permission to do something in the future.

EXAMPLES                    Standard Dialect

Yes, you *may go* to the movies this afternoon.

Yes, you *can buy* that new coat.

   d. COULD, WOULD, and MIGHT usually express possible action occurring in the past or the future. That action is usually dependent on something else taking place first, and for this reason COULD, WOULD, and MIGHT are often preceded or followed by an *if* or *when* clause. (See Section V, Chapter 3, for an explanation of clauses.)

EXAMPLES                    Standard Dialect

I *could go* to Hawaii [if I had the money].

If you bought the tickets, I *would take* you to the football game.

[When you ask me nicely], I just *might help* you with your homework.

When I was a teenager, I *could smoke* at home if I wanted to.

e. CAN expresses the ability to do something, both in the present and in the future.

EXAMPLES                    Standard Dialect

I *can play* the piano very well.
I *can go* with you tomorrow.

Because modal phrases like *could have* and *would have* are not always pronounced the way they are written, students often spell them in an unconventional manner.

EXAMPLES    Unconventional Spelling        Conventional Spelling

I *could of* won the prize.
                                            I *could have* won the prize.
I *coulda* won the prize.

## Summary: Past Modals

| Unconventional Spelling | Conventional Spelling |
|---|---|
| I { could of / coulda } gone. | I *could have* gone. |
| I { should of / shoulda } gone. | I *should have* gone. |
| I { would of / woulda } gone. | I *would have* gone. |
| I { might of / mighta } gone. | I *might have* gone. |
| I { must of / musta } gone. | I *must have* gone. |

## Recognition Drill

The sentences below have modal verbs in conventional and unconventional spelling. Some have community dialect forms of main verbs. Underline the verbs and mark SD, CS next to each sentence that has standard dialect verb forms and conventional spelling. The first three have been done for you.

_____ 1. We could of gone to the movies last night.

SD, CS 2. Tom should have begun his trip to China earlier.

_____ 3. The ice musta broken under the weight of the car.

_____ 4. Gertrude might have told it all.

_____ 5. Muriel and Maurice musta gone all the way to San José.

_____ 6. Clotilda complained that Cosmo should have come later.

_____ 7. Alphonso musta fell for Alma.

_____ 8. Ramona musta sayed to Reginald that it was all over.

_____ 9. Without the life jackets, we woulda sunk.

_____ 10. With money I woulda done many lovely things.

_____ 11. We coulda gone to the movies last night.

_____ 12. Tom shoulda began his trip to China earlier.

_____ 13. The ice must of broke under the weight of the car.

_____ 14. Gertrude mighta telled it all.

_____ 15. Muriel and Maurice must have gone all the way to San José.

_____ 16. Clotilda complained that Cosmo shoulda come later.

_____ 17. Alphonso must have fallen for Alma.

_____ 18. Ramona must have said to Reginald that it was all over.

_____ 19. Without the life jackets, we would have sank.

_____ 20. If I had money, I would have many lovely things.

_____ 21. We could have gone to the movies last night.

_____ 22. Tom should of begun his trip to China earlier.

_____ 23. The ice must have broken under the weight of the car.

_____ 24. Gertrude might of told it all.

_____ 25. Muriel and Maurice must of went all the way to San José.

_____ 26. Clotilda complained that Cosmo should of come later.

_____ 27. Alphonso must of fell for Alma.

_____ 28. Ramona must of said to Reginald that it was all over.

_____ 29. Without the life jackets, we would have sunk.

_____ 30. With money I woulda did many lovely things.

_____ 31. Without the life jackets, we would of sank.

_____ 32. If I had studied for the exam, I coulda passed it.

_____ 33. If you had fed the dog, he would have left the candy alone.

_____ 34. I mighta come over last night if you had asked me.

_____ 35. I must have eaten the whole jar of peanuts.


## Conversion Drill

Convert each sentence that you did not mark SD, CS in the above exercises into the standard dialect in conventional spelling.


## Pattern Practice

In the following sentences insert the modal given in the margin together with the appropriate form of HAVE to form the modal recent past. The first two have been done for you.

WOULD     1. If the nurse had taken the patient's temperature, she <u>would</u> <u>have</u> detected that he

was sick.

SHOULD     2. We <u>should</u> <u>have</u> taken her to the hospital.

MUST     3. If surgical instruments were used, they _____ _____ been sterilized.

MIGHT     4. The driver of the vehicle _____ _____ been drunk.

MUST     5. Ariadne _____ _____ turned into a spider.

COULD     6. If she had, she _____ _____ caught me in her web.

SHOULD     7. You _____ _____ come to the party!

WOULD     8. We _____ _____ given you a lot to eat and drink.

MIGHT 9. If we had planned the house well, we_____ _____included stairs to the

second floor.

MUST 10. We_____ _____been out of our minds.

COULD 11. At least we_____ _____built a ladder.

SHOULD 12. The architect_____ _____warned us.

WOULD 13. If the police had seen him, he_____ _____been arrested for speeding.

MIGHT 14. Then the accident_____ _____been prevented.

MUST 15. He_____ _____been driving over eighty miles per hour.

COULD 16. At this speed he_____ _____overturned.

SHOULD 17. If she didn't catch the chicken pox, she_____ _____.

WOULD 18. Ludovico_____ _____died for Countess Genevra.

MIGHT 19. The flowers_____ _____bloomed if you had watered them.

MUST 20. The King of Tunis_____ _____heard about Ludovico.

COULD 21. He_____ _____cut off his head, but he didn't.

SHOULD 22. Perhaps he_____ _____because Ludovico was his competition.

WOULD 23. Marjean_____ _____loved the trip to Disneyland.

MIGHT 24. There, she_____ _____forgotten her troubles.

MUST 25. Eve_____ _____tempted Adam.

COULD 26. He_____ _____resisted her, but he didn't.

SHOULD 27. Adam_____ _____refused the apple.

WOULD 28. Then Eve_____ _____sinned all alone.

MIGHT 29. If only Adam and Eve hadn't sinned, what_____ _____happened to the

human race?

MUST 30. She_____ _____been a beautiful woman.

## Conversion Exercise

In the following sentences circle compound modal verb forms written in unconventional spelling and community dialects.

1. We could of been friends with Malvina.
2. But Malvina shoulda been more friendly to us.
3. She mighta invite us over to her house for apple cider and ginger snaps on Halloween.
4. We woulda gone too, but we didn't get an invitation.
5. Malvina musta been feeling depressed that night.
6. What a great party that coulda been.
7. I woulda gotten dressed up as one of the three bears.
8. Leonard coulda worn a Cinderella costume.
9. And Malvina mighta been Little Red Riding Hood.
10. We shoulda had a Halloween party.

Now rewrite these sentences using compound modal verb forms in the standard dialect. Use paragraph form.

_____

_____

_____

_____

_____

_____

_____

_____

_____

_____

_____

# *USED TO* AND MODAL SUBSTITUTES

**22**

There are several two- and three-word verbs that are often not pronounced the way they are written, and therefore, students often spell them in an unconventional manner. Some of these also have community dialect variations in their formation. These two- and three-word verbs are *used to, have to, have got to, be able to, ought to,* and *be supposed to.* All of them except *used to* can be used as substitutes for modals.

1. *Used to* is often pronounced *use to* or *useta,* and therefore is sometimes spelled that way.

EXAMPLE

| Unconventional Spelling | Conventional Spelling |
| --- | --- |
| I $\left\{\begin{array}{l} \textit{use to} \\ \textit{useta} \end{array}\right\}$ go to school. | I *used to* go to school. |

Notice that *used to* plus the base form of the main verb is often a substitute for the simple past or the distant past.

EXAMPLES

Standard Dialect, Conventional Spelling

I *went* to school before I started working.
I *had gone* to school before I started working.
I *used to* go to school before I started working.

2. *Have to* and *has to* are often pronounced *hafta, havta,* and *hasta* and therefore are sometimes spelled that way.

EXAMPLES

| Unconventional Spelling | Conventional Spelling |
| --- | --- |
| I $\left\{\begin{array}{l} \textit{hafta} \\ \textit{havta} \end{array}\right\}$ go to school. | I *have to* go to school. |
| He *hasta* go to school. | He *has to* go to school. |

Notice that *have to* and *has to* can substitute for the modal *must*.

EXAMPLES

### Standard Dialect, Conventional Spelling

I *must* go    to school.     He *must*   go to school.
I *have to* go to school.     He *has to* go to school.

In some community dialects *has to* is used instead of *have to* and *have to* is used instead of *has to*. (The rules for using *has* and *have* are the same as those we described in Chapter 7.)

EXAMPLES

| Community Dialect,<br>Conventional Spelling | Standard Dialect,<br>Conventional Spelling |
|---|---|
| I *has to* go. | I *have to* go. |
| He *have to* go. | He *has to* go. |

| Community Dialect,<br>Unconventional Spelling | Standard Dialect,<br>Unconventional Spelling |
|---|---|
| I *hasta* go. | I $\left\{ \begin{array}{l} hafta \\ havta \end{array} \right\}$ go. |
| He $\left\{ \begin{array}{l} hafta \\ hasta \end{array} \right\}$ go. | He *hasta* go. |

3. *Have got to* and *has got to* are often pronounced *have gotta* and *has gotta*, and therefore are sometimes spelled that way.

EXAMPLES

| Unconventional Spelling | Conventional Spelling |
|---|---|
| $\left\{ \begin{array}{l} \text{I } have \\ I've \end{array} \right\}$ *gotta* go to school. | $\left\{ \begin{array}{l} \text{I } have \\ I've \end{array} \right\}$ *got to* go to school. |

Notice that *have got to*, like *have to*, can substitute for the modal MUST.

EXAMPLES

### Standard Dialect, Conventional Spelling

I *must*      go to school.
I *have got to* go to school.

## Summary: *USED TO* and Modal Substitutes

| Community Dialect, Unconventional Spelling | Standard Dialect, Unconventional Spelling | Community Dialect, Conventional Spelling | Standard Dialect, Conventional Spelling |
|---|---|---|---|
| I { use to / useta go } go | | I *used to* go | |
| I { hafta / havta } go  he hasta go | | I *have to* go  he *has to* go | |
| I gotta go  he gotta go | I have gotta go  he has gotta go | I got to go  he got to go | I *have got to* go  he *has got to* go |
| | | I be able to go  I able to go  I is able to go | I *am able to* go |
| I { oughta / oughter } go | | I *ought to* go | |
| I be suppose to go  I suppose to go  I is suppose to go | I am suppose to go | I be supposed to go  I supposed to go  I is supposed to go | I *am supposed to* go |

## Recognition Drill

Underline the modal substitutes in the following sentences. Then mark SD next to each sentence written in the standard dialect, conventional spelling. The first three have been done for you.

USED TO

__SD__ 1. We <u>used to love</u> ice cream.

_____ 2. Joanie <u>useta go</u> with Ronald.

_____ 3. Three years ago I <u>use to hate</u> school.

_____ 4. Parnell useta play basketball.

_____ 5. Our football team used to win all the games.

_____ 6. I used to dream of April showers.

_____ 7. But May flowers use to come before April showers.

_____ 8. Murdoch useta live in Montgomery, Alabama.

_____ 9. Kirk use to eat pizza for breakfast.

_____ 10. The Greyhound bus use to schedule fifteen trips a day between New York and

Philadelphia.

_____ 11. Roger used to call me every night.

_____ 12. Nathan useta go to school in Harlan, Kentucky.

_____ 13. An apple a day use to keep the doctor away.

_____ 14. A clove of garlic used to keep my friends away.

_____ 15. Russell useta brush his teeth after every meal, but he stopped.

_____ 16. My father used to tell me: "Neither a borrower nor a lender be."

_____ 17. My mother useta make me wash my hands before I ate.

_____ 18. Luke use to wiggle his ears like a rabbit.

_____ 19. Humpty Dumpty use to sit on a wall.

_____ 20. I used to dream of a white Christmas.

HAVE TO

_____ 1. You have to see my new Easter outfit.

_____ 2. Bayard and Jasper havta go to work.

_____ 3. Carl and Kenneth has to go to school.

_____ 4. Hiram and Horace have to go to the dentist.

_____ 5. Carrie have to come to Toronto with me for the weekend.

_____ 6. Thurston hasta go to the hospital for a kidney operation.

_____ 7. Stephen and Sheldon hasta do a book report together.

_____ 8. Cassandra hasta meet her mother at the airport at 3 P. M.

_____ 9. The dishes hasta be washed.

_____ 10. Dogs havta scratch their fleas.

_____ 11. We have to fall in love before spring.

_____ 12. The boys think they have to play pool every Saturday night.

_____ 13. The boys think they hasta play pool every Saturday night.

_____ 14. You havta eat oysters on the half shell.

_____ 15. You have to eat oysters on the half shell.

_____ 16. We has to water the grass once a week.

_____ 17. We have to water the grass once a week.

_____ 18. But we hasta water the flowers once a day.

_____ 19. But we have to water the flowers once a day.

_____ 20. She hafta mend her broken heart.

_____ 21. My grandmother hasta control her excessive drinking of gin and tonic.

_____ 22. Fat people have to stop eating.

_____ 23. Thin people hafta start eating.

_____ 24. To make the Olympic swimming team, Pat hafta swim in the pool every day for seven hours.

_____ 25. The boys hasta conform to the team code.

HAVE GOT TO

_____ 1. You have gotta have heart; all you really need is heart.

_____ 2. You've got to have heart.

_____ 3. When you gotta go, you gotta go.

_____ 4. When you've got to go, you've got to go.

_____ 5. I gotta be me.

_____ 6. I have got to be me.

_____ 7. Myron has got to have a fur coat.

_____ 8. I've gotta have all _B_'s to get into medical school.

_____ 9. I have got to have all _B_'s to get into medical school.

_____ 10. Aurelia is gotta sharpen all her yellow pencils before she starts doing her homework.

_____ 11. My little brother, Alfonzo, have gotta glue his model airplane together.

_____ 12. We have gotta wash our new green and white Cutlass Supreme.

_____ 13. I have got to get more gas for my car.

_____ 14. She has got to borrow money from me every week.

_____ 15. Darlene have gotta go back home for a weekend visit.

## OUGHT TO

_____ 1. You oughta be in the movies because you are so handsome.

_____ 2. You should be in the movies.

_____ 3. We oughter serve elegant French wine with every meal.

_____ 4. Aunt Sadie oughta let the corn bread rise just a little bit longer.

_____ 5. Every happily married man ought to take his wife out to dinner once a week.

_____ 6. Brunhilde oughter lower her voice.

_____ 7. Bessie's voice is so soft she ought to raise it.

_____ 8. The whole choir oughta sing in tune.

_____ 9. The Wayne school band ought to march in step.

_____ 10. Our football team oughta win with all the support we are giving them.

_____ 11. After what he did to her she oughter slap him.

_____ 12. After what he did to her, she ought to slap him.

_____ 13. After what he did to her, she oughta cook him a big meal.

_____ 14. Food prices ought to go down.

_____ 15. Roast beef oughter cost fifty cents per pound.

## BE SUPPOSED TO

_____ 1. Sam is supposed to see the draft board tomorrow.

_____ 2. Bob is supposed to cut the lawn.

_____ 3. Vettina suppose to mend her hem.

_____ 4. Sentences supposed to have a subject and a verb.

_____ 5. All cars are supposed to have six wheels, four on the ground.

_____ 6. I suppose to start supper now.

_____ 7. My little sister is suppose to set the table.

_____ 8. My brother suppose to wash the dishes.

_____ 9. Daddy is suppose to be home by now.

_____ 10. Chloette is supposed to be the best ice skater in our crowd.

_____ 11. Randolph suppose to take her to the rink.

_____ 12. They is suppose to sweep the rink clean before they skate.

_____ 13. My Uncle Oliver supposed to pinch my Aunt Opal to keep her awake.

_____ 14. He supposed to pay attention to painting the house.

_____ 15. Nicolette is suppose to be the prettiest girl in the class.

BE ABLE TO

_____ 1. George be able to eat three pizzas in an hour.

_____ 2. Sheldon can do all the exercises in this book.

_____ 3. The hospital is able to hold three hundred patients.

_____ 4. Pat can help in the operating room.

_____ 5. She also be able to quiet the patients when they are upset.

_____ 6. She is able to comfort them.

_____ 7. Bertie able to pass out trays.

_____ 8. Once she has finished her training, she able to give medication.

_____ 9. Engineers can work in the Peace Corps.

_____ 10. They able to help people rebuild their homes after the war.

_____ 11. They can teach uneducated people how to improve their water supply.

_____ 12. Vernon be able to work in the Peace Corps because he is a nurse.

_____ 13. Cathy able to work in the Corps because she is a doctor.

_____ 14. Many people are able to help each other if they look for a way.

_____ 15. The cleaning crew can wash the school floors in two hours.

## Conversion Drill

Convert each sentence that you did not mark SD in the above exercises into the standard dialect, using conventional spelling.

## Substitution Drill

The following sentences use the modal *must*. In each sentence, substitute the appropriate form of *have to* or *have got to* for *must*, using the standard dialect and conventional spelling. The first one has been done for you.

1. She must wear a flower in her hair to go to San Francisco.

   She has to wear a flower in her hair to go to San Francisco. _____

2. You must be a football hero to get along with your girl.

   _____

3. You must hang up my clothes on hangers so they don't get wrinkled.

   _____

4. The cook must put the baking powder in the cake before it will rise.

   _____

5. General Motors must make lots of modifications on its cars.

   _____

6. Winthrop must get a haircut before he gets his picture taken.

   _____

7. I must get a new suit before I go for my job interview.

   _____

8. We must all love one another before we die.

   _____

9. You must have one of your beautiful New Year's Eve parties.

_____

10. Fe Fe must go back to Nebraska to take care of her sister and mother.

_____

11. Bible salesmen must meet new people every day if they want to sell their Bibles.

_____

12. Consuella must buy a wedding gown.

_____

13. You must drink at least eight glasses of water a day on this diet.

_____

14. Cathy must feed her baby vitamins.

_____

15. We must take at least a thirty-minute break every morning before we begin to work.

_____

The following sentences use the simple past or the recent past of the main verb. In each sentence, substitute *used to* for the simple past or recent past, using the standard dialect and conventional spelling. The first one has been done for you.

1. The wind had blown hard.

   The wind used to blow hard.

2. Dishes broke easily until the invention of plastic dishes.

_____

3. Santa Claus had brought me presents.

_____

4. I bought popsicles.

_____

5. My cat caught mice.

_____

6. My Aunt Zenobia had come to visit us twice a year.

_____

7. We exchanged our Christmas gifts on Christmas Eve.

_____

8. We went on a picnic every Sunday in August.

_____

9. My father took us to the zoo every spring.

_____

10. He let us feed the tigers.

_____

The following sentences use the modals *must, can,* and *should.* In each sentence substitute one of the appropriate two- or three-word helping verbs for the modal, using standard dialect and conventional spelling. The first one has been done for you.

1. U. of M. should go to the Rose Bowl.

U. of M. ought to go to the Rose Bowl. _____

2. Americans must conserve energy.

_____

3. They should cut down on their gasoline consumption.

_____

4. The attorney must get more evidence.

_____

5. He must find the gun the killer used.

_____

6. He should look behind the garage.

_____

7. What is more important, he must find the killer.

_____

8. The man that stole my color T.V. should go to jail.

_____

9. Secretariat can run a mile in thirty-seven seconds.

_____

10. I can run a mile in an hour and a half.

_____

11. Now she should run after Donald.

_____

12. And Ronald must run after her.

_____

13. They all should stop running.

_____

14. They must stop playing games at their age.

_____

15. Ronald and Rosie should settle down and get married.

_____

16. Donald must find himself a new girlfriend.

_____

17. Marlene can make him happy.

_____

18. She must have her picture in the paper.

_____

19. Deer hunters should wear orange.

_____

20. Donna Jean's father is so rich he must build a bank for his money.

_____

21. Nurses must read thermometers carefully.

_____

22. They also must read bloodpressure gauges.

_____

23. Registered nurses must undergo strict training.

_____

24. Durette can help others by being a good nurse.

_____

25. Henry should become a doctor.

_____

26. He should take more biology courses.

_____

27. Lisette must train longer before she skates for the Olympics.

_____

28. Perhaps she should wait another year before trying out.

_____

29. I must scold my baby for eating cookies.

_____

30. We must provide a quiet place for our students to study.

_____

31. Joshua can do his homework sitting on the stairs at school.

_____

32. We should read more Shakespeare plays in our English class.

_____

33. I can do anything you can do better.

_____

34. Parzival always can fight better than anybody else.

_____

35. I can be anything I want to be.

_____

36. You should marry the person you love.

_____

37. You must have a meaningful relationship.

_____

38. You should be in pictures.

_____

39. The philosopher said that we must live with uncertainty.

_____

40. We should remember that the only two certainties are death and taxes.

_____

# INFINITIVES

## 23

The verb phrases we have looked at so far consist of one or more helping verbs plus a main verb. There are, however, some verb phrases that consist of two main verbs. In those cases, you use the appropriate form of the first main verb (preceded by any helping verbs), followed by *to* plus the base form of the second main verb. This combination of *to* + base form is called an infinitive.

EXAMPLES                    Standard Dialect

He *wants to study* Latin.
They *asked to go* home early.
They *had wanted to ask* the teacher a question.

Note that other words can come between the first main verb and the infinitive.

EXAMPLES                    Standard Dialect

He *forced* me *to drive* him home.
The teacher *required* us *to do* our homework.

Community dialects can differ from the standard dialect in three ways:
1. The forms of the first main verb or the combination forms can vary in the same way we discussed in earlier chapters.

EXAMPLES

| Community Dialect | Standard Dialect |
|---|---|
| I *done asked* him *to do* his homework. | I *have asked* him *to do* it. |

2. Because "want to" is often pronounced "wanna" or "wanta," students often spell the words that way.

EXAMPLES

| Community Dialect | Standard Dialect |
|---|---|
| I $\begin{Bmatrix} wanna \\ wants \end{Bmatrix}$ go. | I *want to go*. |

3. Some community dialects, instead of using the base form of the verb with *to*, add an ending to it.

EXAMPLES                           Community Dialect

We asked him *to paid* the bill.
Mary always allows her baby *to sucks* his thumb.

Summary: Infinitives

| Community Dialect | Standard Dialect |
|---|---|
| He done wanted to go. | He *has wanted to go.* |
| He $\left\{ \begin{matrix} \text{wanta} \\ \text{wanna} \end{matrix} \right\}$ go. | He *wants to go.* |
| He wants to walks. | He *wants to walk.* |
| He wanted to walked. | He *wanted to walk.* |

## Recognition Drill

Underline the infinitive phrases (main verb plus the infinitive) in each of the following sentences. Then mark SD next to each sentence written in the standard dialect. The first three have been done for you.

_____ 1. I <u>done took</u> him <u>to make</u> the fence.

__SD__ 2. I <u>have taken</u> him <u>to make</u> the fence.

_____ 3. I <u>done taken</u> my cousin Lonnie <u>to see</u> the movie.

_____ 4. I have taken my cousin Lonnie to see the show.

_____ 5. I done told Mary to go home.

_____ 6. I have told Mary to go home.

_____ 7. He have decided to go to the basketball game.

_____ 8. He has decided to go to the basketball game.

_____ 9. Maria has employed Floyd to cut the grass.

_____ 10. Maria done employ Floyd to cut the grass.

_____ 11. I done decided to get myself together.

_____ 12. I have decided to get myself together.

_____ 13. Lavinna done decided to become a Catholic.

_____ 14. Lavinna have decided to become a Catholic.

_____ 15. Lavinna has decided to become a Catholic.

_____ 16. Lemuel hate to tell Nettie that it was all over.

_____ 17. Lemuel hated to tell Nettie it was all over.

_____ 18. Etta done chose to apologize to Delmar for her obnoxious behavior at the party last Saturday night.

_____ 19. Etta has chosen to apologize to Delmar for her obnoxious behavior at the party last Saturday night.

_____ 20. Mimi done persuade Miranda to go downtown with her.

_____ 21. Mimi had persuaded Miranda to go downtown with her.

_____ 22. We done told Sonia to go on a vacation.

_____ 23. We have told Sonia to go on a vacation.

_____ 24. They done convinced me to try to get into Harvard University.

_____ 25. They have convinced me to try to get into Harvard University.

_____ 26. I wanna do the puzzle.

_____ 27. My brother wanta do the puzzle.

_____ 28. You wanna do it.

_____ 29. She wanta do it.

_____ 30. She want to do it.

_____ 31. The dog wanna do the puzzle.

_____ 32. We all want to do it.

_____ 33. They all wanna do it.

_____ 34. What do they wanna do?

_____ 35. They want to sing.

_____ 36. What do they want to sing?

_____ 37. They wanna sing "I wanna be happy."

_____ 38. I want to get a college education.

_____ 39. I wanta get a college education.

_____ 40. I wanna be around to pick up the pieces when somebody breaks your heart.

_____ 41. The teacher ought to ask his students for their evaluation of his class.

_____ 42. The students want to accepted his advice.

_____ 43. The twins want to accept the gift.

_____ 44. The new people on the staff have to asks for more information.

_____ 45. The kitten needed to belonged to someone.

_____ 46. Their sick uncle was forced to stay in the hospital.

_____ 47. Uncle Bill didn't want to remain in the hospital.

_____ 48. Our new couch was supposed to lasted a lifetime.

_____ 49. I can see that it is beginning to wear out already.

_____ 50. The sun appears to moves around the earth but it does not.

_____ 51. Burton had money to burned.

_____ 52. The chicken was forced to cross the road.

_____ 53. His mother taught him to fights his own battles.

_____ 54. The minister told the prisoner to sin no more.

_____ 55. The weather started to changed around six o'clock.

_____ 56. The train wheels began to turns.

_____ 57. The sunshine made Joe want to travel.

_____ 58. Once the old prospector turned eighty, he began to find gold.

_____ 59. The little boy tried to ride his bike in the street, but his brother stopped him.

_____ 60. She was told not to violate the speed laws.

_____ 61. The police cadets are taught how to write a report.

_____ 62. Tammy Lou learned how to rows a boat before she was eight.

_____ 63. Bruce managed to drived three miles with a flat tire.

_____ 64. The team fought to regain its lead.

_____ 65. When the fire siren sounds all the dogs begin to howl.

_____ 66. The Democrats have been trying to unites.

_____ 67. The Republicans are working to win.

_____ 68. Maud Muller has to mow the meadow.

_____ 69. Opal Winans has to opened the window.

_____ 70. Ruthie Shaw has to runs from her own shadow.

## Conversion Drill

Convert each sentence that you did not mark SD in the above exercise into the standard dialect using infinitive phrases.

## Pattern Practice

Complete the following sentences by inserting the appropriate form of the first main verb and the infinitive form of the second main verb. The first two have been done for you.

DECIDE/DELAY      1. Pierre <u>decided to delay</u> his trip to Paris.

WANT/RECEIVE      2. Adolph <u>wanted to receive</u> a valentine from Amy.

LIKE/CALL      3. Lyon <u>liked to call</u> Susie names.

DECIDE/DYNAMITE      4. Adrian and the radicals had _____ the fish house.

WANT/LOVE      5. Cliff always _____ Blanche.

PREFER/HATE      6. Edna _____ rather than to love her piano teacher.

WANT/TALK      7. For a long time I have _____ to Ernestine about a personal

         matter.

TAKE/GO      8. We have _____ a fancy _____ to Nassau.

WANT/FRACTURE      9. He did not _____ his elbow.

WANT/FULFILL      10. Mary _____ her dreams.

LIKE/GAMBLE      11. Felix _____ every cent away.

START/GREASE      12. Our auto mechanic, Lambert, _____ my 1941

         Dodge.

LOVE/IMAGINE      13. I _____ the two of us canoeing down the river on a

         Sunday afternoon.

SEEM/HOPE      14. You _____ for the best.

DECIDE/FEAR      15. He _____ the worst.

PREFER/IGNORE      16. Joe _____ the insult.

COME/INQUIRE      17. My girlfriend, Peaches, _____ about the disc jockey job.

SEEM/INTEREST      18. Bertram _____ Beverly.

SEEM/INTERPRET      19. Ursula _____ Justin's love letter erroneously.

TRY/ISOLATE      20. The doctor _____ the problem.

TRY/KIDNAP      21. Pauline _____ my sneakers.

WANT/MAINTAIN      22. We _____ a proper relationship.

SEEM/MANAGE      23. Hugh and Humbert _____ the house better.

TRY/WIN      24. My uncle _____ .

WISH/PERFORM      25. Mable _____ a belly dance at the party.

START/PERSPIRE      26. George _____ at the altar.

DECIDE/PLAN      27. We _____ the trip to Turkey more carefully.

TRY/PRECEDE      28. The bride _____ the bridesmaid.

WANT/PRACTICE 29. Lois _____ what she preached.

RUSH/ARREST 30. The police _____ the dope peddlers.

DECIDE/RAID 31. The police _____ the go-go bar.

WANT/RECEIVE 32. The go-go dancers did not _____ stiff sentences.

TRY/RECOLLECT 33. Grandpaw _____ many things from his youth.

DECIDE/OFFER 34. Herman _____ Pearl the job.

WANT/REFUSE 35. Valery _____ the offer.

HURRY/REDUCE 36. Giovanna _____ her weight from 200 to 100 pounds.

START/SCATTER 37. The sparrows _____ the seeds in the garden.

TRY/SEIZE 38. The cat _____ the kitten by the neck.

BEGIN/SUSPECT 39. We _____ that DeWitt was the Peeping Tom.

WANT/TRY 40. Yolanda, Yvette, and Yvonne _____ harder.

RUSH/VALIDATE 41. The License Bureau didn't _____ my driver's license.

COME/VALUE 42. He _____ her life more than his.

OFFER/WRESTLE 43. The mailman, Elbert, _____ the Irish wolfhound.

WISH/YIELD 44. The raccoons did not _____ in battle to the skunks.

PERFORM/PLEASE 45. I had _____ my duty _____ my mother.

WANT/MEET 46. We _____ you in Atlanta.

DECIDE/VISIT 47. Zenia _____ her grandmother in Texas.

REFUSE/BE 48. Danny had _____ on the social committee.

WANT/GO 49. Hartford _____ to Spain for the Christmas holiday.

ORDER/QUIT 50. The doctor _____ Sam _____ his job.

| PROMISE/PAY | 51. Bertha _____ me back the money she borrowed. |

| EXPECT/BE | 52. We _____ the examination _____ harder than it really was. |

| TEACH/PLAY | 53. Gary's father _____ me _____ football. |

| WANT/PERFORM | 54. Jane _____ the music she wrote at the party. |

| WANT/FEEL | 55. I _____ important. |

| TRAIN/DO | 56. Matthew _____ his dog, Lassie, _____ four tricks. |

| WANT/GET | 57. I _____ to know you. |

| TRY/WIN | 58. Our team _____ the basketball championship. |

| PRACTICE/BECOME | 59. John _____ a great pianist. |

| WANT/BE | 60. I _____ the best student in English. |

## Conversion Exercise

In the following sentences circle verbs written in community dialects.

1. Charles done wanted to go to Florida for Christmas.
2. Tina done tried to persuades Charles to goes to the mountains.
3. Charles done told Tina that he loved to go swimming in the sun and loved the beach.
4. Tina done hated to telled Charles that she loved to climbs mountains and enjoy nature, and if Charles done chose to go to Florida, then he could just go by himself.
5. Tina done persuaded Charles to go to the mountains.

Now rewrite these sentences in the standard dialect. Use paragraph form.

_____

_____

_____

_____

_____

_____

_____

# PASSIVE FORMS OF VERBS 24

The sentences we have studied so far are "active" sentences: the subject of the sentence performs an action and the object of the sentence receives the effect of the subject's action. In a "passive" sentence just the opposite is true: the subject is passive, that is, it is acted upon by the object. The object is either in a prepositional phrase or omitted altogether.

EXAMPLES:

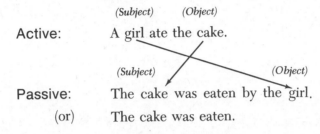

                        *(Subject)*        *(Object)*

Active:        A girl ate the cake.

                    *(Subject)*              *(Object)*

Passive:     The cake was eaten by the girl.

(or)         The cake was eaten.

Notice that in the standard dialect you do four things to change an active sentence into the passive.

1. Reverse the subject and object.
2. Put *by* in front of the original subject.
3. Insert some form of the verb BE—the appropriate form will be in the same tense as the main verb in the active sentence.
4. Add the compound past form of the main verb.

Thus in "A girl ate the cake" and "John kicks the ball" we perform these four steps.

| | | |
|---|---|---|
| 1. The cake | the girl. | 1. The ball | John. |
| 2. The cake | by the girl. | 2. The ball | by John. |
| 3. The cake *was* | by the girl. | 3. The ball *is* | by John. |
| 4. The cake *was eaten* by the girl. | | 4. The ball *is kicked* by John. |

Notice that after you put the subject at the end and put *by* in front of it, the whole phrase with *by* plus the subject can be eliminated and the sentence will still make sense.

> The cake *was eaten* by the girl.
> The cake *was eaten*.

In most community dialects, the passive sentence is formed exactly as it is in the standard dialect, except in the following four cases. (The object phrase is in parentheses.)

1. Some community dialects use *been* instead of the standard dialect form of BE.

EXAMPLES

| Community Dialect | Standard Dialect |
|---|---|
| The cake *been eaten* | The cake $\left\{ \begin{array}{c} is \\ was \end{array} \right\}$ *eaten* |
| (by the girl). | (by the girl). |

2. Some community dialects use *get* or *got* instead of a form of BE.

EXAMPLES

| Community Dialect | Standard Dialect |
|---|---|
| The cake *got eaten* | The cake *was eaten* |
| (by the girl). | (by the girl). |
| John *get hit* (by Henry). | John *is hit* (by Henry). |

3. Some community dialects use *been* or *got* together with a different form of the main verb.

EXAMPLES

| Community Dialect | Standard Dialect |
|---|---|
| The cake $\left\{ \begin{array}{c} got\ eat \\ been\ eat \\ been\ ate \end{array} \right\}$ | The cake *was eaten* |
| (by the girl). | (by the girl). |

4. Some community dialects do not use a form of BE or any other helping verb.

EXAMPLES

| Community Dialect | Standard Dialect |
|---|---|
| The cake *eaten*. | The cake *was eaten*. |

## Summary: Passive Sentences

| Community Dialect | Standard Dialect |
|---|---|
| The cake been { eaten / eat / ate } by the girl. | |
| The cake got { eaten / eat / ate } by the girl. | The cake *was eaten* by the girl. |
| The cake { eaten / eat / ate } by the girl. | |

## Recognition Drill

Some of the sentences below are in the active voice of the standard dialect, and others are in the passive voice of the standard dialect. Place an A beside those in the active voice, and a P beside those in the passive voice. The first three have been done for you.

__P__ 1. Gifts are gladly accepted by brides.

__P__ 2. The gold was divided by the pirates.

__A__ 3. The principal recommended Jeffrey for a scholarship.

_____ 4. The whole community benefits from the new recreation hall.

_____ 5. Jeanine was implicated in the scandal by an informer.

_____ 6. The lawyer authorizes the signing of the will.

_____ 7. My battery was ruined by the heavy rain storm.

_____ 8. Jealousy overcomes Irene when she sees Joe with Enna.

_____ 9. My dog was found on Second Boulevard by my brother.

_____ 10. My dad, a lieutenant in the army, is given a furlough every Christmas.

_____ 11. The admissions office notified Bill of his acceptance to the college.

_____ 12. The doctor operated on my brother to remove the splinter in his foot.

_____ 13. The bulls are weighed by the farmer.

_____ 14. The native Americans used arrows for ammunition.

_____ 15. Al bought a secondhand motorcycle.

_____ 16. The former owner gave him an operator's manual for the cycle.

_____ 17. But driving lessons are still needed by Al.

_____ 18. The front wheel was ruined when he drove into an approaching cow.

_____ 19. An excellent supper was cooked by the women of the church.

_____ 20. Almost all the church members attended the dinner.

## Conversion Exercise

Change the following active sentences in the standard dialect into passive sentences in the standard dialect. The first one has been done for you.

1. Nikos won $300 at bingo.

   $300 was won at bingo by Nikos.
   _____

2. He gave the money to Anna.

   _____

3. A man snatched Anna's purse.

   _____

4. Anna called the police.

   _____

5. Anna described the man.

   _____

6. The police caught the man.

   _____

7. The police returned the money to Anna.

   _____

8. Anna gave the money back to Nikos.

_____

9. Nikos put the money in the bank.

_____

10. Anna made Nikos very happy.

_____


## Review Exercise

Notice that the active sentences in the above exercise are all written in simple past time. When you changed them into the passive form, you should have put the helping verbs in the simple past also. Ordinarily a story like this would be told in past time. But if you were relating something happening right now, or if you were writing stage directions for a play, you would tell it in present time.

As a review of present time and also of the passive, go back and change all the active sentences in the above exercise into the present time. Then change them into the passive form. For example, "Nikos _won_ $300 at bingo" would be, in present time, "Nikos _wins_ $300 at bingo." Changed into the passive form it would then become "$300 is won at bingo by Nikos."


## Conversion Exercise

The sentences below are written in the passive form of the standard dialect. Rewrite each sentence in the active form of the standard dialect. The first two have been done for you.

1. The Cadillac was driven by a gorgeous girl.

   A gorgeous girl drove the Cadillac.

2. The Red Wings were beaten by the Hawks.

   The Hawks beat the Red Wings.

3. The branches of the trees are broken by the wind.

   _____

4. The people of Israel were led to the Promised Land by Moses.

_____ 171

5. Little Red Riding Hood was frightened by a wolf.

_____

6. The million-dollar painting was seen by Mr. Gilbert's art class.

_____

7. The Battle of Jericho was fought by Joshua.

_____

8. The program is begun by Lorenzo.

_____

9. The roses are grown by Nasetta.

_____

10. Sir Anthony is entertained by the queen.

_____

11. The knight was hidden under the chicken coop by his sweetheart.

_____

12. The baker is hurt by Spino's jokes about the bread.

_____

13. The house was built by Jack.

_____

14. The hungry boy was fed by Donna.

_____

15. The bride was delighted by the beautiful gifts.

_____

16. My kind-hearted grandfather is known by everyone in town.

_____

17. The nest was woven by the black widow spider.

_____

18. The devil was driven out of Cassandra by the exorcist.

_____

19. All of the slices of bread are spread with peanut butter and jelly by the boys.

_____

20. They are all eaten by the girls.

_____

## Recognition Drill

Underline passive verbs in the following sentences. Then mark SD next to each sentence where passive verbs are in the standard dialect. The first three have been done for you.

_____ 1. Arnold <u>been bitten</u> by a squirrel.

__SD__ 2. The beautiful bride <u>was dressed</u> by her bridesmaids.

_____ 3. Braces <u>been put</u> on Alvira's teeth by the dentist.

_____ 4. Fillings were put in her teeth by the same dentist.

_____ 5. Floyd's bicycle got stolen from the garage by a strange man.

_____ 6. The fender of Sam's new LTD was dent by his girlfriend.

_____ 7. The junk hauled away by the garbage man.

_____ 8. Six babies been born at once to Mrs. Sadie Lewis.

_____ 9. Mrs. Lewis is frightened and delighted by her new sextuplets.

_____ 10. The church bell gets rang in the middle of the night on Halloween by three devils.

_____ 11. Ghosts are seen in the cemetery by the minister.

_____ 12. Linda been passed by the board of cosmetology.

_____ 13. She hired by Michelle's Beauty Salon.

_____ 14. Linda gets praised by her first customer.

_____ 15. The waitress been give a large tip by the old man.

_____ 16. Waldo's appendix got taken out by the doctor.

_____ 17. William's tonsils were taken out by Doctor Brown.

_____ 18. Lamar and Lily got married by the judge.

_____ 19. They were offer a honeymoon to Las Vegas by Lily's rich uncle.

_____ 20. The horse gets ridden by seven different people.

_____ 21. Seven different people been kicked by the horse.

_____ 22. The Christmas carols are sung by the choir.

_____ 23. Gertie got chose by the choir director to sing the solo.

_____ 24. The mad dog was caught by the Englishman.

_____ 25. The wine drunk up by the first three people who came to the party.

_____ 26. Beautiful flowers been grown by Mrs. Lockhart.

_____ 27. Jeannie was asked by Nigel for a date.

_____ 28. Jackie's shoulder touched by the ghost standing behind her.

_____ 29. The doctor is reached by the patients.

_____ 30. The fog horn is heard by people twenty miles away.

_____ 31. Four new blue dishes got broken by my brother.

_____ 32. The wine been brought by the waiter.

_____ 33. The house been built by her own hands.

_____ 34. The red dress got bought by her mother.

_____ 35. The music played by the band.

_____36. The food gets cook by my aunt.

_____37. All the beer been drunk by my friends.

_____38. My stereo system got stole by the thieves.

_____39. The war been fought by the soldiers.

_____40. Her gloves are always forgot by my mother.

_____41. My umbrella been lost in the subway by my grandfather.

_____42. The sin forgiven by the priest.

_____43. My ring got hidden by the squirrel.

_____44. The baby been held by its grandmother.

_____45. The party is heard by all the neighbors.

_____46. The corn got grown by the Indians.

_____47. The story is known by all the people.

_____48. The cocoon gets spun by the caterpiller.

_____49. The tomatoes are planted by my uncle.

_____50. English got taken by twelve people.

_____51. My coat was tore by my dog.

_____52. My old shoes been worn by my little brother.

_____53. The history paper was written in four hours by me.

_____54. The birthday cake is baked by my uncle.

_____55. The comic strip was drawn by the class president.

## Conversion Drill

Convert each sentence that you did not mark SD in the above exercise into the standard dialect in the passive voice.

## Pattern Practice

Insert the appropriate form of the helping verb BE in the following sentences to form the passive voice in the standard dialect. The first two have been done for you.

1. The car <u>was</u> hit in the fog.

2. Postmen <u>are</u> sometimes bitten by dogs.

3. The lost boys _____ found by the neighbors.

4. The bread _____ cut by the baker.

5. The hay _____ raked by the farmer.

6. Babies _____ fed by their mothers.

7. The cold _____ felt by the old lady.

8. The ball _____ passed by Munson.

9. Huff _____ intercepted by Jauron three times.

10. The ball _____ kicked by George Brenda.


## Pattern Practice

Insert the appropriate form of the helping verb BE and the compound past form of the main verb (in the margin) in the following sentences. The first two have been done for you.

BREAK 1. The windows <u>were</u> <u>broken</u> by girls playing baseball.

CATCH 2. The butterflies <u>are</u> <u>caught</u> by the bug man.

CHOOSE 3. The homecoming queen _____ _____ by a committee.

PLAY 4. Bingo _____ _____ by our block club.

TOUCH 5. I _____ _____ by your generous gift.

DIG 6. The grave of the Egyptian mummy _____ _____ up by an archeologist.

SEE 7. The four-car accident _____ _____ by fourteen people.

HEAR   8. The crash _____ _____ by people six blocks away.

LOVE   9. Thomasine _____ _____ by Ernie.

FEED   10. While we were on vacation, the dog _____ _____ by our neighbors.

FIND   11. The lollipops that were hidden _____ _____ by the children.

GRIND   12. The wheat _____ _____ into flour.

HIT   13. The rocket ship _____ _____ by a meteor

PICK   14. The new football players _____ _____ by the National League.

SMELL   15. The flowers _____ _____ by Ferdinand the Bull.

PAINT   16. The fence _____ _____ by Tom Sawyer.

MAKE   17. Beatrice _____ _____ happy by the surprise party.

REPAIR   18. My Mickey Mouse watch _____ _____ by the jeweler.

PREPARE   19. The elegant steak _____ _____ by Pierre.

SCARE   20. Lucy _____ _____ by the thunderstorm.

TEACH   21. Nicole _____ _____ to go to Sunday School by her mother.

SURPASS   22. His mother's cooking skills _____ _____ by Norman.

WRITE   23. The poem _____ _____ by Langston Hughes.

READ   24. Nursery rhymes _____ _____ by Ed to Ted.

LEAD   25. Jack _____ _____ up the hill by Jill.

# SUMMARY OF VERB FORMS 25

So far we have seen that all verbs in standard English except the nine modal helping verbs have several different forms, and that each of these forms has a different use. Let's first review the forms of these verbs.

### Standard Dialect

| Base Form | Infinitive | Simple Present | Simple Past | Compound Past | Progressive |
|---|---|---|---|---|---|
| Regular Verbs: WALK, etc. | *to walk* | *walk, walks* | *walked* | *walked* | *walking* |
| BE | *to be* | *am, are is* | *was, were* | *been* | *being* |
| HAVE | *to have* | *have, has* | *had* | *had* | *having* |
| DO | *to do* | *do, does* | *did* | *done* | *doing* |
| HIT, etc. | *to hit* | *hit, hits* | *hit* | *hit* | *hitting* |
| Other Irregular Verbs: SWIM, etc. | *to swim* | *swim, swims* | *swam* | *swum* | *swimming* |
| Modals: CAN, etc. | — | *can* | — | — | — |

Now let's review the uses of the forms. Remember that there are three verbs in English that can be used as either helping verbs or main verbs. They are BE, HAVE, and DO. Second, remember that there are nine verbs (the modals) that are usually used only as helping verbs. Finally, all the rest of the verbs in the standard dialect can be used only as main verbs.

The following list shows the uses of these various forms and their combinations.

1. To express simple present time, or ongoing action, use simple present form of main verb:

I *have* six parakeets.
He *walks* to school every day.

2. To express simple past time, use simple past form of main verb:

   When I *was* little I *had* six parakeets.
   He *walked* to school every day.

3. To describe an action that began in the past and continues into the present or that occurred in the recent past, use simple present of helping verb HAVE + compound past form of main verb:

   I *have walked* to school every day for six years.

4. To describe an action that was both begun and completed in the distant past, use simple past of helping verb HAVE + compound past form of main verb:

   I *had walked* to school before I bought a car.

5. To express present time, an ongoing action, or future time, use simple present of helping verb BE + *ing* form of main verb:

   I *am driving* to school now.

6. To describe an ongoing action in the past, or something you intended to do in the past, use simple past of helping verb BE + *ing* form of main verb:

   I *was driving* before I lost the muffler.

7. To express various kinds of future—possibility, condition, obligation, or intention, use base form of appropriate modal + base form of main verb:

   I *might drive* again if I get a new muffler.

## Final Review Exercises

Mark an SD next to each of the following sentences that are written in the standard dialect. Then convert the others into the standard dialect. The first three have been done for you.

### PRESENT, PAST, AND RECENT PAST

_____ 1. He go to the store.

   He went to the store.

__SD__ 2. Henry has gone to the ball game.

_____ 3. Flip Wilson buy his blue suede shoes at Gucci's.

Flip Wilson buys his blue suede shoes at Gucci's. _____

_____ 4. Nancy Wilson order her gown at Pucci's.

_____

_____ 5. Hi Karate were Napoleon's favorite cologne.

_____

_____ 6. Ghengis Khan wore Brut cologne.

_____

_____ 7. Julius Caesar use lime-scented English Leather After-shave Lotion.

_____

_____ 8. Spiro Agnew shave with Gillette Blue Blades.

_____

_____ 9. Gladys Knight and the Pips has sang the most popular songs.

_____

_____ 10. President Roosevelt stop the depression in 1933.

_____

_____ 11. President John Kennedy has gave our country moral leadership.

_____

_____ 12. President Johnson pass more civil rights legislation than any other president.

_____

_____ 13. Sidney Poitier has played many starring roles in the movies.

_____

_____ 14. Red Foxx has made us all laugh in "Sanford and Son."

_____

_____ 15. Many people have call President Lincoln "Honest Abe."

_____

_____ 16. Some people have say that George Washington never told a lie.

_____

_____ 17. Aretha Franklin sang like an angel.

_____

_____ 18. The comedian, Bill Cosby, has became a school teacher.

_____

_____ 19. Lucius has worn designer jackets longer than anyone else in our crowd.

_____

_____ 20. Pierre Cardin shirts has always appeal to me.

_____

_____ 21. Peter and Margaret has support the grape boycott.

_____

_____ 22. Thomas Jefferson signed the Declaration of Independence in 1776.

_____

_____ 23. A new book has came out on Marilyn Monroe.

_____

_____ 24. President Theodore Roosevelt walk softly and carry a big stick.

_____

_____ 25. The "Jackson Five" has name the latest dance the Snake.

_____

_____ 26. The Michigan State team intercepted five passes last Saturday.

_____

_____27. My sister Sally has took my wig.

_____

_____28. Walter has sleep in his wig.

_____

_____29. Gorgeous George has begun to wear a wig at the wrestling matches.

_____


## DISTANT AND RECENT PAST

_____ 1. I had saw Tom three days before his car accident.

_____

_____ 2. In 1961 Roger Maris had hitted sixty-one homeruns.

_____

_____ 3. By 1915, Ty Cobb has stole ninety-six bases.

_____

_____ 4. In 1931, Lou Gehrig batted in one hundred eighty-four runs.

_____

_____ 5. In 1920, George Sisler of the St. Louis Cardinals has made two hundred
fifty-seven hits.

_____

_____ 6. In 1927, Babe Ruth hit sixty homeruns.

_____

_____ 7. Joe Namath of the New York Jets has attracted many beautiful girls.

_____

_____ 8. During her lifetime my mother won the British Open twenty times.

_____

_____ 9. During his lifetime my father had washed dishes 8,927 times.

_____

_____ 10. He had also milk the cow every day for 1,560 weeks.

_____

_____ 11. My father have worked hard for us.

_____

_____ 12. Mercury Morris had leap over the linebacker's back.

_____

_____ 13. My dog Calvin has ran away from home.

_____

_____ 14. I had looked for her everywhere.

_____

_____ 15. Every night until midnight our family has sat around the dinner table discussing

politics.

_____

_____ 16. Love has teach me many wonderful things.

_____

_____ 17. Our baseball team has won more games than any other team in the league.

_____

_____ 18. Two ships had pass in the night.

_____

_____ 19. The people of Pittsburgh has renovated the city.

_____

_____ 20. I have lived in San Francisco and New York City.

_____

_____ 21. I have live in St. Louis and Atlanta.

_____

_____ 22. Noreen had experience an unhappy childhood.

_____

_____ 23. Bill's father had drank a lot of milk with each meal.

_____

_____ 24. Hope has ate strawberry, vanilla, and peach melba yogurt for lunch.

_____

_____ 25. We had planned the Christmas party for the members of our office staff.

_____

_____ 26. Margot and Dolores has bought more Dean Martin records than anyone else in

California.

_____

_____ 27. I had ran out of gas on Sunday while exceeding the fifty mile-per-hour speed

limit.

_____

_____ 28. I have passed my mathematics, psychology, and English examinations.

_____

_____ 29. Shawn had found a good baby sitter for her baby.

_____

## BE, DO, AND HAVE

_____ 1. On payday I be the happiest person in the world.

_____

_____ 2. In the library I is always alone.

_____

_____ 3. Every Saturday night I ready for a party.

_____

_____ 4. Clowns are the happiest people in the world.

_____

_____ 5. Cymbline be in love.

_____

_____ 6. Bayard, Benjamin, and Boyd is good in school.

_____

_____ 7. Ichabod Crane is crazy.

_____

_____ 8. I were miserable after our team lost the football game.

_____

_____ 9. Barbara, Betty, and Pete was friends for life.

_____

_____ 10. Last Saturday we had the reception in Holiday Hall.

_____

_____ 11. Sinclair were a dentist for three years.

_____

_____ 12. He was a member of the Assembly of God Church. You was too.

_____

_____ 13. Leon have a Mastercharge credit card.

_____

_____ 14. I has a new custom fur convertible top for my car.

_____

_____ 15. You has many more pots and pans than I.

_____

_____ 16. My dog have a knitted green sweater and red tam.

_____

_____ 17. My motorbike has a bad muffler.

_____

_____ 18. Last night I had the window shades down.

_____

_____ 19. Milano Bakery had a fire and burned all the bread.

_____

_____ 20. The vegetable man had a sale on grapes, cucumbers, and big ripe melons.

_____

# PART II:
# NOUNS AND PRONOUNS

In this section we will be discussing nouns and pronouns. Some examples of nouns are given in the sentences below. (Nouns are in italics.)

EXAMPLES

> That *house* is made of *brick*.
> *John* likes *peppermint*.
> *Mr. Morrison* likes *spearmint*.
> *Motorcycles* have *brakes*.

Nouns, like verbs, are either regular or irregular. Regular nouns are those that make their plural by adding *s* or *es*.

EXAMPLES

> This recipe uses three egg*s*.
> My aunt*s* and uncle*s* always give a lot
>     of birthday present*s*.
> I spent five dollar*s* on gasoline.
> There are three church*es* in that town.
> All the fox*es* had red hair.

Irregular nouns are those that make their plural *without* adding *s* or *es*. Some of them change the spelling instead:

| Singular | Plural |
|---|---|
| The *child* was crying. | The *children* were crying. |
| Each *man* made $5.00 an hour. | All the *men* made at least $5.00. |
| The *goose* laid a golden egg. | The other *geese* were jealous. |
| This table is one *foot* long. | Walk on both *feet*, please. |

Other irregular nouns are the same in both singular and plural.

EXAMPLES

| Singular | Plural |
|---|---|
| A *sheep* strayed from the fold. | Many *sheep* strayed from the fold. |
| I bought just one gold*fish*. | I now have thirteen gold-*fish*. |

Finally, some nouns have only a plural form and no singular form:

**Plural**

All the *people* danced.
The herd had 108 *cattle*.

In this section we will be looking at these and other forms more closely, and we will see how they compare with those in community dialects.

# REGULAR NOUN PLURALS

In the standard dialect, the plural of regular nouns is formed by adding *s*.

EXAMPLES                  Standard Dialect

| Singular | Plural |
|----------|--------|
| book | book*s* |
| cent | cent*s* |
| tree | tree*s* |
| mile | mile*s* |

In some cases an *es* is added. This usually happens when a noun ends in *s*, *z*, *x*, *sh*, or *ch*.

EXAMPLES                  Standard Dialect

| Singular | Plural |
|----------|--------|
| box | box*es* |
| church | church*es* |

With some words that end in *o*, you also add an *es*. Here are some common ones.

EXAMPLES                  Standard Dialect

| Singular | Plural |
|----------|--------|
| potato | potato*es* |
| tomato | tomato*es* |
| hero | hero*es* |
| mosquito | mosquito*es* |

(With some nouns that end in *o*, however, you add only an *s*: for example, piano/piano*s*, Latino/Latino*s*. When you are in doubt, look the word up in your dictionary.)

With some nouns that end in *f* or *fe*, the *f* is changed to *v* and *es* is added.

EXAMPLES          Standard Dialect

| Singular | Plural |
| --- | --- |
| leaf | lea*ves* |
| knife | kni*ves* |

(Other nouns that end in *f* do not change from *f* to *v* in the plural; just *s* is added: for example, roof, roof*s*. When you are in doubt, look the word up in your dictionary.)

With nouns that end in a consonant plus *y*, the *y* is changed to *i* and *es* is added.

EXAMPLES          Standard Dialect

| Singular | Plural |
| --- | --- |
| party | part*ies* |
| library | librar*ies* |

(Nouns that end in a vowel plus *y*, however, are not pluralized this way; just *s* is added: day/day*s*, play/play*s*.)

Some community dialects do not add an *s* or *es* to the noun, especially when the meaning of the sentence shows that the noun is plural.

EXAMPLES

| Singular | Community Dialect Plural | Standard Dialect Plural |
| --- | --- | --- |
| one cent | two cent | two cent*s* |
| one mile | three mile | three mile*s* |
| a book | many book | many book*s* |
| that tomato | those tomato | those tomato*es* |
| this knife | these knife | these kni*ves* |
| one party | two party | two part*ies* |

There are also some unconventional spellings of standard dialect plural forms. Sometimes *es* is used rather than *s*, or *s* rather than *es*.

EXAMPLES

| Singular | Unconventional Plural | Conventional Plural |
| --- | --- | --- |
| this tomato | these tomato*s* | these tomato*es* |
| one piano | two piano*es* | two piano*s* |

Sometimes the *f* is not changed to *v* before *es* is added.

## EXAMPLE

| Singular | Unconventional Plural | Conventional Plural |
|----------|----------------------|---------------------|
| one wolf | two wolf*s* | two wol*ves* |

Sometimes the *y* is not changed to *i* before *es* is added.

## EXAMPLE

| Singular | Unconventional Plural | Conventional Plural |
|----------|----------------------|---------------------|
| one party | fourteen party*s* | fourteen part*ies* |

Finally, some community dialects form plurals differently because the singular form is different from the standard dialect. That is, in some community dialects the last consonant is silent, which leaves the word with an *s* ending (for example, the word *desk* may be pronounced *des*). In such cases, the community dialect will add *es* to form the plural.

## EXAMPLES

| Community Dialect | Standard Dialect |
|-------------------|------------------|
| *des / desses* | *desk / desks* |
| *tes / tesses* | *test / tests* |

### Summary: Plural of Regular Nouns

| Unconventional Spelling | Conventional Spelling |
|-------------------------|-----------------------|
| two cent | two cent*s* |
| two potato<br>two potatos | two potato*es* |
| five piano<br>five pianoes | five piano*s* |
| eleven wolf<br>eleven wolfs | eleven wol*ves* |
| six party<br>six partys | six part*ies* |
| three desk<br>three desses | three desk*s* |

## Recognition Drill

Underline the plural nouns in the following sentences. Then mark CS next to each sentence whose plural nouns are spelled conventionally. The first three have been done for you.

### S Plurals

   **CS**    1. The <u>patients</u> were attended by three <u>nurses</u>.

_____ 2. Don had many <u>problem</u>.

_____ 3. I have seen two <u>flying saucer</u>.

_____ 4. Nick rang the bell five time.

_____ 5. Georgia has sung in the church choir for ten years.

_____ 6. There is a telephone booth two mile up the road.

_____ 7. The bus fare has gone up to forty-five cent.

_____ 8. Consuela has won two thousand dollars in the lottery.

_____ 9. Your tree has grown to three times the size of mine.

_____ 10. Seventy five cent is enough to pay for a dozen egg.

_____ 11. The cost of the fur coat came to four hundred dollar and thirty-nine cent.

_____ 12. Farmer Jack took three pig to market.

_____ 13. Farmer Jack took one pig to three market.

_____ 14. Papa was ninety year old when he died.

_____ 15. The team of mule pulled the wagon up the hill.

_____ 16. We drove our motorbikes at full speed.

_____ 17. How many nickel are in a quarter?

_____ 18. How many quarter are in a dollar?

_____ 19. King Kong threw stone from the cliff.

_____ 20. He knocked over buildings.

_____ 21. And he trampled on car.

_____ 22. Do you believe that monsters exist?

_____ 23. Were there ever such thing as Frankenstein, Dracula, or vampires?

_____ 24. Scientist know that dinosaur once roamed the earth.

_____ 25. They don't believe that dragons ever existed.

_____ 26. Many fact influence their decision.

_____ 27. How many kind of ancient animals have been found?

_____ 28. Things such as needles, pins, and tacks shoul l be kept away from little children.

_____ 29. Stick and stone can break my bone.

_____ 30. But names can never hurt me.

_____ 31. College desks are more comfortable to work o .

_____ 32. That silly robin built two nesses.

_____ 33. There are morning and evening mists that rise ( ver the valleys.

_____ 34. Every winter both boys come down with colds i  their chesses.

_____ 35. Food costs are too high.

_____ 36. How many ghosses live in the haunted house?

_____ 37. Hattie had to take three tesses for her civil servic  exam.

_____ 38. Maybelle put two pork roases in the oven.

_____ 39. Those starlings are pests.

_____ 40. Harlan Brown builds desses for a living.

## ES Plurals

_____ 1. She threw away three of her good dishes with the p iper plates.

_____ 2. How many inchs are in a mile?

_____ 3. Marlene has had three bosses in two years.

_____ 4. The matchs were soaked by the rain.

_____ 5. There have been three fatal crashes at Martin's Corners this month.

_____ 6. The dime store sells boxes and boxes of greeting cards.

_____ 7. Mrs. Hartley has taught Sunday school classes since she joined the church.

_____ 8. Wilma Jean learned how to can tomatos from her cooking teacher.

_____ 9. John Wayne and Cary Grant were both heroes in westerns.

_____ 10. Our boss insists that we wear dresses to work.

## IES Plurals

_____ 1. The batter hit thirteen pop flies in one game.

_____ 2. All citys have several ethnic communitys within them.

_____ 3. Great quantities of blueberries grew on the bushes.

_____ 4. Sharon Lee was involved in all the graduation activitys.

_____ 5. The old man was in his eightys.

_____ 6. I gave the little girl five pennies for a handful of strawberries.

_____ 7. He continued his studies until he was in his fifties.

_____ 8. There are three librarys on campus.

_____ 9. The salesman had visited twenty-nine cities on his rounds.

_____ 10. The tailor killed 300 flys with one blow.

## VES Plurals

_____ 1. Maria has twelve knifes in her silverware drawer.

_____ 2. Beatrice has not taken enough knives to the picnic.

_____ 3. The leaves have fallen from the tree.

_____ 4. The tree has lost all of its leafs.

_____ 5. Please, Mother, we'd rather do it ourselfs.

_____ 6. Then do it yourselves!

_____ 7. Mom bakes fourteen loaves of bread a week for us.

_____ 8. The four of us ate the fourteen loafs Mother bakes.

_____ 9. The wolfs were howling in the canyon.

_____ 10. How many wolves are in the whole pack?

_____ 11. Roberta dusted off all the bookshelfs.

_____ 12. Dr. Jekyll and Mr. Hyde lived two lives.

_____ 13. The squirrels are the thiefs who are stealing the birdseed.

_____ 14. By the age of 101 Mr. Jones had outlived twelve wifes.

_____ 15. During the flood all of our lifes were in danger.

## Pattern Practice

Fill in the blanks in the following sentences with the standard plural forms of the nouns given in the margin. The first two have been done for you.

### S Plurals

TIME        1. How many <u>times</u> have I told you not to do that?

DOG         2. The town has fifteen thousand <u>dogs</u>.

DOLLAR      3. The town has sixteen thousand _____.

DEGREE      4. The little boy's temperature was 101 _____.

NATIVE      5. The _____ on the island drink cocoanut milk.

RIVER       6. All _____ run into the sea.

FIELD       7. As we drove through Iowa, we saw _____ and _____ of corn.

SON/DAUGHTER 8. Willy had five strong _____ and three strong _____.

GIRL        9. Now only three _____ are alive.

PICTURE     10. He has _____ of all eight children on the wall.

DOOR        11. The carpenter hung five _____ in one day.

PAPER       12. Paula delivered the _____ for her sick brother.

VEIL        13. Marianne tried on several _____.

CENT        14. He put fifty _____ in the gum machine.

LATINO        15. Many _____ know two languages.

TYPE          16. They take many _____ of courses.

STREET        17. All the _____ are covered with snow.

TEMPERATURE   18. The nurse took the _____ of the patients in the ward.

THERMOMETER   19. She used six _____ .

THING         20. One of the _____ she had to do was comfort the depressed patients.

KIND          21. She was cheerful to many _____ of people.

NOUN          22. How many _____ are in this sentence?

DETAIL        23. Josephine has many _____ in her paper.

FACTOR        24. Two _____ changed my mind.

TURKEY        25. Our family is so large, we had to buy two _____ for Thanksgiving.

JOURNEY       26. How many _____ have you made to the moon?

CHIMNEY       27. How many _____ do you have on your house?

ATTORNEY      28. The two _____ were arguing fiercely.

KEY           29. I have two _____ to my house.

RADIO         30. Donald has two _____ in his car.

STEREO        31. He also has two _____ ; one is in the car and the other is in the house.

CAMEO         32. We looked at the beautiful _____ in the store window.

PIANO         33. The famous pianist had five _____ in his home.

SOLO          34. Glorinda sang two _____ in church last Sunday.

CELLO/VIOLA   35. The college symphony orchestra had four _____ and three _____ .

PART          36. The machine has two major _____ .

ESKIMO        37. _____ live in cold regions.

BANJO         38. Bob Winans owns two _____ .

SILO          39. Uncle Bert has three _____ on his farm.

TOY 40. I like _____ that wind up.

NEST 41. He knocked down the hornets' _____ behind the barn.

CHEST 42. The coal miners had X-rays made of their _____ .

TEST 43. I could never pass my spelling _____ in grade school.

ROAST 44. We had two corn _____ in one week.

DESK 45. The men in the office sat behind their _____ .

## ES Plurals

BOX 1. My job is to stack cornflake _____ in the supermarket.

INCH 2. How many _____ are in a yard?

MIX 3. I always use cake _____ when I make chocolate cakes.

HERO 4. The Garcia family had two sons who were _____ in the war.

POTATO 5. Diana Joy wanted a bag of _____ for Christmas.

TOMATO 6. My mother's spaghetti sauce was filled with _____ .

KISS 7. Hector gave Luisa seven _____ on Valentine's Day.

WITNESS 8. The defense attorney used twenty-nine _____ .

FOX 9. The little _____ followed their mother into the den.

CHURCH 10. The town has five _____ .

BIRCH 11. The wind blew so hard the tops of the _____ touched the ground.

SASH 12. The flower girls looked lovely in their rose _____ .

RASH 13. All of the children had _____ .

DITCH 14. After the storm the _____ were overflowing with dirty water.

CLASS 15. The _____ were dismissed early.

MATCH 16. It took me twenty _____ to light the campfire.

NOTCH 17. The squirrels build their nests in the _____ of the trees.

PITCH 18. Gregory threw only three warm-up _____ before he started to play.

197

| | |
|---|---|
| DRESS | 19. Gina had at least a dozen _____ in the closet. |
| INCH | 20. Thirty-six _____ makes a yard. |
| KISS | 21. Joe could eat thirteen candy _____. |
| CATCH | 22. Bob only made two _____ during the whole game. |
| MATCH | 23. Riggs liked exhibition tennis _____. |
| PASS | 24. He made three _____ at her before she slapped him. |
| MASS | 25. Father Janez sang three _____ every Sunday morning. |

## IES Plurals

| | |
|---|---|
| LIBRARY | 1. My English teacher owns enough books to fill two _____. |
| PENNY | 2. My bank was filled with _____. |
| BUNNY | 3. My eight _____ had sixteen ears. |
| BABY | 4. They also had thirty _____. |
| ARMY | 5. _____ of ants invaded my kitchen. |
| COUNTRY | 6. Dr. Kissinger has visited _____ all over the world. |
| GROCERY | 7. The _____ are too heavy to carry on the bus. |
| COUNTY | 8. He hiked through twelve _____. |
| PARTY | 9. I went to four _____ on New Year's Eve. |
| LOTTERY | 10. José has won money in three _____. |
| CITY | 11. Twelve _____ are included in the statistics. |
| BODY | 12. They dumped two old car _____ in my nice, neat backyard. |
| DUTY | 13. The two new paramedics performed their _____ well. |
| STUDY | 14. The doctor is doing blood _____ on me. |
| SUPPLY | 15. The bookstore ran out of _____. |
| CAVITY | 16. Daddy, Daddy, I have only two _____. |

BUDDY 17. I went out with some of my old army _____ last night.

BOUNTY 18. The state stopped giving _____ for wolves.

LIBRARY 19. The _____ are all closed on Sunday.

NURSERY 20. The hospital had two _____ .

COUNTRY 21. England and Canada are the two _____ I have visited.

ENEMY 22. The devil has many _____ in our church.

ARMY 23. In World Wars I and II, the _____ of all countries suffered great losses.

GULLY 24. The rain made _____ in the soil.

JURY 25. The judge dismissed two _____ before he was satisfied.

TWENTY 26. In the _____ they danced the Charleston.

THIRTY 27. In the _____ they danced the fox trot and the waltz.

FORTY 28. In the _____ they danced the tango.

FIFTY 29. In the _____ they danced the monkey.

SIXTY 30. In the _____ they danced the twist.

SEVENTY 31. In the _____ they tried the fox trot again.

EIGHTY 32. In their _____ , the old folks talked about their aches and pains.

NINETY 33. In their _____ , they talked about their younger days.

GROCERY 34. In those days the _____ were cheap.

RESPONSIBILITY 35. In those days the _____ were heavy.

## VES Plurals

KNIFE 1. The farmer came after them with two carving _____ .

LEAF 2. They ran and hid under the _____ .

LOAF 3. The bakery wagon carrying _____ of bread rumbled past.

OURSELF 4. We ate _____ sick on the fresh bread.

LIFE   5. Roderigo is living three _____ .

SHELF   6. My dad put up new _____ in the kitchen.

THIEF   7. The bluejays were both _____ .

WIFE   8. The men introduced their _____ to their relatives.

SCARF   9. Isadora Duncan used to wear _____ .

LIFE   10. The twins lived separate _____ but did many things in the same way.

## Conversion Drill

Reread the sentences in the Recognition Drill. Convert each sentence that you did not mark CS into conventional spelling.

## Review Exercises

Using separate paragraphs, describe the following in the standard dialect.

1. the contents of the picture above;
2. the contents of your purse, wallet, pocket, or schoolroom; and
3. the cost of the items on your bill for groceries or school supplies.

# IRREGULAR NOUN PLURALS 2

In the standard dialect there are some irregular nouns whose plurals are not formed by adding *s* or *es*. Instead the spelling of the singular form is changed to form the plural. Since these nouns are irregular, the only way to learn them is by memorizing the ones you don't know, as you did with irregular verb forms. (Remember also to use your dictionary whenever you are in doubt.)

Here is a list of the most common irregular nouns, with their plurals.

|  | Singular | Plural |
|---|---|---|
| **Irregular plurals—spelling changes** | *child* | *children* |
|  | *foot* | *feet* |
|  | *goose* | *geese* |
|  | *man* | *men* |
|  | *mouse* | *mice* |
|  | *ox* | *oxen* |
|  | *tooth* | *teeth* |
|  | *woman* | *women* |
| **Irregular plurals—same as singular** | *fish* | *fish* |
|  | (notice that the names of most fish do not change their plural form) | |
|  | *trout* | *trout* |
|  | *perch* | *perch* |
|  | *moose* | *moose* |
|  | *sheep* | *sheep* |
| **Irregular plurals—no singular form** |  | *cattle* |
|  |  | *people* |

Some community dialects differ from the standard dialect in that they form the plural by adding *s* either to the singular form, or to the irregular plural form.

EXAMPLES

| Singular | Community Dialect Plural | Standard Dialect Plural |
|---|---|---|
| child | childs / childrens | children |
| fish | fishes | fish |

Summary: Irregular Noun Plurals

| Community Dialect | Standard Dialect |
|---|---|
| three childs / three childrens | three children |
| seventeen fishes | seventeen fish |

## Recognition Drill

Underline the plural nouns in the following sentences. Then mark SD next to each sentence whose plural nouns are in the standard dialect. The first three have been done for you.

_____ 1. The <u>childs</u> were crying for their mother.

__SD__ 2. The <u>children</u> were laughing at "Sesame Street" on T.V.

_____ 3. The <u>mans</u> were sick and tired of being out of work.

_____ 4. The women were happy to be back on the job.

_____ 5. The womans brought food to the orphaned children.

_____ 6. The men all helped at the church supper.

_____ 7. The room was six foot by ten foot.

_____ 8. The house was thirty feet by forty feet.

_____ 9. The lot was seventy foots by one hundred foots.

_____ 10. The garden was twelve feets by six feets.

_____ 11. The driveway was sixty feet long.

_____ 12. The Smiths have twenty-four children.

_____ 13. The Marshals have two childrens.

_____ 14. The shop steward told all the mens to stop work.

_____ 15. The people in the crowd helped to push the stalled car.

_____ 16. There were six married womens in the class.

_____ 17. The men loved to discuss the novels they read.

_____ 18. How many geeses do you have in your pond?

_____ 19. I have twenty geese in my pond.

_____ 20. No, you don't because I just shot two of your gooses for our dinner.

_____ 21. Well, I guess I have only eighteen geese in my pond.

_____ 22. By yesterday he had caught three mouses.

_____ 23. Altogether he has caught six mices.

_____ 24. Perhaps by tomorrow he will have caught nine mice.

_____ 25. Twenty peoples registered for the course.

_____ 26. Crowds of people were downtown doing their Christmas shopping.

_____ 27. They looked like sheeps being herded to a new pasture.

_____ 28. The collie was herding over one hundred sheep.

_____ 29. How many trouts did you catch?

_____ 30. I didn't catch any trout, but I did catch two perch.

_____ 31. Perches are good but I prefer catfishes.

_____ 32. Many people don't like catfish or perch.

_____ 33. How many peoples went to the James Brown concert?

_____ 34. I would say about three thousand people were there.

_____ 35. Cattles don't like shrimps.

_____ 36. I lost two tooths in the hay.

_____ 37. Joe had a plate heaped with shrimp for supper.

_____ 38. Edward loaded all his cattle on the truck.

_____ 39. Sheila likes Indian chiefs.

_____ 40. He bought new teeth at the dime store.

## Pattern Practice

Fill in the blanks in the following sentences with the standard plural form of the nouns given in the margin. The first two have been done for you.

CHILD       1. The old woman who lived in a shoe had so many <u>children</u> she didn't know what to

do.

WOMAN       2. Twenty <u>women</u> were promoted in our division.

MAN       3. The _____ were all over thirty years old.

| | |
|---|---|
| FOOT | 4. The cheerleaders jumped five _____ in the air. |
| GOOSE | 5. As the _____ flew towards the north, they cackled loudly. |
| MOUSE | 6. Three blind _____, three blind _____, see how they run. |
| MOOSE | 7. I caught sight of three _____ in the swamp. |
| PEOPLE | 8. They are my _____. |
| PERCH | 9. Al, would you mind buying three _____ at the market? |
| SALMON | 10. In the spring the _____ swim upstream to the place where they were born. |
| SWORDFISH | 11. The men caught two good-sized _____ on their fishing trip. |
| PEOPLE | 12. Many _____ on the pier cheered them when they returned. |
| MOOSE | 13. My grandfather had three _____ heads mounted in his recreation room. |
| SHEEP | 14. _____ follow their leaders even into danger. |
| PEOPLE | 15. _____ learn to think for themselves. |
| TROUT | 16. _____ love cold, fast-moving water. |
| CHILD | 17. A class of school _____ marched down the street. |
| WOMAN | 18. The _____ played marching music. |
| MAN | 19. The _____ carried the flags. |
| CHILD | 20. The little _____ held balloons. |
| MAN | 21. The _____, women, and children were celebrating the Fourth of July. |
| CATTLE | 22. The dog chased the _____ into the corral. |
| TOOTH | 23. He bit their tails with his _____. |
| CHIEF | 24. The department had a conference for fire _____. |
| ROOF | 25. The _____ of the houses were covered with snow. |

## Conversion Drill

Reread the sentences in the Recognition Drill. Convert each sentence that you did not mark SD into the standard dialect.

# REVIEW OF NOUN PLURALS 3

Here is a summary of the ways in which community dialects may differ from the standard dialect in forming plurals.

| | Singular | Community Dialect Plural | Standard Dialect Plural |
|---|---|---|---|
| **Regular** | mile<br>cent<br>boy | mile<br>cent<br>boy | mile*s*<br>cent*s*<br>boy*s* |
| **Irregular** | child<br><br>fish<br>trout<br>goose | child<br>childs<br>childrens<br>fishes<br>trouts<br>gooses<br>geeses | child*ren*<br><br>*fish*<br>*trout*<br>*geese* |

## Pattern Practice

Fill in the blanks with the standard dialect plural form of the nouns in the margin. The first two have been done for you.

INCH          1. He just missed breaking the broad jump record by two <u>inches</u>.

CENT          2. The cost of a quart of milk went up to ninety-five <u>cents</u>.

PEOPLE        3. How many _____ went to the class picnic?

MILE          4. My X113 Jaguar has gone 130 _____ per hour.

TIME          5. How many _____ must a fool fall in love?

TOMATO        6. How many _____ are needed to make one 12-inch pizza?

FOOT          7. How many _____ do dogs have?

WOMAN         8. Fourteen _____ graduated from the School of Education.

DOLLAR    9. John won a million _____ in the Irish Sweepstakes.

GIRL    10. Joe had dates with three _____ one night.

MAN    11. There are nine _____ on a baseball team.

MILE    12. Try walking three _____ in his shoes.

YEAR    13. How many _____ did it take you to finish college?

TIME    14. Georgina has been married sixteen _____ .

DIME/QUARTER    15. I always tip the taxi driver two _____ and three _____ .

BOY    16. Have you seen the _____ in the band?

CUP    17. The cake takes three _____ of sugar.

PAPER    18. I'm three _____ behind in my English course.

CLASS    19. This semester I have four _____ .

TABLE    20. Philippo bought two marble _____ .

CENT    21. He paid one hundred dollars and thirty _____ for each table.

SCHOOL    22. In our district there are seven elementary _____ .

APPLE    23. Eve gave Adam two _____ .

PEOPLE    24. _____ who need _____ are the luckiest _____ in the world.

DOLLAR    25. College professors earn five _____ a week.

THING    26. While I am on my diet I have to avoid sweet _____ .

CENT    27. A hot fudge sundae costs fifty-five _____ .

BOOK    28. I took out four _____ from the public library.

CHAIR    29. For our church meeting we had to borrow extra _____ .

THING    30. How many _____ do you have in your purse?

BOOK    31. Orson ought to take care of his _____ .

BOX    32. Samson must have built these _____ .

| | |
|---|---|
| MAN | 33. Twenty _____ couldn't carry them. |
| TIME | 34. Tessie tried ten _____ to tell him but she didn't have the courage. |
| WOMAN | 35. Martha and Mary were both intelligent _____ . |
| GOOSE | 36. The girls giggled like silly _____ . |
| THING | 37. How many _____ do you have on your mind? |
| KNIFE | 38. The men carried _____ to clean the fish. |
| INCH | 39. The midget was only thirty _____ tall. |
| LEAF | 40. I will have to turn the _____ of the book carefully. |
| FAMILY | 41. Many _____ have reunions during their vacations. |
| FACT | 42. Please give me all of the _____ . |
| POTATO | 43. How many pounds of _____ are in a peck? |
| LIBRARY | 44. The campus has two _____ . |
| KIND | 45. There are many _____ of cheese in the market. |
| STEREO | 46. Four families on our block have bought new _____ . |
| COUNTRY | 47. Airplanes take us to other _____ quickly. |
| TOMATO | 48. The British like fried _____ . |
| DOG | 49. How many _____ are in the dog pound today? |
| PIANO | 50. The piece was for two _____ . |
| KISS | 51. Sherry was blowing _____ into the air. |
| HOUSE | 52. Pete has to paint two _____ this summer. |
| SOLO | 53. The wolves were singing _____ to the moon. |
| CHURCH | 54. Our minister preaches sermons at two _____ . |
| PENNY | 55. _____ don't buy anything anymore. |
| DRESS | 56. Dorrie makes all of her _____ herself. |

| | |
|---|---|
| CAR | 57. The railroad _____ were filled with fruit. |
| MATCH | 58. May I borrow some _____ from you? |
| CAVITY | 59. Brushing your teeth prevents _____. |
| LATINO | 60. Many _____ know of the story of Gregorio Cortez. |
| SCHOOL | 61. The _____ were closed during the teachers' strike. |
| ENEMY | 62. Mr. Wilson was a man without _____. |
| WOLF | 63. German shepherds look like _____. |
| THIRTY | 64. Your granddad will tell you about the depression of the _____. |
| CLASS | 65. Do social _____ still exist in this country? |
| RESPONSIBILITY | 66. My little brothers refuse to take on their _____. |
| RADIO | 67. Why do you need two _____? |
| CHILD | 68. Jesus said, "Suffer the little _____ to come unto me." |
| PEOPLE | 69. All the _____ in the world couldn't make me change my mind. |
| PARTY | 70. There are two major political _____ in the United States. |
| STAIR | 71. He ran up the _____ and down the _____ all day long. |
| FOOT | 72. What has four _____, two ears, and one trunk? |
| CENT | 73. All I need is ten _____ and I will have enough for my bus fare. |
| STORY | 74. You tell too many _____ that have sad endings. |
| QUARTER | 75. Six _____ will buy a six pack. |
| RUG | 76. They had sheepskin _____ all over the house. |
| PAPER | 77. Terry threw the old _____ in the trash. |
| PANTS | 78. My father wears the _____ in the family. |
| DOLLAR | 79. The book cost two _____. |
| MOTHER | 80. The three _____ discussed their children's successes. |

## Review Exercises

Imagine that it is your job to describe a big family reunion for the local newspaper. Describe the numbers of aunts, uncles, cousins, brothers, sisters, and pets. Describe the food they ate, the games they played. Be careful to use plurals in the standard dialect.

Describe the following picture. Be certain to include the numbers of things you see and the activities being performed.

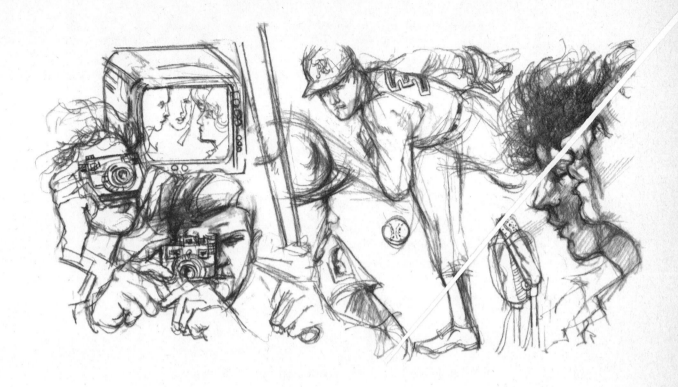

# POSSESSIVE NOUNS (SINGULAR)

# 4

Many times we want to show that one thing is possessed, owned, or part of another thing or person. In the standard dialect, there are three ways of showing this belonging or possession.

1. You can simply use words like *own* and *belong*:

    (with passive verb)   That hat *is owned by* my father.
    (with active verb)    My father *owns* that hat.
    (with active verb)    That hat *belongs to* my father.

2. You can put the thing or person that possesses into a prepositional phrase using *of*:

    the hat *of* my father

3. You can make the noun possessive by adding an apostrophe (') plus an *s* and placing it before the thing that it possesses:

    my father*'s* hat

    If the possessive noun, however, already ends in *s*, you just add an apostrophe (') instead of *'s*:

    Mr. Jones*'* hat

    It is the third type of possession, the possessive noun, that we are going to study in this chapter, because this is the one where the standard dialect differs most from community dialects.

    In some community dialects, the *'s* is not added to the first noun. Possession is shown instead by the order of the two nouns: the first one always possesses the second one, and the second one always belongs to the first.

EXAMPLES

| Community Dialect | Standard Dialect |
|---|---|
| my father hat | my father*'s* hat |
| Mr. Jones hat | Mr. Jones*'* hat |

The difference between the standard dialect and some community dialects is that the standard dialect uses an *'s* or an *'* to show possession or ownership, where the community dialect may not.

## Summary: Possessive Nouns

| Community Dialect | Standard Dialect |
| --- | --- |
| my father hat | my father's hat |
| the teacher book | the teacher's book |
| the fox den | the fox's den |
| Bess hair | Bess' hair |

## Recognition Drill

Underline the singular possessive nouns in the following sentences. Then mark SD next to each sentence whose possessive nouns are in the standard dialect. The first three have been done for you.

_____ 1. Lucy borrowed Mary sweater.

__SD__ 2. My mother had always made her nephew's birthday cake

__SD__ 3. The horse's mane shone in the sun.

_____ 4. Susan rode a boy bike.

_____ 5. My uncle drove my brother car and dented the fender.

_____ 6. The captain was proud of Keith's courage.

_____ 7. Richard new jacket is red velvet.

_____ 8. Miranda's education was interrupted because she couldn't afford a baby sitter.

_____ 9. My baby eyes are blue.

_____ 10. The crowd's attention was caught by the skydiver.

_____ 11. Belinda new coat was fur.

_____ 12. The weatherman's warning was correct.

_____ 13. The thunder's rumble could be heard in the distance.

_____ 14. Paul used Bill bike without his permission.

_____ 15. My grandma was too old to cook my grandpa's meals.

_____ 16. Grandma and Grandpa became my family's responsibility.

_____ 17. We gave them Matthew bedroom to sleep in.

_____ 18. We made our grandparent's last years more comfortable.

_____ 19. The dog's fur bristled when he saw the wildcat.

_____ 20. The book's pages were greasy and torn when he returned it to me.

_____ 21. He should take better care of someone else property.

_____ 22. The car's manual of operation had been lost.

_____ 23. The artist drawings were blown off his desk.

_____ 24. The telephone operator voice was smooth and assuring.

_____ 25. The congregation's offering was large last Sunday.

_____ 26. The ice-cream truck's bell brought out all of the children on the block.

_____ 27. They listened to the driver's warning to look out for the cars.

_____ 28. One child father took him across the street by the hand.

_____ 29. The small table's top had been damaged in moving.

_____ 30. The owner complaint to the moving company was answered promptly.

## Pattern Practice

Fill in the blanks in the following sentences with the standard possessive form of the noun given in the margin. The first two have been done for you.

DIANA      1. <u>Diana's</u> voice was strong and sexy.

CHARLEY      2. The chops were cooked by <u>Charley's</u> aunt.

JACKSON FIVE      3. The _____ performance got rave reviews.

U.C.L.A.      4. Notre Dame broke _____ 88-game streak.

BOBBY THOMSON      5. _____ homer was one of the great moments in base-

ball.

BASEBALL      6. Another of _____ great moments was Bill Maseroske's homer.

SHIP            7. The _____ sails opened to the wind.

PARTY           8. John Kennedy was the _____ choice.

CAT            9. The little gypsy stole the cool _____ money.

FISH           10. He pulled the hook out of the _____ mouth.

STEVE          11. Then he put the fish in _____ bucket.

PAULINE       12. _____ bubble gum stuck to her wig.

WIG            13. The _____ color was bubble-gum green.

GIRL           14. The _____ luck was bad all day.

CAR            15. Next her _____ battery ran down from leaving the lights on.

BOYFRIEND     16. Her _____ tow truck ran out of gas.

GOAT          17. The _____ fur makes me sneeze.

TREE           18. The _____ branches are covered with ice.

CAROL BURNETT   19. _____ show wasn't as funny as usual.

JOHN          20. _____ track record was the fastest in the history of the college.

NEIGHBOR      21. My _____ garden is beautiful.

JOSÉ           22. _____ limousine is pearl gray.

PRESIDENT      23. The _____ car is black.

CHILD         24. The _____ slide has a puddle at the bottom.

BROTHER       25. My _____ new coat is blue corduroy.

BOOK          26. He hid the letter between the _____ pages.

JIM            27. Jacob borrowed _____ car.

ROBIN         28. The bluejay stole the _____ eggs.

FLOOR         29. The boots spoiled the _____ new polish.

TOOTH         30. This _____ filling is gone.

## Substitution Drill

The following paragraph shows possession by using *of* or *of the* constructions. Change them all to possessive nouns.

When she was eighteen, Elizabeth Taylor became the wife of Nicky Hilton. He was the son of Conrad Hilton. Conrad Hilton was, at one time, the husband of Zsa Zsa Gabor. When she was nineteen, Elizabeth Taylor became the wife of Michael Wilding. Wilding is now the husband of Margaret Leighton. Leighton used to be the wife of Laurence Harvey. After divorcing Wilding, Elizabeth Taylor became the wife of Mike Todd, (the former wives of Mike Todd include Joan Blondell), but the death of Todd in a plane crash ended that marriage. Liz then fell in love with Eddie Fisher, the best friend of her late husband. Fisher was the husband of Debbie Reynolds. So Eddie divorced Debbie (who became the wife of Harry Karl) to marry Liz, but Liz soon divorced him to become the wife of Richard Burton. The first wife of Richard Burton, Sybil, became the wife of Jordon Christopher. Eddie became the husband of Connie Stevens. Stevens had been the wife of James Stacey. Stacey had also been the husband of Kim Darby. Stevens and Fisher got divorced. Reynolds and Karl got divorced. Taylor and Burton were separated briefly, got back together, and then were separated again.

## Conversion Exercise

Reread the sentences in the Recognition Drill. Convert each sentence that you did not mark SD into the standard dialect.

# POSSESSIVE NOUNS (PLURAL)

**5**

In the standard dialect, when you want to make a plural noun possessive, you follow the same rule you do for singular nouns: if the plural noun does not end in *s* (for example, *children*), you add *'s* to make it possessive. If the plural noun does end in *s* (for example, *boys*), you add only an apostrophe (*'*).

EXAMPLES                              Standard Dialect

> The children*'s* snowsuits were covered with mud.
> In biology class, the girls*'* grades were better than the boys*'* grades.

Some community dialects do not add the *'s* or the *'*. Instead they show possession simply by word order, as we saw in the last chapter.

EXAMPLES                              Community Dialect

> children snowsuits
> girls grades

If the community dialect plural is different from the standard dialect plural (for example, if *s* is not added to a plural noun), the possessive plural may also be different.

EXAMPLES                              Community Dialect

> childs snowsuits
> girl grades

To convert a community dialect into the standard dialect, choose the standard plural form (see Chapters 1 and 2) and add either *'s* or *'* to make it possessive.

## Summary: Plural Possessives

| Community Dialect | Standard Dialect |
|---|---|
| children snowsuits | |
| childs snowsuits | children's snowsuits |
| child snowsuits | |
| childrens snowsuits | |
| boy grades | boys' grades |
| boys grades | |

## Recognition Drill

Underline the possessive plurals in the following sentences. Then mark SD next to each sentence whose possessive plural nouns are in the standard dialect. The first three have been done for you.

_____ 1. The <u>girls</u> songs were sweet and romantic.

__SD__ 2. The <u>girls'</u> dresses were blue.

_____ 3. The <u>girl</u> voices were clear and in tune.

_____ 4. Marvel looked for the men's department.

_____ 5. He wanted to buy mens' boots.

_____ 6. He also needs three pairs of men baseball shoes for his brothers.

_____ 7. His brothers were young but they wore mans sizes.

_____ 8. The horses tails were braided and tied with ribbons.

_____ 9. The horses' coats were shining from being brushed.

_____ 10. The horse's names were Dobbin, Black Beauty, and Spectator.

_____ 11. The children's appetites were huge after playing all day.

_____ 12. The children playthings were slides, swings, and sandboxes.

_____ 13. The older childrens' games were baseball and basketball.

_____ 14. The very little childs toys were blocks and teddybears.

_____ 15. The citizen's rights were ignored.

_____ 16. The citizens' rights were upheld.

_____ 17. The sheep wool was sold.

_____ 18. The sheep's food was grass.

_____ 19. The sheeps' babies are lambs.

_____ 20. All eight of the two cars' tires were punctured with nails.

_____ 21. Both the car's tires had to be replaced.

_____ 22. The women's doctors were kind and thoughtful.

_____ 23. The womens' babies were well cared for.

_____ 24. The womans breakfasts were brought on trays.

_____ 25. The woman temperatures were taken by one nurse.

_____ 26. The sirens wails could be heard from all parts of the city.

_____ 27. The sirens' sounds meant that there were several big fires in the city.

_____ 28. I hope not many people's homes are burned.

_____ 29. I certainly hope no peoples' lives are lost.

_____ 30. Perhaps all the people lives and homes will be saved.

## Pattern Practice

Fill in the blanks in the following sentences with the standard possessive plural form of the noun given in the margin. The first two have been done for you.

WOMAN      1. The <u>women's</u> stitches were small and even as they worked on the quilt.

CUSTODIAN      2. Fifteen men attended the <u>custodians'</u> meeting.

PARENT      3. The _____ conference was held in Detroit.

FAMILY      4. The two _____ friends attended the funeral.

OCCUPANT      5. Both _____ clothing was lost in the fire.

MAN      6. They assigned her to the _____ ward of the hospital by mistake.

CHURCH　　　　7. These _____ hymns are filled with love.

PEOPLE　　　　8. The _____ interests were being served by the new mayor.

STUDENT　　　9. The _____ complaints resulted in better food at the canteen.

LADY　　　　　10. The _____ eyeglasses had heavier frames.

PAINTER　　　11. The _____ overalls were spattered with rainbow colors.

VEHICLE　　　12. Both _____ back windows were covered with ice.

BABY　　　　　13. The _____ screams could be heard by their mothers every four hours.

AIDE　　　　　14. The _____ voices were soft and comforting as they wheeled the babies to their

　　　　　　　　mothers.

INFANT　　　　15. Now, the _____ cries have stopped.

WOLF　　　　　16. When I camped in the forest, I heard the _____ howls at night.

BIRD　　　　　17. In the morning, I heard the _____ songs.

BOY　　　　　　18. The _____ poker game lasted until three in the morning.

PIGEON　　　　19. I am allergic to the _____ feathers.

CAT　　　　　　20. The _____ fur makes me sneeze.

LADY　　　　　21. Mr. Dino was glad that the _____ photographs had turned out well.

GENTLEMAN　22. The elderly _____ get-togethers were very successful.

EXPERT　　　　23. The karate _____ party was a model of discipline and courtesy.

HOUSE　　　　24. The condemned _____ basements were filled with water.

TEACHER　　　25. The architect ignored the _____ advice about the new school.

## Conversion Drill

Reread the sentences in the Recognition Drill. Convert each sentence that you did not mark SD into the standard dialect.

# REVIEW OF POSSESSIVE NOUNS

**6**

Here is a chart that shows the standard dialect forms for possessive nouns:

| Singular noun, not ending in *s* | add *'s* | the teacher*'s* book |
| Singular noun, ending in *s* | add *'* | the bus*'* window |
| Plural noun, not ending in *s* | add *'s* | the people*'s* rights |
| Plural noun, ending in *s* | add *'* | the dolls*'* house |

## Review Exercise

All of the possessives in the paragraph below use the preposition *of*. Rewrite the paragraph showing possession by using apostrophes. (Watch for both singular and plural possessives.)

The wedding of Sharon was a beautiful affair. The gown of the bride was white velvet, trimmed with the tails of ermines. Her cathedral-length veil was four feet long and touched the feet of the maid of honor. The dress of the maid of honor was deep pink satin. The gowns of the other girls were purple. The bouquets of the bridesmaids were pink roses and the bouquet of the bride was white orchids with one pink rose. The suit of the groom was deep purple with a pink tie and cummerbund. The outfits of the ushers were rose with purple ties and cummerbunds. After the reception the new husband took the arm of his wife and escorted her to the car of a friend who drove them to the airport. They spent their honeymoon on the beaches of Nassau.

# NOUNS FROM VERBS

# 7

There are many nouns that are made from the *ing* form of verbs. When these *ing* words are made into nouns, they do not have helping verbs in front of them as they do when they are used as verbs.

## EXAMPLES

I *was swimming* all day.

(Here *swimming* is a verb, preceded by the helping verb *was*.)

I like *swimming*.

(Here *swimming* is a noun. It has no helping verb, and it is used as an object of the verb *like*.)

*Swimming* is my favorite sport.

(Here *swimming* is also a noun. It is the subject of the sentence.)

I won the race by *swimming* the fastest.

(Here *swimming* is also a noun. It is the object of the preposition *by*.)

There are also many nouns that are made from infinitives. They can often substitute for the *ing* nouns.

EXAMPLES

I like *to swim*.                    (*To swim* is a noun. It is the object of the verb LIKE.)

*To swim* is my favorite sport.      (*To swim* is a noun. It is the subject of the sentence.)

It will be important to remember these nouns made from verbs later, when we discuss sentence patterns. In this chapter, however, there is only one way in which community dialects commonly are different from the standard dialect. Many community dialects do not add *ing* or *to* when they make a noun from a verb.

EXAMPLES

Community Dialect        Standard Dialect

I like swim.             { I like *to* swim.
                         { I like swimm*ing*.

The most common place where this difference occurs is after prepositions.

EXAMPLES

Community Dialect              Standard Dialect

I won the race by swim.       I won the race by

                              swimm*ing*.

Summary:   Nouns from Verbs

| Community Dialect | Standard Dialect |
| --- | --- |
| He was paid for drive a cab. | He was paid for driv*ing* a cab. |
| He was asked drive a cab. | He was asked *to* drive a cab. |

## Recognition Drill

Underline the nouns made from verbs in the following sentences. Then mark SD next to each sentence that is in the standard dialect. The first three have been done for you.

___SD___  1. Justin was paid for <u>going</u> to work.

_____  2. He did Amelia a favor by <u>come</u>.

223

_**SD**_    3. Laverne showed his love for Carol by <u>going</u> home.

_____    4. Robert's Hauling Company was paid for move the company's furniture.

_____    5. By running the mile in 3:58.3 he set a record in 1965.

_____    6. By discover a vaccine for polio, Dr. Salk saved many lives.

_____    7. By limit speed on the highways to 55 miles per hour, many accidents are avoided.

_____    8. New paths were opened in the park for jogging.

_____    9. The car wore out from pull heavy loads.

_____ 10. I earn my paycheck by teaching.

_____ 11. Pastor earns his by preach

_____ 12. Bella likes watching T.V.

_____ 13. She missed the game by wait too long to buy the tickets.

_____ 14. Herman's voice was hoarse from yelling at the umpire.

_____ 15. Miranda's hands were sore from scrub the floor.

## Pattern Practice

Fill in the blanks in the following sentences with a noun (the *ing* form) made from the verbs given in the margin. The first two have been done for you.

ASK      1. Jane could have had a new dress simply by <u>asking</u> for it.

ACCEPT    2. Earl was against <u>accepting</u> the invitation to the rally.

VISIT     3. He embarrassed the Jones by _____ at bedtime.

COME     4. They thanked him for _____ but fell asleep.

CALL     5. He could have saved a trip by _____ on the telephone first.

GROW     6. The fertilizer was intended for _____ green grass.

LAUGH    7. She was angry at their _____ at her.

FALL     8. Fiammetta turned green after _____ into a barrel of green grass.

224

SPELL    9. Rose received a reward for _____ all of the words correctly.

READ    10. Ruthie rewarded Rose for _____ all of the words correctly.

WRITE    11. Romain relied on Rose and Ruth for _____ his letters.

DRIVE    12. Clive earned extra money by_____ a school bus.

RAISE    13. He needed the money for _____ his eleven children.

DANCE    14. Delia showed her delight by_____ around the Christmas tree.

RUN    15. The teacher worked off her anger by_____ around the block.

## Conversion Drill

Reread the sentences in the Recognition Drill. Convert each sentence that you did not mark SD into the standard dialect.

# PRONOUNS

# 8

In the next several chapters we will be dealing with six different kinds of pronouns.

## Personal Pronouns

There are three different types of personal pronouns:

**Type 1** pronouns refer to the speaker of a sentence (*I, me, we, us*).
**Type 2** pronouns refer to the person whom the speaker is addressing (*you*).
**Type 3** pronouns refer to persons and things that the speaker is talking about (*he, him, she, her, it, they, them*). These pronouns can often substitute for nouns, or refer back to a noun previously mentioned:

*My brother* is going steady with three *girlfriends*.
*He* is going to get one of *them* mad at *him* soon.

## Possessive Pronouns

Possessive pronouns are those that show possession or belonging, as do possessive nouns. There are also three types of possessive pronouns, which correspond to the three types of personal pronouns:

**Type 1:** That is *my* book.
          That is *our* book.
**Type 2:** That is *your* book.
**Type 3:** That is *his* book.
          That is *her* book.
          That is *its* book.
          That is *their* book.

Notice that the Type 3 possessive pronouns, like the Type 3 personal pronouns, can substitute for nouns. Possessive nouns that correspond to the possessive pronouns listed in Type 3 above are used in the following sentences:

That is my *brother's* book.
That is *Susan's* book.
That is the *library's* book.
That is the *parents'* book.

## Reflexive Pronouns

Reflexive pronouns are those which reflect back on the subject. Again there are three types:

**Type 1:** I washed *myself*.
          We washed *ourselves*.
**Type 2:** You must wash *yourself*.
          You must all wash *yourselves*.
**Type 3:** He washed *himself*.
          My sister washed *herself*.
          The cat washed *itself*.
          They all washed *themselves*.

## Demonstrative Pronouns

Demonstrative pronouns are those that point to or "demonstrate" a noun —usually an object, event, or person. There are just four demonstrative pronouns in the standard dialect: *this*, *that*, *these*, and *those*. They may be used either alone, or in front of a noun:

*This* cereal tastes wonderful.
*This* is wonderful.
*These* pencils are sharp.
*These* are sharp.

## Relative Pronouns and Question Pronouns

We will not discuss relative pronouns until Part V, Sentence Patterns, and we will not discuss question pronouns (sometimes called WH words) until Part IV, Questions and Negatives. We will just briefly mention them here.

Relative pronouns are those that relate a person or thing in one part of a sentence to the same person or thing in another part of the sentence:

This is the student *who* made the honor roll.
This is the tree *which* was blasted by the tornado.

Question pronouns, or WH words, are sometimes the same as relative pronouns, but have a different purpose—that is, they are used for asking questions:

*Who* is the student in the green dress?
*Which* book did you like the best?

# PERSONAL PRONOUNS  9

As explained in Chapter 8, there are three types of personal pronouns: Type 1 pronouns refer to the speaker; Type 2 pronouns refer to the one spoken to; and Type 3 pronouns refer to the person or thing spoken about.

In the standard dialect, personal pronouns have both subject and object forms. That is, most of them have one form when they act as the subject of a verb, and another form when they act as the object of a verb or a preposition.

|        | Singular | | Plural | |
|        | Subject | Object | Subject | Object |
|--------|---------|--------|---------|--------|
| **Type 1** | I | me | we | us |
| **Type 2** | you | you | you | you |
| **Type 3** | he<br>she<br>it | him<br>her<br>it | they | them |

(Notice that *you* is the same in singular and plural, and in subject and object forms. Notice also that *it* is the same in subject and object forms.)

EXAMPLES Standard Dialect

> *I* am right but *you* are wrong.
>> (*I* and *you* are used as subjects of the verb.)
> My boyfriend likes *me* better than he likes *you*.
>> (*Me* and *you* are used as objects of the verb.)
> The teacher gave the book to *me* before he gave it to *you*.
>> (*Me* and *you* are used as objects of the preposition *to*.)

In some community dialects, the subject and object forms of the personal pronouns are the reverse of the standard dialect.

EXAMPLES

Community Dialect  | Standard Dialect

Bill and *him* gave the book to *you* and *I*.

Bill and *he* gave the book to *you* and *me*.

Summary:  Personal Pronouns

|         | **Community Dialect** | **Standard Dialect** |
|---------|----------------------|----------------------|
| Subject | me, us, him, her, them | *I, we, he, she, they* |
| Object  | I, we, he, she, they | *me, us, him, her, them* |

## Recognition Drill

Underline the personal pronouns in the following sentences. Then mark SD next to each sentence whose personal pronouns are in the standard dialect. The first three have been done for you.

SUBJECT PRONOUNS

_SD_  1. <u>You</u> and <u>I</u> had fun at the roller rink.

_____  2. <u>You</u> and <u>me</u> used to have luck fishing.

_____  3. <u>Them</u> and <u>us</u> all met for a picnic at Washington Park.

_____  4. We joined the PTA.

_____  5. Him and me were both on the football team in high school.

_____  6. He and I bowled together for four years.

_____  7. Her was the star of the girls' baseball team.

3. Hattie and the boys have gone to the fair together.

_____

4. Maria danced like a professional.

_____

5. Jim and Mary Lee ran as if ghosts were after them.

_____

6. Norma and I came from the same town.

_____

7. You and Milton share in a car pool.

_____

8. Our team and your team are an equal match.

_____

9. The garbage collectors come every Tuesday.

_____

10. The bell rang early this Sunday.

_____


## Substitution Drill

Underline the object nouns in the following sentences. Then on the line below rewrite the sentence, substituting the appropriate personal pronoun for the noun in object position. The first two have been done for you.

1. The houses built by the <u>natives</u> were very sturdy.

   The houses built by them were very sturdy.

2. Jennifer began to tell <u>Joe</u> about the <u>day's events</u>.

   Jennifer began to tell him about them.

3. Clarence happened to see Hazel at the next party.

_____

4. We had gone to the class reunion in hopes of seeing our old friends.

_____

5. Geoffrey should have invited our family to his house.

_____

6. The movie showed the boy and the girl happily married in the final scene.

_____

7. Dad took Mother and me to the boat show.

_____

8. The witch doctor tried to cure you and Alicia with a chant.

_____

9. He made Margaret and me laugh.

_____

10. Some old folks believed in witch doctors.

_____

## Pattern Practice

Fill in the blanks in the following sentences with the personal pronouns that best fit the context. (You will have to use both subject and object forms.) The first two have been done for you.

1. Dr. Michael Reese examined the accident victims. <u>He</u> found <u>them</u> severely injured.

2. One girl was unconscious. <u>She</u> had suffered a head injury.

3. The boy was bleeding. _____ had received a cut on the arm.

4. The accident had not been the fault of either _____ or _____.

5. The car had hit _____ while they were on the sidewalk talking.

6. My brother and I witnessed the accident, but the victims were not known by _____.

232

7. I hope that _____ recovered quickly.

8. The little girl was crying. _____ had burst her balloon.

9. _____ and her little brother had been to the zoo.

10. Their mother had shown _____ the elephants.

11. Each of _____ had had a ride on a pony.

12. The bus usually stops at my corner. _____ ride it to work.

13. Yesterday it didn't stop. My neighbor gave _____ a ride.

14. _____ is a very kind man. My wife took _____ a German chocolate cake.

15. My favorite song is "Yearning." The music makes _____ sad.

16. Our favorite old time comedian is Charlie Chaplin. _____ makes _____ laugh.

17. Sue and Rose like cowboy shows. I like _____ too.

18. Rose took Sue and _____ to a John Wayne movie.

19. In return, I took Rose and her brother to the races. They thanked _____.

20. My father is a minister. Some of the parishioners named their babies after _____.

21. Mother is a vestrywoman. Ten girls were named after _____.

22. Since my sister and _____ were named after _____ also, the church is filled with Isaacs and Sarahs.

23. My sister told _____ that _____ wished _____ was the only Sarah.

24. Our parents said they felt sorry for _____.

25. Sarah and _____ will give our children unusual names like Rumpelstiltzken or Nebuchadnezzar.

26. Violet and I asked the teacher to give _____ a *B* and _____ an *A*.

27. Barrett had his appendix out. His appendix had given _____ a stomach-ache.

28. The operation lasted twenty minutes but _____ stayed in the hospital a week.

29. His girlfriend visited _____. He was glad to see _____.

30. His mother brought him cookies but _____ told _____ to take _____ home.

31. His stomach wasn't settled enough to eat _____ .

32. At the end of the week, we picked _____ up at the hospital. He thanked _____ .

33. Pansy Ann won first prize at bingo. They gave _____ to _____ at the end of the

    evening.

34. _____ won a colored T.V. _____ was worth $500.

35. The other players wished that _____ had won _____ .

## Conversion Drill

Reread the sentences in the Recognition Drill. Convert each sentence that you did not mark SD into the standard dialect.

# THE *IT* PRONOUN

# 10

In Chapter 9 we discussed the subject and object forms of the personal pronoun and the community dialect variations of those forms. In this chapter we will discuss one way in which community dialects differ from the standard dialect in their use of the *it* pronoun.

Although *it* is the same whether used as subject or object, in some community dialects it is omitted in the subject position, so that the subject *it* is understood (just as *you* is understood in commands like "Open the door!").

## EXAMPLES

| Community Dialect | Standard Dialect |
|---|---|
| Is going to rain? | Is *it* going to rain? |
| When Joe starts up his motorcycle, is noisy. | When Joe starts up his motorcycle, *it* is noisy. |

## Summary: The *IT* Pronoun

| Community Dialect | Standard Dialect |
|---|---|
| Is raining out. | *It* is raining out. |

## Recognition Drill

Underline the *it* pronouns in the following sentences. Then mark SD next to each sentence written in the standard dialect. The first three have been done for you.

_____ 1. Although the plan is good, is difficult.

___SD___ 2. The ringing of the alarm clock woke him because <u>it</u> was so close to his ear.

_____ 3. No, is not!

_____ 4. When the fire went out, was cold in the room.

_____ 5. "What color is your new blouse?" "Is green."

_____ 6. Although the world is scientifically advanced, is not able to help many of the

people who are sick.

_____ 7. When I visited the country my mother lived in, was very hot.

_____ 8. After I cleaned the house all day, still is dirty.

_____ 9. It needs a new coat of paint to look clean.

_____ 10. Yes, is a happy world when we dance and sing.

_____ 11. While I was watching T.V., it stopped working.

_____ 12. It made me angry that my mother scolded me for coming home late.

_____ 13. Since I failed my test and lost my wallet, was an unhappy day for me.

_____ 14. After twelve innings, we all agreed was the longest game we had ever watched.

_____ 15. Was raining last night?

_____ 16. Perhaps was the wrong day for a visit since no one was home.

_____ 17. Was it a good day for a picnic?

_____ 18. Bravo, was a beautiful performance!

_____19. The race was very exciting since it was won by the horse I bet ten dollars on.

_____20. No, it wasn't a good day for a picnic.

_____21. Was easy to take her picture?

_____22. Was easy to take her picture because she stood so still.

_____23. How is possible to have a flat tire on my new car?

_____24. I drove my new car over a broken bottle and now it has a flat tire.

_____25. You had twenty dollars yesterday and now is all gone.

_____26. Yes, it is all gone because I spent it on food.

_____27. Since you have a large family, it must be difficult to keep up with the housework.

_____28. My daughters all help with the work and then is not so hard.

_____29. "Is the bus stop near here?" "Yes, is across the street."

_____30. After the children were in bed, was quiet.

## Conversion Drill

Convert each sentence that you did not mark SD in the above exercise into the standard dialect.

# POSSESSIVE PRONOUNS 11

Possessive pronouns are those that show possession or belonging. There are two forms of possessive pronouns: one is used before a noun; the other is used to replace a noun phrase. (A noun phrase contains a noun and any words that modify it: for example, _a book, John's book, the red book, John's red book, his red book_, etc.) Like personal pronouns, both forms of possessive pronouns have three types.

| **Form A: Before a Noun** | **Form B: Replacing a Noun Phrase** | |
| --- | --- | --- |
| **Type 1**   This is *my* book. | This is *mine*. | (*singular*) |
|          This is *our* book. | This is *ours*. | (*plural*) |
| **Type 2**   This is *your* book. | This is *yours*. | (*singular or plural*) |
| **Type 3**   This is *his* book. | This is *his*. | (*singular*) |
|          This is *her* book. | This is *hers*. | (*singular*) |
|          This is *its* book. | _____ | (*singular*) |
|          This is *their* book. | This is *theirs*. | (*plural*) |

Notice that *its* does not usually have the B form (it would be very awkward to say "The book is its"). And notice that *his* is the same in both A and B forms.

Both A and B forms of the possessive pronoun can come at the beginning of a sentence as well as at the end.

EXAMPLES        Standard Dialect

| **Form A: Before a Noun** | **Form B: Replacing a Noun Phrase** | |
| --- | --- | --- |
| **Type 1**   *My* book is on the table. | *Mine* is on the table. | (*singular*) |
|          *Our* book is on the table. | *Ours* is on the table. | (*plural*) |
| **Type 2**   *Your* book is on the table. | *Yours* is on the table. | (*singular or plural*) |
| **Type 3**   *His* book is on the table. | *His* is on the table. | (*singular*) |
|          *Her* book is on the table. | *Hers* is on the table. | (*singular*) |
|          *Its* book is on the table. | _____ | (*singular*) |
|          *Their* book is on the table. | *Theirs* is on the table. | (*plural*) |

Possessive pronouns can occupy the same positions as possessive nouns. When it is clear from the context whom you are referring to, you can substitute a possessive pronoun for a possessive noun.

EXAMPLES        Standard Dialect

*Charles'* skis need to be polished.
*His* skis need to be polished.
Those skis are *Charles'*.
Those skis are *his*.

There are two important things to remember about possessive pronouns. First, they never have apostrophes; only possessive nouns have apostrophes. Second, choosing a singular or plural form depends on the person or thing possessing something else, not on the thing that is possessed. For example, in the following sentences the possessive pronoun is often singular when the thing it possesses is plural, and vice-versa:

(*plural*) (*singular*)

*Their school* is right around the corner.

(*singular*) (*plural*)

*My classes* are very interesting this term.

The following chart shows the standard dialect forms of the possessive pronouns compared to the personal pronouns we studied in the last chapter.

| | Personal Pronouns | | Possessive Pronouns | |
|---|---|---|---|---|
| | Subject | Object | Before noun | After noun |
| **Singular** | | | | |
| **Type 1** | *I* | *me* | *my* | *mine* |
| **Type 2** | you | you | your | yours |
| **Type 3** | he | him | his | his |
| | she | her | her | hers |
| | it | it | its | its |
| **Plural** | | | | |
| **Type 1** | *we* | *us* | *our* | *ours* |
| **Type 2** | *you* | *you* | *your* | *yours* |
| **Type 3** | *they* | *them* | *their* | *theirs* |

In some community dialects, the subject or object form of the personal pronoun is used instead of the possessive pronoun to show possession.

EXAMPLES

Community Dialect

That is *they* book.
*Me* father has a birthday today.
Just take *you* time.

Standard Dialect

That is *their* book.
*My* father has a birthday today.
Just take *your* time.

In some community dialects, possessive pronouns that come after the noun have a different form from the one in the standard dialect

EXAMPLES

Community Dialect

That book is *you'n* (*your'n*).
That book is *his'n*.
That book is *her'n*.
That book is *our'n*.

Standard Dialect

That book is *yours*.
That book is *his*.
That book is *hers*.
That book is *ours*.

## Summary: Possessive Pronouns

| Community Dialect | Standard Dialect |
|---|---|
| me book; it is mines | *my* book; it is *mine* |
| you book; it is you'n (your'n) | *your* book; it is *yours* |
| he book; it is his'n | *his* book; it is *his* |
| she book; it is her'n | *her* book; it is *hers* |
| its book | *its* book |
| we book; it is our'n (us'n) | *our* book; it is *ours* |
| they (them) book; it is they'n (their'n) | *their* book; it is *theirs* |

## Recognition Drill

Underline the possessive pronouns in the following sentences. Then mark SD next to each sentence whose possessive pronouns are in the standard dialect. The first two have been done for you.

### FORM A—Before the Noun

__SD__ 1. Mike Williams moved <u>his</u> family from <u>his</u> uncle's house to <u>his</u> own home.

_____ 2. First he took <u>he</u> little boy.

_____ 3. Next he took his wife.

_____ 4. Last he took their furniture.

_____ 5. Maureena, his wife, was happy to move because she wanted her own home.

_____ 6. She told she little boy Marty that he would have a dog to play with.

_____ 7. Mike and Maureena had the big job of moving they belongings.

_____ 8. First she packed all her bedding.

_____ 9. Then she separated her pans from the uncle's pans.

_____ 10. "These enamel ones are me pans," she said, "and the metal ones are he pans."

_____ 11. Then she went through her cupboards and said to herself:

_____ 12. "These are our cups."

_____ 13. "These are you plates."

239

_____ 14. "These are my forks."

_____ 15. "These are his knives."

_____ 16. "I must buy plates and knives for my new house."

_____ 17. The uncle overheard her words and said to himself:

_____ 18. "I will give them me plates so that they won't have to buy new ones."

_____ 19. After they moved, the first thing Marty did was to invite his uncle over.

_____ 20. "See me dog, Uncle," he said.

_____ 21. "Stay to supper and eat from you plates," said his parents.

_____ 22. "You are our first visitor," they said.

_____ 23. "You will bring our house luck."

_____ 24. They called they friends to come over for a party.

_____ 25. Their friends came in their cars and on foot.

_____ 26. It was the best housewarming our uncle had ever seen.

_____ 27. Our friends came early and left late.

_____ 28. The men helped clean up my kitchen.

_____ 29. Me uncle finished off me beer.

_____ 30. The old comb had lost its teeth.

_____ 31. Grandpa must mend the chair now that the children have broken its legs.

_____ 32. The porcupine left it quills in the dog's nose.

_____ 33. The skunk left its smell on the dog's fur.

## FORM B—Replacing the Noun Phrase

_____ 1. The five dogs found the bone in my backyard. "It is mine," each one said.

_____ 2. The red setter said it must be his'n.

_____ 3. The hound said it must be her'n.

_____ 4. The two retrievers said, "It must be our'n."

240

_____ 5. The poodle said, "It must be mines because it is in my backyard."

_____ 6. Then, the setter, hound, and retrievers said, "It must be your'n if it is in your backyard."

_____ 7. My brother said that the bike was his.

_____ 8. I said that the bike was mine.

_____ 9. I said to him that it could not be his'n because it was a girl's bike.

_____ 10. "All right," he said, "since it is a girl's bike it must be yours."

_____ 11. Herman, Paul, and Harry all said that Hermine was theirs.

_____ 12. Herman claimed she was his because he had known her longest.

_____ 13. Paul said that she was his'n because she had promised to date him.

_____ 14. Harry said, "She is mines because I love her the most."

_____ 15. Hermine said to the three of them, "I am not yours, or yours."

_____ 16. "Hermine isn't any of our'n," they complained.

_____ 17. The choice of a boyfriend was her'n.

_____ 18. Hermine finally became mine.

_____ 19. We married; now the house is ours, the baby is ours, and so are the bills.

_____ 20. Now Herman, Paul, and Harry say, "They are all yours, especially the bills."

## Pattern Practice

Fill in the blanks in the following sentences with the standard possessive pronouns that best fit the meaning. The first two in each section have been done for you.

### FORM A—Before the Noun

1. He washed <u>his</u> car.

2. She sewed the rip in <u>her</u> hem.

3. Martha and Bob love _____ little boys.

4. David rode _____ bike to the store.

5. We cut _____ neighbor's grass while he was on _____ vacation.

6. I entered _____ quilt in the state fair.

7. I made _____ cake from a new recipe. Do you like _____ flavor?

8. Somebody stole _____ pet octopus.

9. Now you are going to lose _____ .

10. _____ mother and _____ father are still alive and kicking _____ heels.

11. We are papering _____ kitchen wall.

12. Mom is handing _____ tools to Dad.

13. She wishes she were doing _____ ironing.

14. I lost _____ schoolbooks on the bus.

15. They had _____ name in them.

16. _____ little brother built a bird feeder outside _____ window sill.

17. All kinds of birds come there for _____ food.

18. At night I can hear the wolves calling _____ mates.

19. _____ howls can be heard for miles around.

20. The family car has broken down after doing _____ duty for ten years.

21. _____ new car is plum purple. I love _____ color.

22. The moon cast _____ silver glow over the landscape.

23. The birch tree lost _____ golden leaves.

24. The snow covered both tree and leaves with _____ white flakes.

25. Mike would awaken in the morning and use _____ new sled.

FORM B—Replacing the Noun

1. Farmer Brown said the carrots were <u>his</u>.

2. Peter Rabbit said the carrots were <u>his</u>.

3. Mrs. Brown said they were _____ .

4. I said they were _____.

5. After we had eaten them, we knew they were _____.

6. Mrs. Bradley makes the best apple pies. The ones with the brown crust are _____.

7. Since I gave you that candy, it must be _____.

8. Since you gave me that valentine, it must be _____.

9. Since we paid for the house, it must be _____.

10. Since they bought the dog, it must be _____.

11. Bernard went to the dentist. The groans and screams were _____.

12. Devonne went to the show. All the laughter and shouting was _____.

13. Roland and Matthew practiced karate. The yells were _____.

14. My dad sorted the laundry for the family. The overalls were _____.

15. The girl scout uniform was my sister's. The baseball shirt was _____.

16. The table cloth and towels were _____.

17. He said to my mother, "The next turn at washing clothes is _____."

18. "Then," she said, "the next turn at ironing them is _____."

19. Maybe my sister and I should make the job _____.

20. Eugene said to Maxine, "I'll always be _____."

21. Maxine said to Eugene, "You'll always be _____?"

22. "Then give back to Doreen, Dorette, and Doranne the things that are _____."

23. "The radio, T.V., and car are not _____."

24. "Each gave them as gifts when you promised to be _____."

25. Eugene gave to Doreen the radio that was _____.

26. He gave to Dorette and Doranne the things that were _____.

27. Maxine then said, "I am _____."

28. She was _____. He was _____.

29. Now I have asked Dorette and Doranne, "Will you be _____?"

30. And Doreen has said, "I will be _____."

## Substitution Drill

Underline the possessive nouns in the following sentences. Then on the line below, rewrite the sentence, substituting the appropriate possessive pronoun for each possessive noun. The first two have been done for you.

1. The book's cover was torn.

   Its cover was torn.

2. The man who hit the home run was John's dad.

   The man who hit the home run was his dad.

3. Mrs. Gruber's daughter was a beautiful young lady.

   _____

4. The man's coat was lined with fleece; the woman's was lined with silk.

   _____

5. The players' faces were covered with sweat.

   _____

6. They all admired Marulla's dress.

   _____

7. Adele's party was the biggest.

   _____

8. Morton's house is down the street from Joan's.

   _____

9. Both televisions' picture tubes wore out.

   _____

10. The fire's intensity was so great it melted the furnace.

   _____

11. Roberta's job as a waitress was hard work.

_____

12. The volunteers' uniforms were striped with pink and white.

_____

13. The nurses aid's uniform was blue; the orderly's was gray.

_____

14. The doctors' coats were white.

_____

15. Joseph's coat had many colors.

_____


## Substitution Drill

Below is a short dialogue between two neighbors, Deanna and Samantha. Make it easier to read by substituting the appropriate possessive pronouns (*my, mine, your, yours, our, ours*) for the possessive nouns.

| | |
|---|---|
| DEANNA | Deanna's family is larger than Samantha's. |
| SAMANTHA | Since Deanna's family is always at Samantha's house, I think Samantha's family is larger than Deanna's family. |
| DEANNA | But Samantha's children invite Deanna's over! |
| SAMANTHA | Maybe Samantha's invite Deanna's over, but I don't invite them. Do you really think I want Deanna's four children along with Samantha's four? |
| DEANNA | I'm sorry! Perhaps we could have a cookout in Deanna's backyard so that Samantha's and Deanna's children can play and eat together. |
| SAMANTHA | Great! Samantha's and Deanna's children will love the idea. Deanna's and Samantha's other neighbors may complain about the noise, though. |
| DEANNA | If they do, we will invite their children over to join Deanna's and Samantha's. |
| SAMANTHA | Twelve children all together? |
| DEANNA AND SAMANTHA | On that day we will ask Deanna's and Samantha's husbands to stay at home and we will go out shopping. |


## Conversion Drill

Reread the sentences in the Recognition Drill. Convert each sentence that you did not mark SD into the standard dialect.

# REFLEXIVE PRONOUNS

Reflexive pronouns are pronouns that "reflect back" on the subject of the sentence.

## EXAMPLES

> John did his homework by *himself*.
> John gave *himself* a haircut.

In the standard dialect, reflexive pronouns are formed by adding *self* or *selves* to either the object form of the personal pronoun or to the possessive pronoun. The following chart adds the reflexive pronouns to the personal and possessive pronouns we discussed in Chapter 6.

### Standard Dialect

| | Personal Pronouns | | Possessive Pronouns | | Reflexive Pronouns |
|---|---|---|---|---|---|
| | Subject | Object | Before Noun | After Noun | |
| **Singular** | | | | | |
| **Type 1** | *I* | *me* | *my* | *mine* | *myself* |
| **Type 2** | *you* | *you* | *your* | *yours* | *yourself* |
| **Type 3** | *he* | *him* | *his* | *his* | *himself* |
| | *she* | *her* | *her* | *her* | *herself* |
| | *it* | *it* | *its* | | *itself* |
| **Plural** | | | | | |
| **Type 1** | *we* | *us* | *our* | *ours* | *ourselves* |
| **Type 2** | *you* | *you* | *your* | *yours* | *yourselves* |
| **Type 3** | *they* | *them* | *their* | *theirs* | *themselves* |

Some community dialects form reflexive pronouns by adding *self* to a different form of the personal or possessive pronouns.

EXAMPLES

| Community Dialect | Standard Dialect |
|---|---|
| I want to do it meself. | I want to do it *myself.* |
| You talk to youself. | You talk to *yourself.* |
| He talks to hisself. | He talks to *himself.* |
| They talk to theyselves (theirselves). | They talk to *themselves.* |

Some community dialects use the singular form of *self* with plural pronouns or add *s* to the singular form.

EXAMPLES

| Community Dialect | Standard Dialect |
|---|---|
| They talk to *theyself* (*theirself*). | |
| They talk to *theyself* (*theirselfs*). | They talk to themsel*ves.* |

Finally, some community dialects use the object form of the personal pronoun without adding *self* or *selves.* This is only used with Type 1 pronouns.

EXAMPLES

| Community Dialect | Standard Dialect |
|---|---|
| I bought *me* a new hat. | I bought *myself* a new hat. |
| We got *us* a new car. | We got *ourselves* a new car. |

### Summary: Reflexive Pronouns

| | **Community Dialect** | **Standard Dialect** |
|---|---|---|
| **Singular** | | |
| **Type 1** | me, meself | *myself* |
| **Type 2** | youself | *yourself* |
| **Type 3** | heself, hisself | *himself* |
| | herself | *herself* |
| | itself | *itself* |
| **Plural** | | |
| **Type 1** | us, ourself | *ourselves* |
| **Type 2** | yourself | *yourselves* |
| **Type 3** | theyself, theirself | *themselves* |

## Recognition Drill

Underline the reflexive pronouns in the following sentences. Then mark SD next to each sentence whose reflexive pronouns are in the standard dialect. The first two have been done for you.

__SD__    1. I bought <u>myself</u> a Coke.

_____ 2. We found the way to the store <u>ourselfs</u>.

_____ 3. My brother and I went by ourselves on the train to Toronto.

_____ 4. You will do youself harm if you play with rattlesnakes.

_____ 5. You will make yourself look beautiful if you make up your eyes.

_____ 6. I made meself drunk by drinking apple cider.

_____ 7. I don't understand how he could hurt hisself like that.

_____ 8. He must have driven himself into the ditch.

_____ 9. In my dream, I gave me a million dollars.

_____ 10. All of you will bring yourselfs luck if you throw salt over your shoulder.

_____ 11. I gave meself a cold by getting my feet wet.

_____ 12. He helped hisself out of the trouble he got hisself into.

_____ 13. I filled me up with homemade cookies.

_____ 14. You three boys will help yourselves most by staying in school.

_____ 15. The top spun itself down.

_____ 16. The boys scattered theyselfs over the playground.

_____ 17. The girls giggled among themselves about the way the boys played.

_____ 18. Almadene told herself a big story.

_____ 19. Between themselves, Letty and Lola discovered the secret.

_____ 20. She gradually broke herself into the new routine.

_____ 21. He nearly killed himself laughing.

_____ 22. I gave myself a week at the new job.

_____ 23. I gave me a pat on the back.

_____ 24. In fact, we all gave ourselfs a pat on the back.

_____ 25. We have helped you pull yourself up from a _D_ to a _B_.

## Pattern Practice

Fill in the blanks in the following sentences with the standard form of the reflexive pronouns that best fit the sentence. The first two have been done for you.

1. He hit <u>himself</u> with the hammer.

2. The three of you won the game <u>yourselves</u>.

3. I am sorry you went home alone by _____.

4. The hurricane blew _____ out.

5. Mary Ann made _____ a new dress.

6. Paul built a little house for _____.

7. I gave _____ the cough medicine.

8. They have no one to blame but _____.

9. Earl bought _____ a leather jacket with a fringe.

10. Earlene bought _____ a leather jacket with suede trim.

11. The bear hid _____ in the woods.

12. The baby boy cried _____ to sleep.

13. You have to cure _____ when there is no doctor in the town.

14. I tried to cure _____ of appendicitis but ended up in the hospital.

15. The paperboy delivered the papers for two routes all by _____.

16. My grandma used to plant the vegetable garden _____.

17. Some plants would come up year after year by _____.

18. I wrote the whole book _____.

19. We were frightened because we were all by _____ in the thunderstorm.

20. I would like to have a room to _____ but I have six sisters.

21. He looked admiringly at _____ in the mirror.

22. I kicked _____ for being such a fool.

23. Beth loved sitting by _____ up in a tree.

24. You soldiers distinguished _____ in the army.

25. Did you see _____ on T.V.?

## Conversion Drill

Reread the sentences in the Recognition Drill. Convert each sentence that you did not mark SD into the standard dialect.

# DEMONSTRATIVE PRONOUNS 13

Demonstrative pronouns are those that point to (demonstrate) an object, event, or person. There are four demonstrative pronouns in the standard dialect: *this, that, these,* and *those.*

All demonstrative pronouns fall into the **Type 3** category because, like *a* and *the,* they all come before nouns; or like the personal pronouns *he, she, it,* and *they,* can be substituted for nouns.

EXAMPLES                        Standard Dialect

*This* book is a good one.        *The* book is a good one.
*Those* books are good ones.      *The* books are good ones.
*This* is good.                   *It* is good.
*Those* are good.                 *They* are good.

There are two ways in which some community dialects differ from the standard dialect in the use of demonstrative pronouns.

250

1. Some community dialects use compound forms: *this here, that there, these here,* and *those there.*

EXAMPLES

| Community Dialect | Standard Dialect |
|---|---|
| *That there* book is good. | *That* book is good. |
| *That there* is good. | *That* is good. |

2. Some community dialects use the object form of the Type 3 personal pronouns, *them,* where the standard dialect uses *these.*

EXAMPLES

| Community Dialect | Standard Dialect |
|---|---|
| *Them* books are good. | *Those* books are good. |
| *Them* are good. | *Those* are good. |

### Summary:   Demonstrative Pronouns

| Community Dialect | Standard Dialect |
|---|---|
| That there book is good. | *That* book is good. |
| That there is good. | *That* is good. |
| Them books are good. <br> Them there books are good. | *Those* books are good. |
| Them are good. <br> Them there are good. | *Those* are good. |

## Recognition Drill

Underline the demonstrative pronouns in the following sentences. Then mark SD next to the sentences whose demonstrative pronouns are in the standard dialect. The first three have been done for you.

_____ 1. <u>Them</u> people aren't going anywhere.

_SD_ 2. <u>These</u> foolish things remind me of you.

_____ 3. How much do <u>them there</u> oranges cost?

_____ 4. That's too much money.

_____ 5. Them is bad people.

_____ 6. Do you remember that there lady who weighed 500 pounds?

_____ 7. There will always be them strange people who won't like anything you do.

_____ 8. Them there is supposed to be here, and them here is supposed to be there.

_____ 9. These are the most beautiful flowers I have ever seen.

_____ 10. Those apple trees produce the most delicious apples I've ever tasted.

_____ 11. First you bite them fingernails, then you comb your hair while waiting in the dentist's office for your turn to have them teeth fixed.

_____ 12. Them there relatives of yours are always saying unkind things behind my back and I don't like them.

_____ 13. That there is the best movie I've seen in a long time.

_____ 14. Who are those people you keep talking about?

_____ 15. I'd really like to tell them people to keep their dogs out of my yard.

_____ 16. The prettiest pair of feet I've seen are them there.

_____ 17. I get that there odd feeling when I see you walking down the street.

_____ 18. Have you ever seen them dogs that don't bark?

_____ 19. Them there mountains are hard to climb.

_____ 20. California is that place where people can dream.

## Pattern Practice

Rewrite the following sentences, replacing _the_, _it_, and _they_ with appropriate demonstrative pronouns in the standard dialect. The first two have been done for you.

1. The book is on the table.

   That book is on the table.

2. It is a good one.

   That is a good one.

252

3. They are the kindest people in the world.

   _____

4. It is a difficult problem to solve.

   _____

5. The house is falling apart.

   _____

6. The dogs are not very clean.

   _____

7. It seems like the best thing to do in the situation.

   _____

8. The two boys are *A* students in history.

   _____

9. It doesn't make any sense.

   _____

10. The neighbors are not very considerate.

    _____

11. Have you found it yet?

    _____

12. The aspidistra plant finally flowered.

    _____

13. It's just one of those things.

    _____

14. The mistake was serious.

    _____

15. The homework assignments are due tomorrow.

_____

16. Walt gave Margaret the roses.

_____

17. Take me out to the ball game.

_____

18. I've got to catch the uptown train to take Carrie her present.

_____

19. It's cool.

_____

20. It doesn't matter any more.

_____

## Conversion Drill

Reread the sentences in the Recognition Drill. Then convert those sentences that you did not mark SD into the standard dialect.

# PART III:
# ADJECTIVES AND ADVERBS

# ADJECTIVES

Adjectives are words that describe nouns or pronouns. They most often come before the nouns they describe.

EXAMPLES (Adjectives are in italics)

1. The *green* book is on the *round* table.
2. The *little* boy picked up his *huge brown* dog.
3. *Green*, *red*, and *orange* pillows were scattered on the *bare* floor.

Notice that in sentence 2, there are two adjectives that describe the dog: *huge* and *brown*. If there are more than two adjectives in a row, they are separated by commas, with an *and* before the last one in the series (as in sentence 3: *green*, *red*, and *orange* pillows).

Adjectives can often come after the nouns they describe. In that case, they are always separated by a form of the verb BE or a linking verb (a verb that can be substituted for BE). The most common linking verbs are *seem*, *become*, *grow*, *appear*, *look*, *feel*, *smell*, *taste*, and *sound*.

EXAMPLES                    Standard Dialect

| With BE Verbs | With Linking Verbs |
|---|---|
| 1. The book *is green*. | The book *appears green*. |
| 2. The table *is round*. | The table *seems round*. |
| 3. The boy *is little*. | The boy *looks little*. |
| 4. The dog *is huge* and *brown*. | The dog *grew huge* and *brown*. |
| 5. *The pillows are green*, *red*, and *orange*. | The pillows *shone green*, and *orange*. |
| 6. The floor *is bare*. | The floor *looks bare*. |

Notice that in sentence 4, the word *and* is inserted between the two adjectives. In sentence 5, the three adjectives are separated with commas, and the word *and* is used before the last adjective.

As discussed in Part I, Chapter 5, in some community dialects there is no BE verb between the adjective and the noun it describes.

EXAMPLES                    Community Dialect

The book *green*.
The dog *huge* and *brown*.

To change those community dialects into the standard dialect you either insert the appropriate form of the verb BE (see Part I, Chapters 5 and 6), or insert a linking verb.

## Summary: Adjectives with Linking Verbs

| Community Dialect | Standard Dialect |
|---|---|
| The dog sick. | The dog *is sick*.<br>The dog *appears sick*. |

## Recognition Drill

In the following sentences, underline the adjectives once and the verbs twice. Mark SD beside each sentence written in the standard dialect. The first three have been done for you.

_____ 1. My house <u>big</u>.

_____ 2. She <u>bad</u>.

__SD__ 3. The teacher <u>seems</u> <u>interested</u> in the class.

_____ 4. The room noisy.

_____ 5. Ice cream is good.

_____ 6. Children grow strong when they eat the proper food.

_____ 7. He together.

_____ 8. We cool.

_____ 9. Bertha always sick.

_____ 10. John sometimes tired.

_____ 11. They happy.

_____ 12. She good.

_____ 13. Spring is beautiful.

_____ 14. My new car is expensive and elegant.

_____ 15. Life is exciting.

_____ 16. Ronald smart.

_____ 17. Amy always late.

_____ 18. They rich.

_____ 19. We poor.

_____ 20. English is interesting.

_____ 21. School is fun.

_____ 22. She ready.

_____ 23. John lazy.

_____ 24. She active.

_____ 25. Tony is mad.

_____ 26. Bertha funny.

_____ 27. Marsha sad.

_____ 28. Our flowers grow fast.

_____ 29. Leonard fat.

_____ 30. Dennis skinny.

_____ 31. Larry seems busy.

_____ 32. Curtis is happy.

_____ 33. Arthur is mad.

_____ 34. Toby is funny.

_____ 35. The lemon is bitter.

_____ 36. Ice cream is cold.

_____ 37. The Pontiac Grand Prix is beautiful.

_____ 38. Your assistance is valuable.

_____ 39. The toothbrush is red, white, and blue.

_____ 40. The radio is expensive.

## Conversion Drill

Convert each sentence that you did not mark SD in the above exercise into the standard dialect using standard dialect forms of a linking verb or BE.

## Pattern Practice

The following sentences all have a form of BE between the noun and the adjective. Substitute a linking verb for each BE verb. The first two have been done for you.

1. The sun was very bright.

   The sun appeared very bright.

2. My sister is very smart.

   My sister seems very smart.

3. My uncle's hair is dark.

   _____

4. My vegetable garden is big and wormy.

   _____

5. The pencil sharpener is yellow.

   _____

6. The adventure story is dull.

   _____

7. The cartoon is funny.

   _____

8. The ocean waves are violent and wet.

   _____

9. The desert cactus plants are dry.

   _____

10. The lemon meringue pie is fluffy.

---

## Pattern Practice

The following sentences all have adjectives following linking verbs or a form of BE in the standard dialect. Change them so that adjectives precede the nouns. You'll have to make up new endings to complete some sentences; in others, you will have to combine two or three sentences into one (as in number 2). The first two have been done for you.

1. The man was old.

   The old man limped down the street.

2. The apple was sour and green.

   The tree looked bushy.

   The sour green apple fell off the bushy tree.

3. My shirt was dirty and ripped.

   _____

4. The birds were red and gold.

   The morning was bright and sunny.

   _____

5. My sister is short and dark.

   _____

6. The kitchen is bright yellow.

   _____

7. My station wagon is dark blue and noisy.

   _____

8. My shoes are expensive and comfortable.

   _____

9. The roses are red and fragrant.

   The green vase is on the table.

   _____

10. The lady is lonely and sad.

    _____

11. The snow is soft and white.

    The street is deserted.

    _____

12. The football player is big, blond, and bold.

    The football is hard and brown.

    The football stadium is small and cold.

    _____

13. The lights were dim and soft.

    The chairs were old and rickety.

    _____

14. The girl is smart and sassy.

    Her boyfriend is friendly and handsome.

    _____

15. The mathematics problem is long and involved.

    _____

16. My dog is affectionate and frisky.

    _____

17. My friends are crazy but charming.

    The birthday party was spectacular.

    _____

18. The countryside is scenic and warm.

The picnic food was delicious.

_____

19. The house is big and roomy.

The owner is gracious and generous.

_____

20. The lion is playful.

The lion trainer is fearful.

_____

21. The high fashion model is tall and slender.

The magazine is expensive.

_____

22. My brother is jolly and round.

_____

23. The movie was interesting.

The theatre was downtown.

_____

24. The moon is soft and yellow.

_____

25. Your eyes are dreamy and watery.

The soldier is romantic and adventurous.

_____

26. The dinner was exquisite and nourishing.

The guests were crude and thoughtless.

_____

27. Her mother is thoughtful.

    Her father is bashful.

    _____

28. Your shag carpet is deep, soft, and green.

    _____

29. The blossoms are beautiful and fragrant.

    _____

30. The snow and sleet are thick and sloppy.

    Driving is slow and treacherous.

    _____

# ADJECTIVES FROM VERBS  2

We saw in Part II, Chapter 7, that there are many nouns in English made from verbs. Those nouns are made by using either the *ing* form of the verb or the infinitive (*to*) form. There are also adjectives that are made from verbs—they are made by using either the *ing* form of the verb or the compound past form of the verb.

EXAMPLES                    Standard Dialect

    The *potted* plants were growing fast.
    The *growing* plants sat on the windowsill.
    He gave the *completed* assignment to the teacher.
    A *grown* boy should get his homework in on time.
    A *growing* boy often doesn't get his homework in on time.
    The homework is *finished*.
    The boy is *grown*.

As we saw in Chapter 1, adjectives can either come before the noun they describe, or after BE or a linking verb. The examples above include adjectives in both positions. Notice that when they come after a BE verb they look very much like the passive forms we studied in Part I, Chapter 24. In the following sentence, it is possible to consider *finished* as either a passive verb or as an adjective.

EXAMPLES                          Standard Dialect

My homework is *finished*.


Adjectives made from verbs, however, are sometimes in other positions as well. They are often separated from the noun they describe by other words that come in between, so it may take a little practice to recognize them as adjectives.

EXAMPLES                          Standard Dialect

*Running* down the street, the boy dropped his books.
*Running*, the boy dropped his books.
The *running* boy dropped his books.
*Cooked* before I arrived, the stew was steaming on the stove.
*Cooked*, the stew was steaming on the stove.
The *cooked* stew was steaming on the stove.
Every night the teacher lies awake *thinking* about her classes.
Every night the teacher lies awake *thinking*.
Every night the *thinking* teacher lies awake.


Some community dialects do not include the *ing* ending; some do not put the *ed* ending on adjectives made from the compound past of regular verbs; and some use a different form of the compound past of irregular verbs. These variations occur most often when the adjective is separated from the noun it describes, or follows it.

EXAMPLES

| Community Dialect | Standard Dialect |
|---|---|
| The teacher lies awake just *think* about her students. | The teacher lies awake just *thinking* about her students. |
| The *finish* homework lay on her desk. | The *finished* homework lay on her desk. |
| The money, *stole* from the bank last week, was finally found. | The money, *stolen* from the bank last week, was finally found. |

One of the most frequent kinds of adjectives made from verbs is called the double adjective. That is, a regular adjective is put in front of an adjective made from a verb, and the two together act like one adjective. For example, the compound past form of the verb FASHION is *fashioned*. If you put the adjective *old* in front of it with a hyphen between, you have made a new adjective, *old-fashioned*.

EXAMPLE                                  Standard Dialect

Her *old-fashioned* dress still looked new.

Some double adjectives have a noun as the second part instead of an adjective. For example, the distant past form of the verb WHIP is *whipped*. If you put the noun *cream* after *whipped* and use the two words together in front of another noun, you have created a new adjective.

EXAMPLE                                  Standard Dialect

She made a *whipped-cream* pie.

Notice, however, that *whipped* can be an adjective alone, modifying the noun *cream* as in the following sentence:

She loves to eat *whipped* cream.

Like single adjectives made from verbs, double adjectives made from verbs often differ in community dialects by not using the compound past form for one part of the double adjective.

EXAMPLES

| Community Dialect | Standard Dialect |
|---|---|
| My sister likes whip-cream desserts. | My sister likes *whipped-cream* desserts. |
| My mother is very old-fashion. | My mother is very *old-fashioned*. |

### Summary: Adjectives Made from Verbs

| Community Dialect | Standard Dialect |
|---|---|
| The Sing Nun is a soprano. | The Sing*ing* Nun is a soprano. |
| My homework is finish. | My homework is finish*ed*. |
| He is an old-fashion teacher. | He is an old-fashion*ed* teacher. |

# Adjectives Made from Compound Past Forms of Regular Verbs

## Recognition Drill

Underline the adjectives in the following sentences that have been made from verbs. Then mark SD next to each sentence that is written in the standard dialect. The first three have been done for you.

_____ 1. There was a <u>crook</u> man who walked a <u>crook</u> mile and found a crook.

__SD__ 2. The lady's <u>wrinkled</u> skin showed her age.

_____ 3. The <u>promise</u> gift never arrived.

_____ 4. The allege robber was picked up in the neighborhood bar.

_____ 5. The school principal spoke to the concern parents.

_____ 6. I want fry potatoes and a hamburger.

_____ 7. Manuella's lowered eyes showed her shyness.

_____ 8. There were a dozen ice-cream cones fill with chocolate marshmallow ice cream.

_____ 9. My Aunt Sara bought a hand-painted plate at the rummage sale.

_____ 10. Your braid hair looks pretty.

_____ 11. Everyone admired the newly painted room.

_____ 12. I admired my newly scrub floor.

_____ 13. The lake looks like polished glass.

_____ 14. Harrietta had an impact wisdom tooth.

_____ 15. The finished picture now hung in the art gallery.

_____ 16. The frighten children ran past the cemetery after dark.

_____ 17. I hate burn toast.

_____ 18. I don't like boiled eggs either.

_____ 19. But I love broil pork chops.

_____ 20. Dick walked over my freshly cleaned rug with his muddied boots.

## Pattern Practice

Fill in the blanks in the following sentences with adjectives made from the verbs given in the margin. In cases of double adjectives, the noun or adjective that combines with the verb-adjective is given in the sentence. The first two have been done for you.

BAKE  1. The freshly <u>baked</u> cookies smelled delicious.

CHEW  2. Ralph spanked the puppy when he found his <u>chewed</u> slipper.

SHARPEN  3. The box was filled with newly _____ pencils.

TRAIN  4. The _____ bears were very comical.

LOAD  5. The heavily _____ truck moved very slowly up the hill.

DRESS  6. Everyone at the reception was beautifully _____ .

BOIL  7. How many hard _____ eggs did you bring?

COOK  8. _____ potatoes taste better than raw ones.

LOVE  9. Grandma was the best _____ member of our family.

MIDDLE-AGE  10. The _____ man dyed his hair black.

FILL  11. The children's balloons, _____ with hydrogen gas, floated out of reach.

RUST  12. I won't buy a car with a _____ body.

FINISH  13. The _____ product is handsome.

CURL  14. With _____ hair and a velvet jacket with lace frills, he catches our eyes.

FROST  15. With a _____ windshield, I couldn't drive very far.

ICE  16. Betty Ann loves cakes _____ with chocolate mocha frosting.

PANEL  17. The new neighbors had _____ walls in their family room.

VARNISH  18. The freshly _____ floors look like new.

USE  19. The _____ car market is strong these days.

MARRY  20. The _____ men played against the bachelors at the church picnic.

STEREOTYPE  21. Lucy plays _____ roles.

PLOUGH        22. The _____ snow was heaped at the curbs.

SALT          23. The _____ streets were safe to drive on.

RESPECT       24. Our _____ doctor retires from his practice next month.

ATTEMPT       25. The plane's _____ landing was not successful.

DESIRE        26. The long _____ car was sitting in the driveway.

ASSEMBLE      27. The _____ crowd cheered the mayor.

BATTER        28. The _____ motorbike was carried home in a pick-up truck.

WORRY         29. The _____ mother waited for her son to come home from boot camp.

SHINE/PRESS   30. She was delighted when she saw him in his _____ shoes and well

              _____ uniform.


## Adjectives Made from Compound Past Forms of Irregular Verbs

### Recognition Drill

In the following sentences, underline the adjectives that are made from verbs. Then mark SD next to each sentence that is written in the standard dialect. The first three have been done for you.

_____ 1. The fall snow was clean and shining in the sun.

__SD__ 2. The half-grown boy was trying to dress like a man.

__SD__ 3. The spoken word is as powerful as the written word.

_____ 4. The stole truck was found hidden in the gulley.

_____ 5. The hand-woven Indian blanket is beautiful.

_____ 6. The broke rake must be mended.

_____ 7. We are God's chosen people.

_____ 8. The forgot toys were rusted from the rain.

_____ 9. The half-eaten food was left on their plates.

268

_____ 10. We all have hidden faults.

_____ 11. The newly risen sun dried the dew from the grass.

_____ 12. The hard rid horses were dusty and sweating.

_____ 13. The freshly mow hay smelled sweet.

_____ 14. The fallen trees blocked the road.

_____ 15. The fell snow looked soft.

## Conversion Drill

Convert each sentence that you did not mark SD in the above exercise into the standard dialect.

## Pattern Practice

Fill in the blanks in the following sentences with adjectives made from the verbs given in the margin. The first two have been done for you.

FREEZE     1. They skated on the <u>frozen</u> pond.

GROW     2. Lady is a full <u>grown</u> beagle.

HIDE     3. The _____ truth was seen in the eyes of the doctor.

WEAVE     4. Today our clothes are made from machine _____ cloth.

FALL     5. After the storm, we cleared away the _____ tree limbs.

MOW     6. The un_____ grass made the house look abandoned.

FORGET     7. After the exam, the _____ answers came back to him.

BLOW     8. Her wind-_____ hair had to be smoothed down.

BEAT     9. The badly _____ team drove home in silence.

DRIVE     10. The soldiers, _____ by the enemy, were exhausted.

STEAL     11. I took a _____ nap while the children were out playing.

CHOOSE     12. Teaching is my _____ field.

EAT     13. The worm_____ apples lay on the ground.

HIDE    14. The _____ money was discovered in a cave.

BREAK   15. Virginia's _____ arm was put in a splint.


## Adjectives Made from Compound Past Forms of Regular and Irregular Verbs

### Recognition Drill

Underline the adjectives made from verbs in the following sentences. Then mark SD next to each sentence written in the standard dialect. The first three have been done for you.

_____ 1. The puppy is <u>grow</u>.

__SD__ 2. The plane was <u>flown</u>.

_____ 3. The race was <u>finish</u>.

_____ 4. The car is repair.

_____ 5. The error is correct.

_____ 6. The mistake was forgiven.

_____ 7. The man was shook.

_____ 8. The ladies were seated.

_____ 9. The man's eye was swole.

_____ 10. The battle is won.

_____ 11. Nothing is left.

_____ 12. The sun is risen.

_____ 13. The job was attempt.

_____ 14. The house is built.

_____ 15. The game is played.

### Conversion Drill

Convert each sentence that you did not mark SD in the above exercises into the standard dialect.

## Pattern Practice

Fill in the blanks in the following sentences with adjectives made from the verbs in the margin. The first one has been done for you.

LOSE        1. The treasure is <u>lost</u>.

HIDE        2. The chests of gold are _____ .

FINISH      3. The search is _____ .

HATE        4. The enemy was _____ .

FORGET      5. All anger is _____ .

SETTLE      6. The peace terms are _____ .

SENTENCE    7. The war leaders are _____ .

RELEASE     8. The prisoners are _____ .

BUILD       9. The houses were newly _____ .

LAY         10. The tile was freshly _____ .

PAINT       11. The walls were brightly _____ .

FURNISH     12. The rooms were _____ .

OCCUPY      13. The houses are _____ .

INVITE      14. Friends are _____ .

DRINK       15. Toasts are _____ .

Rewrite the sentences above, placing the adjective before or after the noun and making up the remainder of a new sentence. The first one has been done for you.

1. The lost treasure must be on this island. _____

2. _____

3. _____

4. _____

5. _____

6. _____

7. _____

8. _____

9. _____

10. _____

11. _____

12. _____

13. _____

14. _____

15. _____


## Adjectives Made from ing *Forms of Verbs*

### Recognition Drill

In the following sentences underline the adjectives that have been made from verbs. Then mark SD next to each sentence that is written in the standard dialect. The first three have been done for you.

_____ 1. Madison just sits at his desk <u>think</u> about Belinda.

__SD__ 2. A <u>driving</u> rain slowed down the traffic.

__SD__ 3. Jacqueline froze, <u>fearing</u> the big dog coming down the sidewalk.

_____ 4. Our university observatory has a new reflect telescope.

_____ 5. The train go from Detroit to New York has been discontinued.

_____ 6. The buy power of the dollar has dropped.

_____ 7. The recording industry makes millions of dollars.

_____ 8. Water running over the rocks makes a pretty sound.

_____ 9. Water drip from the faucet makes a disagreeable sound.

_____ 10. Children starving in Biafra need our help.

_____ 11. Dark clouds usually signal approaching storms.

_____ 12. Women knitting remind me of my grandmother.

_____ 13. In the bar I was surrounded by people drink beer.

_____ 14. Sleeping bags are great on a camping trip.

_____ 15. The sign at the show said "Standing room only."

_____ 16. Come home late last night, I lost my way.

_____ 17. Justine was frightened standing alone at the bus stop.

_____ 18. Wake so early, I am tired by nine P.M.

_____ 19. The waves were beautiful, break and roll.

_____ 20. Speed down the highway, the car made it in record time.

_____ 21. The boys became good friends sharing their gossip at lunch.

_____ 22. Writing to his family every week, the soldier kept up his wife's spirits.

_____ 23. The student learned a new language studying two hours every night.

_____ 24. The moon made us feel romantic shine over the trees.

_____ 25. Hitting his home runs, Hank Aaron builds his record game by game.

_____ 26. I can see fish leaping in the water.

_____ 27. Filling up on mosquitoes, the fish won't bite.

_____ 28. The ghost wandered through the castle, moan and groan.

_____ 29. The congregation prayed kneel at the altar rail.

_____ 30. He heard the church bells ringing in his ears during the whole ride.


## Conversion Drill

Convert each sentence that you did not mark SD in the above exercise into the standard dialect.


## Pattern Practice

Fill in the blanks in the following sentences with _ing_ adjectives made from verbs given in the margin. The first two have been done for you.

JUMP       1. The <u>jumping</u> events came last on the sports program.

PASS       2. Paula decided her poverty was just a <u>passing</u> problem.

PULL        3. The puppies _____ at the slipper tore it apart.

HUM         4. The _____ noise grew louder as he approached the bees' nest.

BAKE        5. Zina entered her peach pie into the _____ contest.

BUY         6. Then she went on a _____ spree.

FALL        7. When Arthur saw the _____ leaves, he bought a new rake.

SING        8. The _____ Six came down for a concert.

BUILD       9. The little boy's birthday package contained _____ blocks.

FRY         10. The _____ chicken smelled delicious.

SLITHER     11. _____ snakes scare me.

ACHE        12. _____ feet come from standing on cement floors all day.

SIGH        13. Maria loved to hear the _____ gypsy strings.

HANG        14. We went to visit the _____ gardens of Babylon.

COME        15. The bride and groom are certain to be happy in the _____ years.

PAY         16. Marvin went through life _____ all his bills on time.

LEAD        17. _____ her down the street, the seeing eye dog acted as Mary's eyes.

MAKE        18. I feel very proud _____ my own clothes.

SEE         19. Constance walked with her head in the clouds _____ only the blue sky.

GIVE        20. Florence worked very hard _____ up much of her free time.

SHOOT       21. Carl is out in the field _____ pheasant for dinner.

SING        22. They went through their adventures _____ .

SIT         23. _____ at his desk, the teacher corrected five hundred themes.

FREEZE      24. _____ over during the night, the pond became a lovely skating rink.

FORGET      25. Archibald became a big joke by _____ his own name.

COME/GO     26. The relatives make me nervous, constantly _____ and _____ .

KEEP        27. Randall is a great man in a crisis, always _____ things under control.

274

BRING    28. I remember Chester always _____ home stray kittens.

BURST    29. The water main down the street _____ from the cold weather looks like a

geyser.

CHOOSE    30. Edgar became rich _____ his investments wisely.


## REVIEW: Adjectives Made from ing and Compound Past Forms of Verbs

### Recognition Drill

Underline each adjective made from a verb in the following sentences.
Then mark SD next to each sentence written in the standard dialect. The first
three have been done for you.

_SD_    1. The <u>rattling</u> window kept us up all night.

_____    2. The <u>stutter</u> student was unable to complete the speech.

_SD_    3. Very often the <u>spoken</u> word has less power than the <u>written</u> word.

_____    4. Touch third base, I kept running and I scored the winning run in the baseball

play-off game.

_____    5. Assume I am right, I will go on to the next mathematics problem.

_____    6. Realizing my mistake, I went on to do the problem over again correctly.

_____    7. We are tire.

_____    8. The paintings were exhibit in the library.

_____    9. The composition Tom did in the English class was publish in the local newspaper.

_____    10. After accidently mentioning the party to Debra, I had to invite her.

_____    11. The stole television set was found by the police.

_____    12. In the movie, the ambush marines finally defeated the enemy.

_____    13. The hid treasure chest was found by the children play hide-and-seek.

_____ 14. Tell us what the next assignment would be, the English teacher let us go early.

_____ 15. Bertha is a loving person when she is in the mood.

_____ 16. The threatened undercover agents went into hiding.

_____ 17. Remember that I had to buy a loaf of bread for dinner, I had to drive all the way

back downtown to the store.

_____ 18. Aunt Margie's unexpect arrival surprised me.

_____ 19. Your charming smile has made me fall in love with you.

_____ 20. Realizing the difficulties, I still would like to go to college.

_____ 21. Sandra is ignore Tom's insults.

_____ 22. They were insist that the children be home by 10 P.M.

_____ 23. Our trusting dog is always fool.

_____ 24. I am just realize how much you mean to me.

_____ 25. The smoke oven contained a burn turkey.

_____ 26. When I heard about Mary and Mike, I was tremble.

_____ 27. Their broken hearts will never be mended.

_____ 28. Stop feel sorry for yourself; you are a grow man now.

_____ 29. The froze vegetables tasted good.

_____ 30. The chose volunteers commenced their latrine duty.

## Conversion Drill

Convert each sentence that you did not mark SD in the above exercises
into the standard dialect.

# ADVERBS

You will remember from Chapter 1 that adjectives are words that describe nouns. Adverbs are similar to adjectives, except that they describe verbs, adjectives, or other adverbs.

EXAMPLES            Standard Dialect

He ran *quickly*.           (*Quickly* describes the verb *ran*.)

He is a *very* hard worker.     (*Very* describes the adjective *hard*.)

He ran *very quickly*.         (*Very* describes the adverb *quickly*.)

Often you can distinguish adverbs from adjectives because they sometimes end in *ly*.

EXAMPLES            Standard Dialect

| **Adjectives** | **Adverbs** |
| --- | --- |
| *quick* | *quickly* |
| *sweet* | *sweetly* |
| *soft* | *softly* |
| *smooth* | *smoothly* |

There are some words that end in *ly*, however, that can be either adjectives or adverbs. The most common ones are *only* and *early*.

EXAMPLES            Standard Dialect

I lost my *only* pair of gloves.      (*adjective*)
There are *only* three pieces of pie left.    (*adverb*)

There are other words that do not end in *ly* that can also be either adjectives or adverbs. Some of the most common of these are *far, fast, little, right*, and *straight*.

EXAMPLES            Standard Dialect

He is a *fast* driver.     (*adjective*)
He drives *fast*.     (*adverb*)

There is one set of adverbs and adjectives that are often used differently in community dialects from the way they are used in the standard dialect. They are *well* and *good*. In the standard dialect, *well*, like the words listed above, can be either an adjective or an adverb, but in each case it has a different meaning. *Good*, however, is only an adjective.

**EXAMPLES**                    Standard Dialect

He is a *good* singer.          (*adjective*)
He sings *well*.                (*adverb* meaning "talented")
He is *well*. (He feels *well*.)  (*adjective* following linking
                                  verb, meaning "healthy")

Some community dialects use *good* as an adverb.

**EXAMPLE**

Community Dialect          Standard Dialect

He sings *good*.           He sings *well*.

There are many other instances where community dialects use adjective forms when the standard dialect uses adverb forms—especially after action verbs.

**EXAMPLES**

Community Dialect          Standard Dialect

He runs *quick*.           He runs *quickly*.
She sings *beautiful*.     She sings *beautifully*.

Just the opposite thing happens when you use a linking verb or a form of BE. In that case, community dialects sometimes use adverbs where the standard dialect uses adjectives.

**EXAMPLE**

Community Dialect          Standard Dialect

She appears *healthily*.   She appears *healthy*.

Notice that *appears* in the above sentence is a linking verb (it can be replaced by a form of BE: "She *is* healthy") and therefore in the standard dialect an adjective follows it rather than an adverb. Remember, however, that APPEAR can also be used as an action verb. In that case an adverb, not an adjective, would follow.

**EXAMPLE**                    Standard Dialect

She appeared *suddenly*.

278

## Summary: Adverbs and Adjectives

| Community Dialect | Standard Dialect |
|---|---|
| *with action verbs* ||
| He runs quick. (*adjective*) <br> He sings good. (*adjective*) | He runs *quickly*. (*adverb*) <br> He sings *well*. (*adverb*) |
| *with linking verbs* ||
| He looks hungrily. (*adverb*) | He looks *hungry*. (*adjective*) |
| *with* BE ||
| He is swiftly. (*adverb*) | He is *swift*. (*adjective*) |

## Recognition Drill

### With Action Verbs

Underline action verbs twice, and adverbs once in the following sentences. Then mark SD next to each sentence whose adverbs are written in the standard dialect. The first three have been done for you.

_____ 1. He <u>aggravated</u> the problem <u>bad</u>.

_____ 2. We <u>did</u> our work <u>cheerful</u>.

\_\_SD\_\_ 3. Barbara <u>loves</u> Bobby <u>deeply</u>.

_____ 4. Myrtle sings the blues beautifully.

_____ 5. They walk soft through the library.

_____ 6. Crazy Rosie beat the dog mercilessly.

_____ 7. Vera answered the teacher scornful.

_____ 8. The lions attacked the deers fierce.

_____ 9. We defend our leaders brave.

_____ 10. Kathy strongly opposed the busing plan.

_____ 11. I handled the difficult situation smooth.

_____ 12. The mathematics teacher explained the difficult problem slow.

_____ 13. On Christmas Eve the stars shined bright.

_____ 14. Arthur plays the piano very sweet.

_____ 15. James always speaks loud at the YMCA meetings.

_____ 16. My mother traveled extensively through New Mexico and Arizona.

_____ 17. The doctor recommended that we eat moderate.

_____ 18. You should use your time profitable.

_____ 19. I studied intense for the history test.

_____ 20. Our cat responds to us very indifferent.

_____ 21. The minister said we should live our lives religious.

_____ 22. Sam does his job very creative.

_____ 23. The football captain is built very powerfully.

_____ 24. I am learning English grammar gradual.

_____ 25. Jake can play the piano and harmonica simultaneously.

_____ 26. I took his place temporary.

_____ 27. Roberta will be gone indefinite.

_____ 28. He especially notices her teeth.

_____ 29. Barbara ran continuous for three minutes.

_____ 30. I thought originally we were to meet uptown.

## Conversion Drill

Convert each sentence that you did not mark SD in the above exercise into the standard dialect.

## Recognition Drill

### With Linking Verbs and BE

Underline linking verbs and BE forms twice, and adjectives once in the following sentences. Then mark SD next to each sentence whose adjectives are written in the standard dialect. The first three have been done for you.

_SD_   1. I <u>am</u> <u>sick</u>.

_____   2. My dog <u>appears</u> <u>listlessly</u>.

_____   3. Gertrude <u>feels</u> <u>happily</u>.

_____   4. His homework seems well.

_____   5. I feel sleepily.

_____   6. The plants appear wildly.

_____   7. Your new Italian shoes look spectacularly.

_____   8. My drawings are symmetrically.

_____   9. Larry's silence appears unchangeably.

_____ 10. Marvin appears hesitantly.

_____ 11. The pink bubble gum is sticky.

_____ 12. Our family life appears weakly.

_____ 13. My love for strawberry shortcake is increasing.

_____ 14. Linda's fear of the dark was distressingly.

_____ 15. The yellow and orange patterns in my necktie look striking.

_____ 16. Mary Jane's performance in the school drama appeared amazingly.

_____ 17. When I am sick, I am miserable.

_____ 18. When I am angry, I am cruel.

_____ 19. The price of hamburgers and hotdogs today appears excessively.

_____ 20. Her curiosity seems amazing.


## Conversion Drill

Convert each sentence that you did not mark SD in the above exercises into the standard dialect.

## Pattern Practice

### With Action Verbs

For each sentence below there is an adjective and an adverb given in the margin. Fill in the blank with the form that is appropriate in the standard dialect. The first two have been done for you.

QUICK/QUICKLY          1. He runs quickly.

GOOD/WELL              2. He did his homework well.

UNCOMMON/UNCOMMONLY     3. Grace's rose garden is _____ beautiful.

WONDERFUL/WONDERFULLY   4. Bertha has a _____ outgoing personality.

FRIGHTFUL/FRIGHTFULLY   5. Death leaves us all _____ alone.

GLARING/GLARINGLY      6. Your hatred of Ruth is _____ obvious.

REMARKABLE/REMARKABLY   7. Henry is a _____ gifted and talented jazz musician.

INDEFINITE/INDEFINITELY 8. I am leaving home _____.

INTENSE/INTENSELY      9. Joan loves John _____.

GOOD/WELL             10. We know each other very _____.

SOFT/SOFTLY           11. I walked with her _____ through the moonlight.

EXTRAVAGANT/EXTRAVAGANTLY 12. We _____ spent all our money in Paris.

FEARFUL/FEARFULLY     13. The children explored the haunted house _____.

TERRIBLE/TERRIBLY     14. Our telephone bills were _____ expensive.

MISERABLE/MISERABLY   15. Everybody felt bad because Tony performed _____ in the dance contest.

COURTEOUS/COURTEOUSLY 16. The Bible salesman should treat his customers _____.

GRACEFUL/GRACEFULLY   17. She dances _____.

282

COMPASSIONATE /        18. Treat those who are less fortunate than we are
COMPASSIONATELY

_____.

HONORABLE / HONORABLY        19. The general told the soldiers that they should live

_____.

INNOCENT / INNOCENTLY        20. Bertha behaves _____.

LEGAL / LEGALLY        21. You certainly can earn money _____.

COLD / COLDLY        22. Jerry deals with people _____.

COMFORT / COMFORTABLY        23. I can enroll in four courses a semester

_____.

PERFECT / PERFECTLY        24. Let me make this _____ clear.

DEFINITE / DEFINITELY        25. We _____ think you are wrong.

## Pattern Practice

### With Linking Verbs and BE

For each sentence below there is an adjective and an adverb given in the margin. Fill in the blank with the form that is appropriate in the standard dialect. The first two have been done for you.

SICK / SICKLY        1. He looks <u>sick</u>.

GOOD / WELL        2. He appears <u>well</u> and healthy.

HARMONIOUS / HARMONIOUSLY        3. Their relationship appears _____.

BITTER / BITTERLY        4. The purple grapes were _____.

BOISTEROUS / BOISTEROUSLY        5. Our family always appears _____ in public.

GRAVE / GRAVELY        6. Trudy looks _____ today.

FLUENT / FLUENTLY        7. Her knowledge of French is _____.

LIGHT / LIGHTLY        8. Her eyes are _____ in comparison to mine.

SLOW / SLOWLY        9. Roy's running of the 100-yard dash is _____.

| | |
|---|---|
| GRADUAL/GRADUALLY | 10. My cousin's physical growth is _____ . |
| GREAT/GREATLY | 11. The difference between Ray and Roger is _____ . |
| INTERNAL/INTERNALLY | 12. Winifred's reactions to pain are always _____ . |
| COMPLETE/COMPLETELY | 13. On July 23 my vacation will be _____ . |
| ORIGINAL/ORIGINALLY | 14. The song he wrote seemed _____ . |
| STRONG/STRONGLY | 15. Gladys' arms appear _____ . |
| NATURAL/NATURALLY | 16. My singing of the Star Spangled Banner is _____ . |
| FINAL/FINALLY | 17. The boss' decision seems _____ . |
| REGULAR/REGULARLY | 18. Jody's visits to the hospital are _____ . |
| SUDDEN/SUDDENLY | 19. Louis' appearance was _____ . |
| OVERWHELMING/<br>OVERWHELMINGLY | 20. The desire to see you was _____ . |

# COMPARING ADJECTIVES 4

When you want to compare one adjective with another, there are two ways you can do it.

1. You can use *more* before the adjective if you are comparing two things, or *most* if you are comparing three or more things.

EXAMPLES                    Standard Dialect

This dress is *more* fashionable than my old dress.
That dress is the *most* fashionable of all my dresses.

2. You can add the ending *er* to the adjective if you are comparing two things, or *est* if you are comparing three or more things.

Standard Dialect

This dress is new*er* than my old dress.
That dress is the new*est* of all my dresses.

If the adjective already ends in *e*, however, then you only add *r*, or *st*.

EXAMPLES                    Standard Dialect

This dress is cut*er* than that one.
That dress is the cut*est* one of all.

If the adjective or adverb ends in *y*, then you change the *y* to *i* before adding *er* or *est*.

EXAMPLES                    Standard Dialect

This dress is pretty.
That dress is prett*ier* than this one.
That dress is the prett*iest* of all.

Notice that, like all adjectives, comparative forms can come after the words they describe as well as before.

EXAMPLES                    Standard Dialect

That is a *pretty dress*.           That *dress* is *pretty*.
That is a *prettier dress*.         That *dress* is *prettier*.
That is the *prettiest dress*.      That *dress* is the prettiest.

How do you know when to use *more* or *most*, and when to use the endings *er* or *est*? You usually use *er* or *est* with words of one syllable and sometimes of two syllables. With longer words you usually put *more* or *most* in front of them instead of *er* or *est* at the end.

EXAMPLES                    Standard Dialect

That teacher is nic*er* than this one.
That teacher is the nic*est*.
This teacher is *more* demanding than that one.
This teacher is the *most* demanding.

In some community dialects, both *more* or *most* and *er* or *est* are used together. In the standard dialect, only one is used: *more* or *most*; or *er* or *est*.

EXAMPLES

Community Dialect              Standard Dialect

That is the *more* loud*er*       That is the loud*er* boy of
  boy of the two.                   the two.
That is the *most* loud*est*      That is the loud*est* boy.
  boy.

## Summary: Comparing Adjectives

| Community Dialect | Standard Dialect |
|---|---|
| more louder | loud*er* |
| most loudest | loud*est* |
| more beautifuller | *more* beautiful |
| most beautifullest | *most* beautiful |

## Recognition Drill

In the following sentences underline the adjectives that compare. Then mark SD next to each sentence written in the standard dialect. The first three have been done for you.

_____ 1. The second trumpet player sounds <u>more louder</u> than the first.

\_\_SD\_\_ 2. The first trumpet player is the <u>most talented</u>.

\_\_SD\_\_ 3. The drummer has the <u>hardest</u> work and makes the <u>most</u> noise.

_____ 4. The third horn is more out of tune than the fourth horn.

_____ 5. The conductor has a more faster beat than the drummer.

_____ 6. The band is the most dull I have ever heard.

_____ 7. The audience, however, was one of the most happiest I have ever seen.

_____ 8. Their team had won the biggest game of the season.

_____ 9. They thought their band was the greatest.

_____ 10. I think my college has the finest liberal arts school.

_____ 11. The classes are the most smallest.

_____ 12. The instructors are the handsomest.

_____ 13. The buildings are the most beautifullest.

_____ 14. The standards of education are the most highest.

_____ 15. The students are the nicest group I have ever met.

_____ 16. My skates are more better than your skates.

_____ 17. My bike is better than your bike.

_____ 18. I don't know which one of you two is more boastful.

_____ 19. But I do know which one is most silliest.

_____ 20. Joseph gave Yvonne the most beautiful diamond she had ever seen.

_____ 21. She told him that it was brighter than the brightest star.

_____ 22. They agreed to have the most splendid wedding the town has ever seen.

_____ 23. The bridesmaids would be prettiest.

_____ 24. The dancing would be most merriest.

_____ 25. The food would be the tastiest.

_____ 26. They would honeymoon in the finest motel in Niagara Falls, U.S.A.

## Conversion Drill

Convert each sentence that you did not mark SD in the Recognition Drill into the standard dialect.

## Pattern Practice

Fill in the blanks with the appropriate comparative forms of the adjectives in the margin. (Use _er_ or _est_ endings, or use _more_ or _most_ in front of the adjective.) The first one has been done for you.

LIGHT/EASY 1. The <u>lighter</u> the load, the <u>easier</u> is the road.

UGLY/KIND 2. The _____ man has the _____ face.

WET/GREEN 3. The _____ climate makes the _____ grass.

SMOOTH/SOFT 4. The kitten's fur was _____ and _____ .

ROUGH/CURLY 5. The dog's coat was _____ and _____ .

MAGNIFICENT 6. Andrew thinks the skydivers are _____ .

TOUGH 7. Mark claims the Green Berets are _____ .

IMAGINATIVE 8. Tony says the army cooks are _____ .

WEAK 9. The engineer warned the builder that the top girders were _____ .

MUSHY 10. My cornmeal mush is _____ than yours.

# COMPARING ADVERBS

5

You can usually compare adverbs in the same way you compare adjectives—either with *more* and *most*, or with *er* and *est* endings. The same rules apply to choosing them and spelling them, as applied to adjectives in the last chapter. Here are some examples with adverbs that compare.

EXAMPLES                    Standard Dialect

It's raining *more* heavily today than it has in several years.
It rained *most* heavily three years ago.
He runs fast*er* than I do.
He runs the fast*est* of all.

There are two kinds of variations in community dialects.

1. Some community dialects use both *er* or *est* and *more* or *most*, as we saw with adjectives.

EXAMPLES                    Community Dialect

He runs *more* fast*er* than I do.
He runs the *most* fast*est*.

2. Some community dialects put the *er* or *est* endings on the adjective forms rather than the adverb forms, or put *more* or *most* in front of adjective forms. Sometimes they also use *more* or *most* in addition to the *er* and *est* ending.

EXAMPLES

| Community Dialect | Standard Dialect |
|---|---|
| He runs quick*er* than I do.<br>He runs *more* quick than I do.<br>He runs *more* quick*er* than I do. | He runs *more* quick*ly* than I do. |

## Summary: Comparing Adverbs

| Community Dialect | Standard Dialect |
|---|---|
| more faster | fast*er* |
| most fastest | fast*est* |
| quicker | |
| quickest | |
| more quick | *more* quick*ly* |
| most quick | *most* quick*ly* |
| more quicker | |
| most quickest | |

## Recognition Drill

Underline the comparative adverbs or adverb phrases in the following sentences. Then mark SD next to each sentence written in the standard dialect. The first two have been done for you.

_____ 1. The second trumpet player plays <u>more louder</u> than the first.

__SD__ 2. The first trumpet player plays the <u>most brilliantly</u> of the group.

_____ 3. The drummer pounds more noisily.

_____ 4. The conductor beats most noisily.

_____ 5. The band plays more bad than any other I have heard.

_____ 6. The audience looks most happy because the team has won the game.

_____ 7. The chief walks braver into battle than his men.

_____ 8. However, his men act more cooly than the enemy.

_____ 9. The battle is won more quick because of the men's coolness.

_____ 10. Of all the hostesses I know, she behaves the most gracious.

_____ 11. Her home is the most beautiful decorated of any I have ever seen.

_____ 12. College students behave more mature in class than high-school students do.

_____ 13. The kittens tumble about more playful now that their eyes are open.

_____ 14. The police siren wails more mournfully than the ambulance.

_____ 15. Dion performed the job the most sloppiest of the three men.

_____ 16. He would have worked more happy if he had known he was appreciated.

_____ 17. The choir sang more joyously on Easter.

_____ 18. The chorus sang more joyous on Christmas.

_____ 19. The choir and the chorus sang most merrily on their trip to Washington.

_____ 20. The stars shone more beautiful on the night of their wedding.

_____ 21. As the paper deadline grew close he typed more and more furiously.

_____ 22. She worked most intensely the hour before the class started.

_____ 23. Red pop goes down more smoothly and sweetly than any other.

_____ 24. After it blew a tire, the speeding car moved more slow.

_____ 25. Since he came close to being hit, he watches the crossings more careful.

_____ 26. I think you have done your job most carelessly.

_____ 27. The most well-trained nurse sterilized her instruments very thoroughly.

_____ 28. The children played more free on the playground.

_____ 29. When she saw I had a dog, the little girl approached more shy.

_____ 30. Leontyne said Joe dresses the most fashionable of all her boyfriends.

## Conversion Drill.

Convert each sentence that you did not mark SD in the above exercises into the standard dialect.

## Pattern Practice

In the margin before each sentence is an adjective. Change each adjective into an adverb and make it comparative, either adding *er* or *more*, or *est* or *most*, whichever fits best in the sentence. The first one has been done for you.

290

GREEDY  1. Of all the animals, the squirrel ate the <u>most greedily</u>.

QUICK  2. When the birds arrived, he ate _____ than they could.

STUPID  3. Spot behaved _____ than any other dog in the dog school.

RAPID  4. The others all learned _____ than he did.

SERIOUS  5. Cynthia took her job _____ of all the girls.

FURIOUS / HASTY  6. The _____ the bull bellowed, the _____ the crowd backed off.

ANGRY  7. He roared the _____ of all the bulls.

SAD  8. Of all those graduating, Celia and Dave said good-bye the _____.

FREQUENT  9. They wrote their mother _____ this year than ever before.

GORGEOUS  10. My roses have bloomed _____ than ever before.

EVEN  11. Life goes _____ when we are together.

SLOW  12. Of all the children, Stella grew the _____.

GENTLE  13. The teacher treated the worst of all his students the _____.

HOPEFUL  14. The mountain climbers looked _____ at the summit now that they were so near.

FEARFUL  15. But they looked _____ at its smooth walls.

GRAND  16. The African chief walked _____ than his captors.

BRIGHT  17. The golden ornaments of the Inca chief shone _____ than the sun.

INTRICATE  18. The Spaniards crowded in closely to see which of his necklaces was the _____ made.

SWEET  19. John treated Susie _____ than he did any other girl.

CRUEL  20. The cat treated this tiny mouse the _____ of any mouse that she had caught.

# COMPARING IRREGULAR ADJECTIVES; COMPARING IRREGULAR ADVERBS

## 6

There are a few adjectives and adverbs that are irregular in their comparative forms. They are *less* and *least*; *better* and *best*; *worse* and *worst*.

## LESS AND LEAST

*Less* and *least* can be used as both adjectives and adverbs. When used as adjectives they are the comparative forms of *little* when *little* means "small amount."

EXAMPLES                    Standard Dialect

John has *little* time to do his homework.
Jack has *less* time than John.
James has the *least* time of all.

When you use *little* to mean "small size" rather than "small amount," however, you add *er* and *est* to *little*.

EXAMPLES                    Standard Dialect

John is a *little* boy.
Jack is *littler* than John.
James is the *littlest* of all.

*Less* and *least* can also be used as adverbs. When they are used as adverbs, they have the opposite meaning of *more* and *most*.

EXAMPLES                    Standard Dialect

John is *less* hungry than Jack.
James is *least* hungry of all.

An adjective that is similar to *little/less/least* but which has a different use is *few/fewer/fewest*. *Few* is used to show a small number of things that can be counted, where *little* is used to show a small amount of something that cannot be counted.

We can see this difference with the nouns *hour* and *energy*. *Hour* is a noun that can be counted (one hour, two hours, three hours, etc.); but *energy* cannot be counted. With *hour*, therefore, you use *few* (and *fewer* and *fewest*); but with *energy* you use *little* (and *less* and *least*).

EXAMPLES                                    Standard Dialect

I have a *few hours* left before my train leaves.
He has *fewer hours* than I do.
She has the *fewest* hours.

I have *little energy*.
He has *less energy* than I do.
She has the *least energy*.

Some community dialects use *few*, and especially *less* or *least*, to mean small amount rather than small number.

EXAMPLES                                    Community Dialect

I have *little hours* left.
He has *less hours* left.
She has the *least hours* left.

Some community dialects use *lesser* and *leastest* where the standard dialect uses *less* and *least*.

EXAMPLES                                    Community Dialect

He has *lesser* hours left.
She has the *leastest* hours left.

## BETTER AND BEST

*Better* and *best* can also be used as both adjectives and adverbs. When they are used as adjectives, they are the comparative forms of *good*.

EXAMPLES                                    Standard Dialect

She is a *good* student.
Her sister is a *better* student.
Their cousin is the *best* student in the family.

*Better* and *best* can also be used as adverbs, when they are the comparative forms of *well* meaning "healthy."

EXAMPLES                                    Standard Dialect

She is feeling *well* today.
She will feel *better* tomorrow.
She will feel *best* in about a week.

*Better* and *best* can also be used as adverbs when they are the comparative forms of *well* meaning "how something was done."

EXAMPLES                     Standard Dialect

She plays the piano *well*.
Her husband plays the piano *better*.
Her father plays the piano *best* of all in the family.

The only variations in community dialect are like those we discussed in Chapter 4. Sometimes *more* or *most* is used together with *better* or *best*.

EXAMPLES                     Community Dialect

Sarah plays the piano *more better* than John.
Suzanne plays the piano the *most best* of all.

## WORSE AND WORST

*Worse* and *worst* can also be used as either adjectives or adverbs. When used as adjectives they are the comparative forms of the adjective *bad*.

EXAMPLES                     Standard Dialect

The theme I wrote last week is a *bad* one.
The theme I wrote this week is *worse*.
It is the *worst* of all my themes.

When used as adverbs, *worse* and *worst* are the comparative forms of the adverb *badly*.

EXAMPLES                     Standard Dialect

I wrote that theme *badly*.
I wrote this one *worse*.
It is the *worst* written theme of all.

In some community dialects, *worse* and *worst*, like *better* and *best*, are preceded by *more* or *most*.

EXAMPLES                     Community Dialect

He wrote that theme *more worse* than I did.
He wrote that theme the *most worst* of all.

Some community dialects use the forms *worser* and *worsest* where the standard dialect uses *worse* and *worst*.

EXAMPLES                     Community Dialect

He writes *worser* than I do.
He writes the *worsest* of all of us.

## Summary: Irregular Comparative Forms of Adjectives and Adverbs

| Community Dialect | Standard Dialect |
|---|---|
| John has least books. | John has the *fewest* books. |
| John has less books. | John has *fewer* books. |
| John has lesser money. | John has *less* money. |
| John has leastest money. | John has the *least* money. |
| John has more better shoes. | John has *better* shoes. |
| John has most best shoes | John has the *best* shoes. |
| John has a worser cold. | John has a *worse* cold. |
| John has the worsest cold. | John has the *worst* cold. |

## LITTLE AND FEW

### Recognition Drill

Underline the comparative forms of *little* and *few* in the following sentences. Then mark SD next to each sentence written in the standard dialect. The first two have been done for you.

___SD___ 1. We have <u>fewer</u> minutes left in the game than you do.

_____ 2. She has <u>lesser</u> control of her temper than I have.

_____ 3. My Vega is more littler than your Pinto.

_____ 4. Did you notice how lesser people were at the party on Saturday than there have

ever been?

_____ 5. There is lesser space in this closet to put your clothes in.

_____ 6. There is few land left for the Indians than there used to be.

_____ 7. Only the littlest part of the city is unpolluted.

_____ 8. They have fewer books than we do.

_____ 9. Wilt's dog is more littler than mine.

_____ 10. The most least thing you should be concerned about is what these people think

of you.

## Pattern Practice

In the following sentences, fill in the blanks with the standard dialect comparative forms of *little* and *few*. The first two have been done for you.

1. Our family owns the <u>littlest</u> house on the block.

2. Your garage is <u>littler</u> than ours.

3. I study the _____ hours of all my friends.

4. Junior's watch cost _____ than Sonny's.

5. Even the _____ kindness goes a long way.

6. Some people are _____ fortunate than others.

7. The unemployed people are the _____ fortunate of all.

8. You always get _____ than you expected when you go for a bargain.

9. You have _____ days than you think to get your work done.

10. That is the _____ important consideration of all.

## Conversion Drill

Reread the sentences in the Recognition Drill. Then convert each sentence that you did not mark SD into the standard dialect.

## GOOD AND WELL

## Recognition Drill

Underline the comparative forms of *good* and *well* in the following sentences. Then mark SD next to each sentence whose irregular forms are in the standard dialect. The first two have been done for you.

_____ 1. I can do anything <u>more better</u> than you.

__SD__ 2. I can do some things <u>best</u> of all.

_____ 3. Do you really think you are better than I am?

_____ 4. She is really a better person than I thought.

_____ 5. You're more better off without him.

_____ 6. Love is more better than hate.

_____ 7. Love is the best answer to our problems.

_____ 8. Who does best in grammar—you or I?

_____ 9. She is really the better dancer of the two.

_____ 10. We know that you do your best every time.

## Pattern Practice

In the following sentences, fill in the blanks with the standard dialect comparative forms of *good* and *well*. The first two have been done for you.

1. Snoopy is a <u>better</u> runner than Sherman.

2. I work <u>best</u> by myself.

3. The doctor thinks she will get _____ soon.

4. Who is the _____ student in your class?

5. I don't feel any _____ today.

6. I expect to feel _____ tomorrow.

7. I know I am the _____ singer in the group.

8. I know it is _____ to pull myself together than to feel sorry for myself.

9. The _____ way to deal with the problem is to forgive him for what he has done

   to you.

10. Who is the _____ of the two runners on the team?

## Conversion Drill

Reread the sentences in the Recognition Drill. Then convert each sentence that you did not mark SD into the standard dialect.

## BAD AND BADLY

### Recognition Drill

Underline the comparative forms of *bad* and *badly* in the following sentences. Then mark SD next to each sentence in the standard dialect. The first two have been done for you.

_____ 1. A toothache is <u>worser</u> than a headache.

__SD__ 2. Loving you has made me a <u>worse</u> person than I was before.

_____ 3. Sitting next to you is the worsest thing that could have happened, because now I

am distracted by your enchanting eyes.

_____ 4. What is the worst thing that has ever happened to you?

_____ 5. Mrs. Kritchmalnick has a worser temper than Mrs. Humptydumpty.

_____ 6. He is a much worser person than I ever thought.

_____ 7. Which is worser—working days or working nights?

_____ 8. Can something be worser than worst?

_____ 9. Allesandro is doing the worsest thing when he decides to run away from his

problems.

_____ 10. My boyfriend is my worsest problem.

### Pattern Practice

In the following sentences, fill in the blanks with the standard dialect comparative forms of *bad* and *badly*. The first two have been done for you.

1. I feel <u>worse</u> when I'm alone than when I'm with you.

2. He is the <u>worst</u> composition writer in the world.

3. Do you feel _____ before or after you exercise?

4. Something _____ happened to me.

5. You can say that this is the _____ that has ever happened, but things can still

   get _____ .

6. That's the _____ movie I've seen in a long time.

7. Barbara is the _____ dancer in the world.

8. Henry is even a _____ dancer than Mary.

9. What is the _____ thing you can say about me?

10. Ice cream and beer is the _____ possible combination at a party.

## Conversion Drill

Reread the sentences in the Recognition Drill. Then convert each sentence that you did not mark SD into the standard dialect.

## Recognition Drill

Underline the irregular adjective and adverb forms of *little*, *few*, *good*, *well*, *bad*, and *badly*. Then mark SD next to each sentence whose irregular forms are in the standard dialect. The first two have been done for you.

_____ 1. What is the <u>most best</u> thing that ever happened to you?

_____ 2. He has the <u>worsest</u> looking teeth in the world.

_____ 3. I have more fewer things to tell you than I did last week.

_____ 4. Johnny is the more better of the two basketball players.

_____ 5. What is the most best thing you've ever done for anybody?

_____ 6. I am more worser off than you.

_____ 7. Who has it better—rich men or poor men?

_____ 8. I have fewest friends than you.

_____ 9. Who makes the better pizza—you or I?

_____ 10. I wish you the best in your future.

## Pattern Practice

In the sentences below, fill in the blanks with one of the following words: *less, least, few, fewer, better, best, worse, worst*. The first two have been done for you.

1. She does things with the <u>least</u> amount of effort.

2. You are no <u>better</u> for having known him.

3. You made a _____ impression on the boss than I did.

4. Mattie and Cora are the _____ students in the class.

5. I don't think any _____ of you, knowing what you have done.

6. The _____ you do in this matter, the _____ off you'll be.

7. _____ words were never spoken.

8. He is the _____ possible person you could have chosen for the job.

9. If you could only make _____ comments when you give a speech, people might

   not fall asleep.

10. Connie is really the _____ teacher in the world.

## Conversion Drill

Reread the sentences in the Recognition Drill. Then convert each sentence that you did not mark SD into the standard dialect.

# PART IV:
# QUESTIONS AND
# NEGATIVES

So far in this book we have studied the way individual words (verbs, nouns, pronouns, adjectives, and adverbs) are used in sentences. In this section and the next we will be studying the larger units of phrases, clauses, and sentences—both how they are connected to each other, and how words are arranged within them.

In this particular section we will deal with how questions and negative statements are formed. In earlier sections most of the examples and exercises were positive statements. Because the standard and community dialects have different ways of forming questions and negative statements, we will compare them in order to see more clearly how to form the standard dialect patterns. Before we compare them, however, we will first look at the standard dialect.

# TYPES OF QUESTIONS

## 1

There are two common types of questions that we must distinguish in the standard dialect: yes/no questions, and WH questions.

1. Yes/no questions are those that can be answered with a simple *yes* or *no*, or with *yes* or *no* plus a restatement of the question.

EXAMPLE                    Standard Dialect

Did you pass the chemistry exam?
(*Yes*, I passed the chemistry exam.)

2. WH questions are those that require some specific information to answer them, instead of a simple yes or no. They are called WH questions because they begin with words that start with *wh* (with one exception, *how*): *who, whose, where, when, why, what, which,* and *how.*

EXAMPLES                   Standard Dialect

*Which* book did you read?
*Why* do you live so far away from school?
*How* did you get so much money?

# YES/NO QUESTIONS

In the standard dialect, there are three ways to make yes/no questions from a statement:

1. If the statement has a helping verb, you form a yes/no question by moving the helping verb to the beginning of the sentence and replacing the period with a question mark.

He *can* go with you.

*Can* he       go with you?

My sister *is* singing in the choir.

*Is* my sister       singing in the choir?

2. If the statement does not have a helping verb, you have to give it one, by inserting a form of DO, moving it to the beginning, and replacing the period with a question mark.

My uncle      *has*     three dogs.

My uncle *does*   *have*    three dogs.

*Does* my uncle      *have*    three dogs?

Notice that when you insert a form of DO, you put it in the same time as the main verb, and then change the main verb back to the base form. For example, in the sentence above, *has* is in present time. When you insert a form of DO, you put DO in present time and change *has* back to its base form, HAVE:

my uncle       *has*

my uncle *does*   *have*

Then you form the yes/no question by moving the helping verb *does* to the beginning of the sentence:

*Does* my uncle       have three dogs?

If you begin with a main verb in past time, then the form of DO will also be in past time.

My uncle      *had*    three dogs.

My uncle *did*   *have*   three dogs.

*Did* my uncle      *have*    three dogs?

3. There is one kind of sentence in which you don't need a helping verb at all in order to make a yes/no question: that is when the main verb is a form of BE. In that case, you simply move the form of BE to the beginning of the sentence.

His father *is* a plumber.

*Is* his father    a plumber?

## Pattern Practice

Make each of the following statements (S) into a question (Q) by following the rules above. The first two have been done for you.

1.  S   You have seen that movie three times.

    Q   _Have you seen that movie three times?_

2.  S   My brother went to the state university.

    Q   _Did my brother go to the state university?_

3.  S   His mother is a great cook.

    Q   _____

4.  S   I saw Thomas at the football game.

    Q   _____

5.  S   They are going to the Shakespeare festival in Canada this summer.

    Q   _____

6.  S   The pictures of your cousin's baby are beautiful.

    Q   _____

7.  S   The teacher's aides took the fourth and sixth grade classes to the zoo.

    Q   _____

8.  S   She has always been afraid of mice.

    Q   _____

9.  S   Florence is Carl's best friend.

    Q   _____

10. S   Amy misses Phil.

    Q   _____

11. S   Edward's summer job seems very interesting.

    Q   _____

12. S  Beverly sees Roberta's dog every day.

    Q _____

13. S  She congratulated me on my success.

    Q _____

14. S  That rare and magical sensation is love.

    Q _____

15. S  Peter and Paula know the story of Daniel and the Lion.

    Q _____

16. S  The party was a failure.

    Q _____

17. S  Jerry's father was elected the new mayor of Los Angeles.

    Q _____

18. S  They pleaded their own case in court today.

    Q _____

19. S  The Bible says, "Honor thy father and thy mother."

    Q _____

20. S  Some of the lions in the zoo are very nervous.

    Q _____

21. S  Good manners are always in fashion.

    Q _____

22. S  Arthur's salary was raised to forty-seven cents an hour.

    Q _____

23. S  Toby nicked his front tooth playing baseball.

    Q _____

24. **S** David wrinkled his new $30 Oleg Cassini white-on-white cotton dress shirt.

   **Q** _____

25. **S** John has a lot of style.

   **Q** _____

26. **S** The bells are ringing for me and my girl.

   **Q** _____

27. **S** Alfi knows what it's all about.

   **Q** _____

# WH QUESTIONS

# 3

In the standard dialect, WH questions can be formed in three ways:

1. Substitute a WH word for some word or words in the beginning of the statement.

EXAMPLE                    Standard Dialect

My brother ate all the neighbor's apples.

*Who*    ate all the neighbor's apples?

EXAMPLE                    Standard Dialect

My brother ate all the neighbor's apples.

{ *Whose*
  *Which*    brother ate all the neighbor's apples?
  *What* }

2. a. Make the statement into a yes/no question.
   b. Put a WH word at the beginning.

EXAMPLE                     Standard Dialect

My brother ate all the neighbor's apples.

a.    *Did* my brother eat all the neighbor's apples?

b.
$\begin{cases} Why \\ When \\ How \\ Where \end{cases}$ *did* my brother eat all the neighbor's apples?

3. a. Make the statement into a yes/no question.
   b. Substitute a WH word for some word or words in the statement.
   c. Move the WH word to the front (along with whatever noun it may modify).

EXAMPLE                     Standard Dialect

My brother *ate* all the neighbor's apples.

a. *Did*      my brother *eat* all the neighbor's apples?

b. *Did*      my brother *eat*              *what*?

c. *What did* my brother *eat*?

EXAMPLE                     Standard Dialect

My brother *ate* all the neighbor's apples.

a. *Did* my brother *eat* all the neighbor's apples?

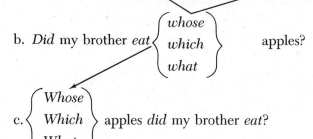

b. *Did* my brother *eat* $\begin{cases} whose \\ which \\ what \end{cases}$ apples?

c. $\begin{cases} Whose \\ Which \\ What \end{cases}$ apples *did* my brother *eat*?

## Pattern Practice

Turn the following statements into WH questions, using the WH words given at the beginning of each line. The first two have been done for you.

1.  **S**  Your boyfriend is a freak.

    **Q**  Why  is your boyfriend a freak? _____

    **Q**  Whose  boyfriend is a freak? _____

307

2. **S** We are moving to the west coast.

   **Q** When <u>are we moving to the west coast?</u>

   **Q** Why <u>are we moving to the west coast?</u>

   **Q** Where <u>are we moving?.</u>

3. **S** I like rock and roll music.

   **Q** What_____

   **Q** Which_____

   **Q** Who_____

4. **S** Margaret and Mabel like to watch wrestling matches on T.V.

   **Q** Who_____

   **Q** What_____

   **Q** Which_____

   **Q** Why_____

   **Q** Where_____

5. **S** My dog prefers to eat spaghetti and drink Coca-Cola.

   **Q** What_____

   **Q** Which_____

   **Q** Whose_____

   **Q** Who_____

   **Q** How_____

   **Q** Why_____

6. **S** You can study with the radio playing.

   **Q** Who_____

   **Q** What_____

   **Q** How_____

**Q** Where_____

7. **S** Philadelphia is the fifth largest city in the United States.

   **Q** Which_____

   **Q** What_____

   **Q** Where_____

8. **S** The Baptist Church was formed in England in 1609.

   **Q** When_____

   **Q** Where_____

   **Q** Which_____

   **Q** What_____

   **Q** Why_____

   **Q** How_____

9. **S** The oldest living trees in the world are the bristlecone pines found in California's White Mountains.

   **Q** Which_____

   **Q** What_____

   **Q** Where_____

10. **S** The earth is the fifth largest planet and the third from the sun.

    **Q** Which_____

    **Q** Where_____

    **Q** What_____

11. **S** The state of Utah is composed of twenty-nine counties with a population of 1,059,273.

    **Q** Which_____

    **Q** What_____

12.  **S**  In 1804 Lewis and Clark explored the Northwest Territory of the United States.

    **Q**  When_____

    **Q**  Who_____

    **Q**  Which_____

    **Q**  What_____

    **Q**  Why_____

13.  **S**  In 1972 John McKay of USC was voted the College Football Coach of the year.

    **Q**  Who_____

    **Q**  When_____

    **Q**  What_____

    **Q**  How_____

    **Q**  Why_____

14.  **S**  The life expectancy of people in the United States is seventy-one years.

    **Q**  Whose_____

    **Q**  What_____

    **Q**  Where_____

    **Q**  Why_____

15.  **S**  O'Hare Airport in Chicago is the busiest airport in the country with 641,429 take-offs and landings in a year.

    **Q**  Which_____

    **Q**  What_____

    **Q**  Why_____

16.  **S**  In 1970 an average of 1,800 gallons of water per day were used by the public in the United States.

    **Q**  When_____

**Q** What_____

**Q** Why_____

17. **S** Ethel was named after her mother's best friend.

    **Q** Who_____

    **Q** Why_____

    **Q** Whose_____

18. **S** To be or not to be is the question!

    **Q** What_____

    **Q** Which_____

    **Q** Why_____

    **Q** How_____

19. **S** I wish I could dance like my sister Kate!

    **Q** Whose_____

    **Q** Why_____

    **Q** How_____

    **Q** Who_____

20. **S** Beverly's husband believes in love.

    **Q** Whose_____

    **Q** What_____

    **Q** Why_____

21. **S** The Air Force was started on August 1, 1907, as the Aeronautical Division of the

    Signal Corps., U. S. Army.

    **Q** When_____

    **Q** What_____

    **Q** Which_____

**Q** How_____

**Q** Why_____

22.  **S**  Ronald's cousin's birthday is tomorrow.

**Q** Whose_____

**Q** Which_____

**Q** When_____

**Q** Why_____

23.  **S**  The Pacific Ocean is 64,186,300 square miles.

**Q** Which_____

**Q** What_____

24.  **S**  The Pentagon, headquarters of the Department of Defense, is the world's largest office building, and was completed on January 15, 1943.

**Q** What_____

**Q** Which_____

**Q** When_____

**Q** Where_____

25.  **S**  The National Shrine of the Immaculate Conception in Washington D. C. is the largest Catholic Church in the United States.

**Q** Which_____

**Q** What_____

**Q** Where_____

26.  **S**  Arlington National Cemetery is the site of the Tomb of the Unknown Soldier and was established June 15, 1864.

**Q** Which_____

**Q** What_____

**Q** When_____

**Q** Where_____

**Q** Whose_____

27. **S** Easter is the chief festival of the Christian year, celebrating the resurrection of Jesus.

**Q** Which_____

**Q** What_____

**Q** Whose_____

**Q** Why_____

# QUESTIONS AND INDEFINITE PRONOUNS

# 4

In Part II we studied four kinds of pronouns: personal, possessive, reflexive, and relative. All of those pronouns refer to a specific person, thing, or event. There is another group of pronouns that are called indefinite pronouns, which we will study in this chapter because they are important in forming sentences.

Indefinite pronouns are those which refer to something that is not specifically identified. They include *some*, *any*, *each*, *one*, *none*, and combined forms like *somebody*, *everybody*, *nowhere*, *anything*, etc. The ones we'll be most concerned about in this chapter are the *some* and *any* forms, since they are the ones that most often are used differently in standard and community dialects. Here is a list of them:

| | |
|---|---|
| *some* | *any* |
| *someone* | *anyone* |
| *somebody* | *anybody* |
| *somewhere* | *anywhere* |
| *somehow* | *anyhow* |
| *sometime* | *anytime* |
| *someway* | *anyway* |

In the standard dialect, forms of *some* are usually (though not always) used in statements; forms of *any* are used in questions (and, as we will see in a later chapter, in negative statements).

EXAMPLES                    Standard Dialect

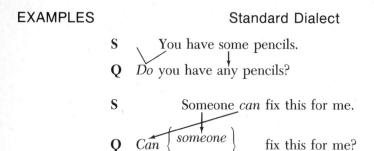

S      You have some pencils.

Q   *Do* you have any pencils?

S      Someone *can* fix this for me.

Q   *Can* { *someone* / *anyone* }   fix this for me?

Notice that when you ask someone a question, the person who answers will often have to change the pronouns.

EXAMPLE

Q   *Can you*      fix this for *me*?

A   Yes, *I* *can* fix this for *you*.

## Pattern Practice

Answer the following yes/no questions with a *yes* statement. (Remember that you might have to change pronouns, as in number 1.) The first two have been done for you.

1. **Q**  Do you have any stamps?

   **S**  Yes, I have some stamps. _____

2. **Q**  Can anyone bring a corkscrew to the party?

   **S**  Yes, someone can bring a corkscrew to the party. _____

3. **Q**  Do you know anyone who is interested in ice skating?

   **S**  _____

4. **Q**  Do you know anybody who sells used cars?

   **S**  _____

5. **Q**  Did anyone complete the homework assignment?

   **S**  _____

6. **Q**  Does John have any relatives in New York?

   **S**  _____

7. **Q**  Can anybody come to the party?

   **S**  _____

8. **Q**  Can you lend me any of your old James Brown records?

   **S**  _____

9. **Q**  Are we having any dessert for dinner tonight?

   **S**  _____

10. **Q**  Isn't there anyone who can help us get rich?

    **S**  _____

11. **Q**  Wasn't there any way to avoid the accident?

    **S**  _____

12. **Q**  Haven't you found any time to help with the housework?

**S**  _____

13  **Q**  Is there any way I can help ease the pain?

**S**  _____

14. **Q**  Can't you locate the psychology book anywhere?

**S**  _____

15. **Q**  Doesn't anyone know the way to Ohio?

**S**  _____

16. **Q**  Do you have any time to volunteer your services to the Boy Scouts?

**S**  _____

17. **Q**  Can you afford to contribute any money to the Red Cross?

**S**  _____

18. **Q**  Haven't you made any new friends in your neighborhood?

**S**  _____

19. **Q**  Is there any way I can avoid facing your aunt?

**S**  _____

20. **Q**  Haven't you been able to find your keys anywhere?

**S**  _____

21. **Q**  Do you know anyone who knows anything about English grammar?

**S**  _____

22. **Q**  Do you have any extra dishes I can borrow for my party?

**S**  _____

23. **Q**  Did Rachel's dog have any puppies?

**S**  _____

24. **Q**  Haven't they any time to attend the meeting next Friday?

**S**  _____

25. **Q**  Is there any way we can go to Mexico next summer?

**S**  _____

# INDIRECT QUESTIONS

In a direct question the speaker either directly addresses the listener, or directly quotes a question which he asked himself or which someone else asked (in the latter case, quotation marks are always put around the question).

EXAMPLES                Standard Dialect

Direct Question
1. Is Richard going with Olga?

Direct Question Quoted

2. She asked me, "Is Richard going with Olga?"
3. I wondered, "Is Richard going with Olga?"

An indirect question differs from a direct question in that it is a report of a question asked by the speaker or someone else, but is not directly quoted. The question part is always preceded by an introductory word like *if*, *whether*, or one of the WH question words we studied in Chapter 3.

EXAMPLES                Standard Dialect

Indirect Question

4. She asked me if Richard was going with Olga.
5. I wondered if Richard was going with Olga.

Compare the first example with the corresponding quoted question on the preceding page.

> 2. She asked me, "Is Richard going with Olga?"
> 4. She asked me if Richard was going with Olga.

First, notice that the verb in the quoted part of number 2 is in present time (*is*), but in number 4 it is in past time (*was*). That's because present time verbs in direct questions often become past time verbs in indirect questions. In the case of modals, *can* in direct questions becomes *could* in indirect questions; *will* becomes *would*; *shall* becomes *should*; and *may* becomes *might*.

EXAMPLE                    Standard Dialect

> She asked me, "*Can* Richard go with Olga?"
> She asked me if Richard *could* go with Olga.

Another important difference is that the quoted question always has quotation marks around it. The reported (indirect) question does not.

One of the most important differences is in the word order. Look again at sentences 1, 2, and 3:

> 1. Is Richard going with Olga?
> 2. She asked me, "Is Richard going with Olga?"
> 3. I wondered, "Is Richard going with Olga?"

In all three, the question has the helping verb *is* before the subject *Richard*.

So the pattern is

helping verb→subject→main verb

Now look again at sentences 4 and 5:

4. She asked me whether Richard was going with Olga.
5. I wondered whether Richard was going with Olga.

In these indirect questions the helping verb comes after the subject. So the pattern is

subject→helping verb→main verb

There is another important difference between direct and quoted questions on the one hand, and indirect questions on the other. The indirect question begins with one of the following words: *if*, *whether*, or any of the WH words we discussed in Chapter 3. Now it's easy to spot an indirect question if it has *if* or *whether*. If it has one of the WH words, however, you have to depend on the other three properties of indirect questions in order to distinguish them from direct questions (that is, the use of past time instead of present, the lack of quotation marks, and especially the **subject→helping verb→main verb** word order).

EXAMPLES                    Standard Dialect

> Where is Richard going?
> She asked me, "Where is Richard going?"
> She asked me where Richard was going.

Finally, there is one more difference that affects only questions with pronouns. Compare the following sentences:

> She asked me, "Do *you* want to go with *me*?"
> She asked me if *I* wanted to go with *her*.

Notice that the subject of the first question ( *you* ) is a **Type 2** pronoun and the object (*me*) is a **Type 1** pronoun. In the second question, however, the subject (*I*) is a **Type 1** pronoun and the object (*her*) is **Type 3**. This change in pronouns occurs only when the person or persons referred to in the first part are the same as the person or persons referred to in the second part of the question.

In some community dialects, the question word order is used in *both* direct and indirect questions, and *if* or *whether* is not used.

EXAMPLES

| Community Dialect | Standard Dialect |
|---|---|
| I asked, "Is she going to college?" | I asked, "Is she going to college?" |
| I asked *is she going* to college. | I asked *whether she was going* to college. |

| Community Dialect | Standard Dialect |
|---|---|
| I wondered, "Does she want to go?" | I wondered, "Does she want to go?" |
| I wondered *did she want* to go. | I wondered *if she wanted* to go. |
| I asked, "What does he want for dinner?" | I asked, "What does he want for dinner?" |
| I asked, "*What did he want* for dinner. | I asked *what he wanted* for dinner. |

### Summary:   Indirect Questions

| Community Dialect | Standard Dialect |
|---|---|
| I wondered did he want to go. | I wondered *if* he *wanted* to go. |

## Recognition Drill

The following are indirect questions. Mark SD next to those that are written in the standard dialect. The first three have been done for you.

_____  1. Luisa asked Lucy had she made her own dress.

\_\_SD\_\_  2. Brother Francis wonders whether the birds will come for their seed today.

_____  3. The German professor asked the class did they learn their lesson.

_____  4. The political scientist wondered was the government deteriorating.

_____  5. The animal doctor inquired whether the dog had a toothache.

_____  6. The witch ponders has she really cast a spell on him.

_____  7. Little Red Riding Hood asked her grandmother whether the wolf had visited her.

_____  8. Eve asked Adam did he eat the apple pie.

_____  9. The Queen asked Jason did he bring her the golden fleece.

_____ 10. The children's mother asked them whether they had put their boots on.

_____ 11. My little brother asked is there a Santa Claus.

_____ 12. My little niece wonders whether she was born under a cabbage leaf.

_____ 13. Scientists ponder whether there is life on Mars.

_____ 14. The refugees asked did the Red Cross bring food.

_____ 15. I asked my daughter was she on a diet.

_____ 16. Matthew wondered is the bacon done.

_____ 17. Mark wondered whether there was none.

_____ 18. Luke wondered had the race been run.

_____ 19. John wondered whether Mark had won.

_____ 20. Zebedee pondered did the answers come to Matthew, Mark, Luke, and John.

_____ 21. The young men in the class asked the pretty teacher was she married.

_____ 22. She asked them whether it was any of their business.

_____ 23. She wondered did they have something in mind.

_____ 24. The policeman asked was I speeding.

_____ 25. I asked the policeman whether he had clocked me.

_____ 26. He inquired was I on my way to a fire.

_____ 27. I wondered whether I had been speeding.

_____ 28. I had been pondering was my paycheck going to last through the week.

_____ 29. He asked whether I had my license.

_____ 30. I asked myself whether I had left it at home or lost it. I wondered whether I was

in trouble.

_____ 31. I asked where the new girl in the class came from.

_____ 32. I asked where did the new girl in the class come from.

_____ 33. Griselda wondered when she would have her children returned to her.

_____ 34. Griselda wondered when would her children be returned to her.

_____ 35. Mateo wondered why everyone was being so kind to him.

_____ 36. Mateo wondered why was everyone being kind to him.

_____ 37. He asked what they knew that he didn't know.

_____ 38. He asked what did they know that he didn't know.

_____ 39. She asked them when they were going to be engaged.

_____ 40. She asked them when were they going to be engaged.

## Pattern Practice

The following exercises contain both direct and indirect questions, all in the standard dialect. Change the direct questions to indirect questions, and the indirect questions into direct questions, keeping them all in the standard dialect. The first one in each section has been done for you.

## DIRECT TO INDIRECT

1. He asked, "Can you fix this shoe for me?"

   <u>He asked if I could fix the shoe for him.</u>

2. Three year old Jimmy asked, "Can I send my baby brother back?"

   _____

3. Everytime Belinda goes to the store she asks, "Can I have some gum?"

   _____

4. The astronomer asks, "Does the universe have limits?"

   _____

5. The little child asks, "How big is the sky?"

   _____

6. The philosopher inquires, "What is the nature of God?"

   _____

7. Joe asks, "What does God look like?"

   _____

8. Mrs. Brookinson wonders, "How will I afford the groceries at these high prices?"

_____

9. Bettina asks, "May I have permission to go to the show on Saturday?"

_____

10. Her mother asks, "Which young man is taking you?"

_____

11. Bettina inquires, "Does it make any difference?"

_____

12. Pablo asks Bettina, "Will you go to the drive-in with me?"

_____

13. She asks him, "What picture is showing?"

_____

14. He asks, "What difference does it make when the popcorn is good?"

_____

15. Billie Mae asked Jimmy, "Why do you feel high when the sun is on your shoulder?"

_____

16. Jimmy Dell asked her, "Why do you feel romantic when the moon is out?"

_____

17. They both wondered, "How do the sun, moon, and stars affect us?"

_____

18. The professor asked Reverend Jones, "Do you believe in the devil?"

_____

19. Reverend Jones asked the professor, "Do you ever commit sin?"

_____

20. The reverend asked the professor, "Will you come to the next revival meeting on Thursday?"

_____


## INDIRECT TO DIRECT

1. The bus driver inquired where my fare was.

   The bus driver inquired, "Where is your fare?"
   _____

2. I asked him whether I could ride free since I had forgotten my fare.

   _____

3. He asked me whether I knew that he would be fired if he let me ride free.

   _____

4. I wondered how I would get to school.

   _____

5. A lady asked me whether she could loan me the fifty cents for the fare.

   _____

6. I thanked her and asked her why she was so kind.

   _____

7. I also asked her where she lived so I could repay her.

   _____

8. I wondered how many nice people there are in the world.

   _____

9. Pauletta asked me what sign I was born under.

   _____

10. She asked me if I was an Aquarius.

    _____

11. I asked her if she was a Capricorn.

_____

12. I wondered whether we could get along together.

_____

13. Allison asked me whether Dennis was born at the conjunction of Mars and Venus.

_____

14. She asked if those signs made him loving and aggressive.

_____

15. The men wondered whether the young ladies saw them coming when they started to giggle.

_____

16. John questioned whether the horses had been doped.

_____

17. He wondered if the race had been fair.

_____

18. He inquired whether the officials investigated the race.

_____

19. He asked whether the neighbors would turn down their radio.

_____

20. They asked whether he would turn down his television.

_____

## Conversion Drill

Reread the sentences in the Recognition Drill. Convert each sentence that you did not mark SD into the standard dialect, keeping the indirect question form.

# MAKING NEGATIVE
# STATEMENTS WITH *NOT*

# 6

The most common way of making a statement negative in the standard dialect is by adding *not*; this can be done in one of three ways, similar to the three ways of making questions that were listed in Chapter 2:

1. If the statement has a helping verb, you insert a *not* (or the contraction of *not, n't*) after the helping verb.

EXAMPLE                          Standard Dialect

My brother *is*      having a good time.

My brother *is not* having a good time.

My brother *isn't*   having a good time.

2. If the statement does not have a helping verb or a BE verb, you must add a helping verb (a form of DO) before you can insert the *not*.

EXAMPLE                          Standard Dialect

My brother         has three rabbits.

My brother *does*      have three rabbits.

My brother *does not* have three rabbits.

My brother *doesn't*   have three rabbits.

Remember (from Chapter 2) that when you insert a form of DO, you give it the tense that the main verb had and you change the main verb back to its base form.

3. If there is no helping verb, but the main verb is a form of BE, add *not* after the BE form.

EXAMPLE                          Standard Dialect

My brother *is*    sick today.

My brother *is not* sick today.

My brother *isn't*   sick today.

In the standard dialect, it is common to use a contracted form with negatives. We used the example of "he isn't" above, which is a contracted (or shortened) form of "he is not." Notice that an apostrophe (') is always inserted to show where something was left out in the contraction. Contractions only occur when there is a helping verb, or when there is a form of BE as the main verb.

In positive statements, the subject is usually contracted with the helping verb of BE form.

EXAMPLE                    Standard Dialect

He *is* going.
He*'s* going.

In negative statements, however, the subject may be contracted with the helping verb or BE form, or the helping verb or BE form may be contracted with not.

EXAMPLE                    Standard Dialect

He *is* not going.      or      He *is not* going.
He*'s* not going.                He *isn't* going.

With most BE forms, either one is possible; with *I am*, however, only the first is a possibility, as the following chart shows.

|  | Positive | Negative | Negative |
|---|---|---|---|
| **Type 1 pronouns as subject** | *I am* going. <br> *I'm* going. | *I am* not going. <br> *I'm* not going. | *I am not* going. <br> (no contraction) |
|  | *We are* going. <br> *We're* going. | *We are* not going. <br> *We're* not going. | *We are not* going. <br> *We aren't* going. |
| **Type 2 pronouns as subject** | *You are* going. <br> *You're* going. | *You are* not going. <br> *You're* not going. | *You are not* going. <br> *You aren't* going. |
| **Type 3 pronouns as subject** | *He is* going. <br> *She is* going. <br> *It is* going <br><br> *He's* going. <br> *She's* going. <br> *It's* going. | *He is* not going. <br> *She is* not going. <br> *It is* not going <br><br> *He's* not going. <br> *She's* not going. <br> *It's* not going. | *He is not* going. <br> *She is not* going. <br> *It is not* going. <br><br> *He isn't* going. <br> *She isn't* going. <br> *It isn't* going. |
|  | *They are* going. <br> *They're* going. | *They are* not going. <br> *They're* not going. | *They are not* going. <br> *They aren't* going. |

With the modal helping verbs and HAVE, you use one form of contraction in positive statements and a different one in negative statements. In positive statements, the subject, of course (since there is no *not*), must be contracted with the helping verb.

EXAMPLES                  Standard Dialect

I will go.                      I have gone.

*I'll*   go.                    *I've*   gone.

In negative statements, however, the helping verb is almost always contracted with *not*.

EXAMPLES                  Standard Dialect

I *will not* go.               I *have not* gone.

I *won't*   go.               I *haven't*   gone.

(Notice the irregular spelling of *won't*.)

Occasionally in your reading you may find the subject contracted with a modal helping verb or the helping verb HAVE ("I'll not go" or "I've not gone"); but you will probably find that the book was printed in Great Britain. "I'll not go" is common in British dialects; in the standard American dialect, however, "I won't go" is the accepted form.

DO is never contracted with the subject; therefore, when you use DO with *not*, you always contract the DO form with *not*.

EXAMPLE                  Standard Dialect

I *do not* go.

I *don't* go.

### Summary: Contractions with DO, HAVE, and Modal Helping Verbs

| | Positive | Negative |
|---|---|---|
| **Modals** | I *will* go. / *I'll* go. | I *will not* go. / I *won't* go. |
| **HAVE** | I *have* gone. / *I've* gone. | I *have not* gone. / I *haven't* gone. |
| **DO** | I *do* go. (no contraction) | I *do not* go. / I *don't* go. |

## Pattern Practice

Rewrite each of the following sentences, using a contraction.

1. Paul is not coming.

_____

2. The train is not running on standard time.

_____

3. We are not calling Dad long distance.

_____

4. You are not paying for the bill.

_____

5. Vela is not paying for the bill.

_____

6. It is not going to be paid for by all of us.

_____

7. I am not making good money working for the gas company.

_____

8. Daryn has not been a good husband.

_____

9. They have not been gentle people all their lives.

_____

10. You have not taken me for granted for too long.

_____

11. We have not taken several trips together.

_____

12. I have not had too much fried chicken.

_____

13. He has not had too many chips.

_____

14. The supper has not been too satisfying.

_____

15. We will not have to leave now.

_____

16. I am not sorry.

_____

17. I will not do the same for you some day.

_____

18. Do you not think she will forgive us?

_____

19. The day will not come when Sharon will forgive us.

_____

20. I would not go even if I had the money.

_____

Community dialects can differ from standard negative dialect forms in several ways:

1. Many community dialects use *ain't* as a substitute form for many contractions, including *aren't*, *isn't*, and *won't*.

EXAMPLES

| Community Dialect | Standard Dialect |
|---|---|
| I *ain't* going. | I'*m not* going. |
| He *ain't* going. | He *isn't* going. |

| Community Dialect | Standard Dialect |
|---|---|
| You *ain't* going. | You *aren't* going. |
| You *ain't* go. | You *won't* go. |
| You *ain't* go (gone). | { You *didn't* go. |
| | { You *haven't* gone. |

(It is interesting to note where *ain't* comes from. If you look back at the chart of BE contractions you'll remember that "I am not" is the only negative BE form that can't contract the helping verb and the *not*—there is no such thing as "I amn't." But in older British dialects of English, as well as in many today, that was a common contraction, though it was usually spelled "en't" or "ain't." So *ain't* began as a contraction for *am not* and then spread as a substitute for many other contractions.)

2. Negative statements in community dialects can differ from the standard dialect in the same ways the positive statements do as we showed in earlier chapters—that is, they may use a community dialect form of the helping verb instead of the standard form.

EXAMPLES

| Community Dialect | Standard Dialect |
|---|---|
| he *do not* | he *does not* |
| he *don't* | he *doesn't* |
| I *has not* gone. | He *has not* gone. |
| I *hasn't* gone. | He *hasn't* gone. |

3. Some community dialects use *no* where the standard dialect uses *not*.

EXAMPLES

| Community Dialect | Standard Dialect |
|---|---|
| He is *no* running. | He is *not* running. |
| He does *no* run. | He does *not* run. |

Summary:   Negative Statements with *NOT*

| Community Dialect | Standard Dialect |
|---|---|
| I ain't gone | I *didn't* go (I *haven't* gone) |
| he ain't go | he *won't* go |
| I's not | *I'm* not |
| he haven't | he *hasn't* |
| it is no raining out | it is *not* raining out |

## Recognition Drill

Underline the negative words in the following sentences. Then mark SD next to the negative statements that are written in the standard dialect. The first two have been done for you.

__SD__    1. My little sister <u>won't</u> go to the store for me.

__SD__    2. She will <u>not</u> do anything I ask her to do.

_____    3. Our family ain't buying a used car.

_____    4. Dexter ain't eaten for days.

_____    5. Tina ain't gone yet.

_____    6. Tamara's not dating Darryl Lee.

_____    7. I isn't the biggest one in the family now that my little brother Christopher has grown up.

_____    8. My brother did not try out for the basketball team but he should have.

_____    9. He haven't had time.

_____    10. We hasn't sung together in years.

_____    11. Rosemary hasn't ridden her horse for a month.

_____    12. Odille won't go home.

_____    13. Ruth will not let her stay here.

_____    14. I'm not green with envy over your beautiful new dress.

_____    15. You aren't ugly; you're beautiful.

_____    16. Hugo isn't kind to you.

_____    17. The secretary of the club don't write the minutes.

_____    18. I'm not going skating.

_____    19. That dog will not let me train her to the leash.

_____    20. I'm writing poetry.

_____    21. I is not a red hot mama.

_____ 22. You ain't either.

_____ 23. I'm the last son still at home.

_____ 24. Mother won't let me work in the coal mines.

_____ 25. But I'm not looking for a safer job.

_____ 26. You're not brave enough for me.

_____ 27. Billy is not coming home on furlough.

_____ 28. Butch ain't going to do it.

_____ 29. I's not a good citizen because I ain't voted.

_____ 30. Dwight has no paid his parking ticket.


## Pattern Practice

Change each of the following positive statements into a negative statement, first with *not*, and second with the contraction *n't*. The first two have
been done for you.

1. That corkscrew will open the bottle of wine.

   That corkscrew will not open the bottle of wine.
   _____

   That corkscrew won't open the bottle of wine.
   _____

2. Grandmother is smoking her pipe again.

   Grandmother is not smoking her pipe again.
   _____

   Grandmother isn't smoking her pipe again.
   _____

3. The grape jelly is delicious.

   _____

   _____

4. I am the next Miss America.

   _____

   _____

5. Bobette was angry.

_____

_____

6. The dogs will be in the dog pound.

_____

_____

7. The grass next door was green.

_____

_____

8. Martha has a gorgeous wardrobe.

_____

_____

9. Stephen had the chicken pox.

_____

_____

10. Victor will have three thousand dollars in the bank by next Friday.

_____

_____

11. The bank had twenty million dollars in assets.

_____

_____

12. The baby girls have beautiful eyes.

_____

_____

13. The house has walls made of brick.

_____

_____

14. The dish is filled with blue flowers.

_____

_____

15. Grandpa will soon have a long gray beard.

_____

_____

16. The gypsy had a head full of stories.

_____

_____

17. The church has three bells in the tower.

_____

_____

18. He's a strange character.

_____

_____

19. They're new people in town.

_____

_____

20. We're the oldest family in town.

_____

_____

21. You're the town marshall.

_____

_____

22. She's a fine woman.

_____

_____

23. It's a hard job.

_____

_____

24. The Grove Real Estate bought the building.

_____

_____

25. The roof needed repair.

_____

_____

26. The wind blew off the shingles.

_____

_____

27. The stairs broke.

_____

_____

28. The children went home from the party.

_____

_____

29. Their parents saw them coming across the street.

30. The children began shouting to their parents.

_____

_____

_____

## Conversion Drill

Reread the sentences in the Recognition Drill. Convert each sentence that you did not mark SD into the standard dialect.

---

# MAKING NEGATIVE STATEMENTS WITH *NO*

# 7

The standard dialect has another common way of making a statement negative: that is, by inserting the adjective *no* before the noun that you want to make negative (replacing any articles or number adjectives already there, like *a*, *the*, *many*, *some*, etc.).

### EXAMPLES          Standard Dialect

| Positive | Negative |
|----------|----------|
| He has *a* house. | He has *no* house. |
| He has *many* houses. | He has *no* houses. |

Notice that these are alternate forms to the *not* or *n't* forms discussed in Chapter 5. Compare the above examples with their *n't* forms:

### Standard Dialect

| Positive | Negative |
|----------|----------|
| He *has* a house. | He *doesn't have* a house. |
| He *has many* houses. | He *doesn't have many* houses. |

In some community dialects, both *not* (*n't*) and *no* are used together.

EXAMPLE                                   Community Dialect

He *doesn't* (*don't*) have no house.

Summary: Negative Statements with *NO*

| Community Dialect | Standard Dialect |
|---|---|
| He { doesn't / don't } have no house. | { He *doesn't* have *any* house. / He has *no* house. } |

## Recognition Drill

Underline the negative words in the following sentences. Then mark SD next to each sentence that is written in the standard dialect. The first three have been done for you.

__SD__ 1. The poor old man has <u>no</u> home.

_____ 2. I <u>ain't</u> got <u>no</u> home.

_____ 3. Marshalleen <u>don't</u> have <u>no</u> car.

_____ 4. Freddie hasn't no marshmallow candy.

_____ 5. La Veen hasn't no yo-yo.

_____ 6. The train has no whistle.

_____ 7. The valley has no river running through it.

_____ 8. The trees ain't got no fruit this year.

_____ 9. The roads have no ice on them.

_____ 10. I ain't got no allowance left.

_____ 11. Those clouds haven't no rain in them.

_____ 12. The picture had no frame.

_____ 13. The gasoline station hadn't no gas.

_____ 14. Maybelle ain't got no false teeth.

_____ 15. She has no teeth at all.

_____ 16. The T.V. has no antenna.

_____ 17. The car ain't got no engine.

_____ 18. The library ordered no new books.

_____ 19. The bookstore hasn't no paper.

_____ 20. The A & P don't have no fresh vegetables today.


## Pattern Practice

Change each of the following positive statements into a negative statement in the standard dialect by inserting *no*. The first two have been done for you.

1. He has a car.

   He has no car.
   _____

2. The house has big windows.

   The house has no big windows.
   _____

3. That family has dogs.

   _____

4. The farmer had many cows.

   _____

5. That house has a key.

   _____

6. The well has water.

   _____

7. All summer they had had rain.

   _____

8. Mr. and Mrs. Powers wanted children.

   _____

9. The Davis family had money.

_____

10. This typewriter has keys.

_____

11. Lana owned books for school.

_____

12. The airplane flew with wings.

_____

13. My car has gas.

_____

14. My girlfriend has hair on her head.

_____

15. My boyfriend has brains.

_____

## Pattern Practice

Change each of the following positive statements into a negative statement in the standard dialect, first by using *not* or *n't*, and then by using *no*. The first two have been done for you.

1. Marietta threw the boxes away.

    Marietta didn't throw the boxes away.

    Marietta threw no boxes away.

2. Charlie wanted a lot of presents for Christmas.

    Charlie didn't want a lot of presents for Christmas.

    Charlie wanted no presents for Christmas.

3. Bonnie bought a brown hat.

_____

_____

4. Peter picked pickled peppers.

_____

_____

5. Charlie Brown ate peanuts.

_____

_____

6. The sailors dated the girls.

_____

_____

7. The cherry pickers held a strike.

_____

_____

8. We bought lettuce at the market.

_____

_____

9. Hansel and Gretel killed the witch.

_____

_____

10. Humpty Dumpty sat on a wall.

_____

_____

11. Humpty Dumpty had a great fall.

_____

_____

12. Humpty Dumpty was an egg.

_____

_____

13. There were ghosts in the attic.

_____

_____

14. There was a burglar in the cellar.

_____

_____

15. The dog gave a bark.

_____

_____

16. The burglar stole the washing machine.

_____

_____

17. My wife makes me wash the dishes.

_____

_____

18. Agatha and her dad moved furniture.

_____

_____

19. I contributed an antique lamp to the rummage sale.

_____

_____

20. Olar Cass collects bottles.

_____

_____

## Conversion Drill

Reread the sentences in the Recognition Drill. Convert each sentence that you did not mark SD into the standard dialect.

# MAKING NEGATIVE STATEMENTS WITH *ONLY, HARDLY,* AND *SCARCELY*

# 8

In addition to *no* and *not* (or *n't*), there are three other words that are often used to make a sentence negative in the standard dialect: *only* (meaning "no more than" or "nothing but"), *hardly,* and *scarcely* (both meaning "almost no").

EXAMPLES                 Standard Dialect

       I have *hardly (scarcely)* any money.
          (Meaning: I have *almost no* money.)
       I have *only* three books.
          (Meaning: I have *no more than* three books.)

In the standard dialect, you usually don't use more than one negative word in a clause or simple sentence—thus you never use *not* (*n't*), or *no* with *hardly, scarcely,* or *only.* In many community dialects, however, you use *no, n't,* and *ain't* with *hardly, only,* and *scarcely.*

| Community Dialect | Standard Dialect |
| :--- | :--- |
| I *ain't got hardly no* money. | I *have hardly any* money. |

Some community dialects use *but* as a negative word where the standard dialect uses *only*, in addition to inserting *n't*.

**EXAMPLES**

| Community Dialect | Standard Dialect |
| :--- | :--- |
| I *ain't got but* three books. | I *have only* three books. |

Summary: Negatives with *ONLY*, *HARDLY*, and *SCARCELY*

| Community Dialect | Standard Dialect |
| :--- | :--- |
| I ain't got hardly no money. | I *hardly have any* money. |
| I ain't got but three books. | I *only have* three books. |

## Recognition Drill

Underline the negative words in the following sentences. Then mark SD next to each negative statement that is in the standard dialect. The first two have been done for you.

   **SD**    1. We have <u>hardly</u> enough gas to get us to the gas station.

_____ 2. Ethelred the Unready had <u>scarcely</u> <u>no</u> courage in battle.

_____ 3. The bulb doesn't hardly fit in the socket.

_____ 4. The trucker only had three more miles to go.

_____ 5. The old gray mare ain't got but three legs to go on.

_____ 6. There isn't scarcely no man alive who knew Abraham Lincoln.

_____ 7. Abraham Lincoln only had a few years of schooling.

_____ 8. I didn't hardly go near the flowers.

_____ 9. The bee tree ain't got hardly no honey this year.

_____ 10. The fire siren ain't hardly got no sound.

_____ 11. The artist only received three dollars for his painting.

_____ 12. Felice ain't got but three pages of her sixty-page paper written.

_____ 13. Anna had scarcely paid for her sewing machine when she broke it.

_____ 14. Elizabeth ain't got hardly no ironing done.

_____ 15. Catherine had hardly raised her children when she had to raise her grandchildren.

_____ 16. We ain't eaten together but three times this year.

_____ 17. The fruit man ain't got hardly no bananas today.

_____ 18. The graduating class only has three hundred seniors.

_____ 19. They collected scarcely two thousand dollars for their trip to Nassau.

_____ 20. The herb doctor hasn't got but three patients.


## Pattern Practice

Using the negative word in the margin, make each of the following positive statements into a negative statement in the standard dialect. The first two have been done for you.

SCARCELY   1. I have three dollars in my pocket.

I have scarcely three dollars in my pocket. _____

ONLY   2. I have one year left of college.

I have only one year left of college. _____

HARDLY   3. We have pictures on our walls.

_____

SCARCELY   4. She felt the pain in her shoulder.

_____

ONLY   5. Darnelle is the doctor on the expedition to the North Pole.

_____

HARDLY   6. This is the way to dance the twist.

_____

ONLY    7. Harold is the artist in the family.

_____

SCARCELY    8. The crops have had rain this year.

_____

ONLY    9. We had two feet of snow last winter.

_____

HARDLY    10. He was twenty-one when he went to war.

_____

## Conversion Drill

Reread the sentences in the Recognition Drill. Convert each sentence that you did not mark SD into the standard dialect.

# MAKING NEGATIVE STATEMENTS WITH *NEVER* AND *NEITHER . . . NOR*

# 9

Still another way of making a statement negative in the standard dialect is by using the words *never* and *neither...nor*. *Never* is the negative form of *always*, and *neither...nor* is the negative form of *either...or*.

EXAMPLES                    Standard Dialect

**Positive**                        **Negative**

1. He *always* goes to the     2. He *never* goes to the
   library on Fridays.            library on Fridays.
3. He is taking *either*       4. He is taking *neither*
   chemistry *or* physics         chemistry *nor* physics
   this term.                     this term.

(Notice that *neither...nor* is the only case in the standard dialect where you use two negative words together.)

Sentences 1 and 3 can also be made negative by adding *n't* or *not* instead of changing the *always* to *never* or the *either...or* to *neither...nor*.

EXAMPLES            Standard Dialect

**Positive**                  **Negative**

5. He *always* goes to the library.
7. He is taking *either* chemistry *or* physics. this term.

6. He does*n't* *always* go to the library.
8. He is*n't* taking *either* chemistry *or* physics this term.

Notice, however, that the meaning changes when you say *isn't always* instead of *never*. Which negative form you choose, then, will depend on what meaning you want to get across.

Some community dialects use *never* and *neither...nor* together, or in combination with other negative words.

EXAMPLES

Community Dialect         Standard Dialect

He never took *neither* chemistry *nor* physics.
He did*n't* take *neither* chemistry *nor* physics.
He *never* went to *no* football game.

He never took *either* chemistry *or* physics.
He did*n't* take *either* chemistry *or* physics.
He *never* went to *a* football game.

Summary: *NEVER and NEITHER · · · NOR*

| **Community Dialect** | **Standard Dialect** |
|---|---|
| He never had neither money nor friends. | He *never* had *either* money *or* friends. |
| He did*n't* have neither money nor friends. | He did*n't* have *either* money *or* friends. |
| He didn't never know it. | He did*n't* *ever* know it. |

## Recognition Drill

Underline the negative words in the following sentences. Then mark SD next to each sentence whose negative forms are in the standard dialect. The first three have been done for you.

_____ 1. He <u>never</u> knew <u>nothing</u> about it.

__SD__ 2. Kate did<u>n't</u> ever remember receiving the letter.

<u>SD</u>  3. His father <u>never</u> knows where James goes after school.

_____  4. I like neither ice cream nor candy.

_____  5. Douglas don't never do nothing right.

_____  6. Our old house didn't have neither wallpaper nor carpets.

_____  7. We didn't never miss those things neither.

_____  8. We never spent our time either worrying or caring about them.

_____  9. We didn't never think we missed them.

_____ 10. In fact, we didn't ever think about them.

_____ 11. Antonio didn't never know the meaning of love.

_____ 12. Antonio had neither happiness nor good luck.

_____ 13. Antonio never thought about anybody except himself.

_____ 14. Being overweight didn't do no good for Arthur.

_____ 15. Arthur didn't ever think about losing weight.

_____ 16. Arthur never thought about nothing except food.

_____ 17. Now Arthur can't fit into neither his clothes nor his car.

_____ 18. Arthur didn't never have a girlfriend neither.

_____ 19. You should never either give up the struggle or the desire to reach your goal.

_____ 20. Roberta didn't never like doing these exercises in the grammar book, but this

grammar book is the best grammar book in the world.

## Pattern Practice

Make each of the following sentences negative, either by changing *either...or* and *always* to their negative forms, or by inserting *not* or *n't*. The first two have been done for you.

1. I have always been a lover of beautiful shoes.

I have never been a lover of beautiful shoes.
_____

2. I will either buy the best shoes imported from Italy or I will do without shoes.

   I will neither buy the best shoes imported from Italy nor will I do without shoes. _____

3. My friends always criticize me for staring at their shoes.

   _____

4. They tell me I have either fallen in love with their feet or need a doctor.

   _____

5. However, I am the one who always wears the most up-to-date shoes.

   _____

6. My friends have either bad taste or bad manners when they criticize me.

   _____

7. They are always either borrowing my beautiful shoes or looking like fools wearing last year's shoes.

   _____

8. I am always the one they turn to.

   _____

9. They always tell me that story of the old lady who either lived in a shoe or had so many children she didn't know what to do.

   _____

10. I always go to the library on Tuesday nights.

    _____

11. On Wednesday I always read the books I borrowed on Tuesday.

    _____

12. On Thursday night I either visit friends to discuss the books I've read or go back to the library for more books.

    _____

13. I always relax on Friday nights.

_____

14. Saturday is the day I either clean around the house or go shopping.

_____

15. On Sunday I always start my diet.

_____

16. On Monday morning I always have the blues because I have to choose to either jump out of bed or lose my job.

_____

17. It's always a hard choice.

_____

18. Have you ever felt like running away either to Hawaii or Nassau?

_____

19. Have you ever gotten tired of always doing the same old thing day in and day out and wished to get out of the routine or take a long vacation?

_____

20. I always have that feeling on Monday morning.

_____

## Conversion Drill

Reread the sentences in the Recognition Drill. Then convert each sentence that you did not mark SD into the standard dialect.

## 10

# INDEFINITE PRONOUNS IN NEGATIVE STATEMENTS

The indefinite pronouns that we discussed in Chapter 4 (*some, any, each,* and their combined forms like *somebody, anybody,* and *everybody*) have corresponding negative forms. They are as follows:

| Positive | | Negative |
|----------|----------|----------|
| *some* | *any* | *none* |
| *somebody* | *anybody* | *nobody* |
| *someone* | *anyone* | *no one* |
| *something* | *anything* | *nothing* |
| *somewhere* | *anywhere* | *nowhere* |

In the standard dialect, there are two ways of changing a statement from positive to negative when it contains an indefinite pronoun.

1. You can change the positive indefinite pronoun into a negative one.

EXAMPLES                    Standard Dialect

| Positive | Negative |
|----------|----------|
| *Someone* is knocking at the door. | *No one* is knocking at the door. |
| *Anybody* can pass this course. | *Nobody* can pass this course. |
| I'll have *some* of that. | I'll have *none* of that. |

2. You can keep the positive form of the indefinite pronoun and insert a negative word (*not, n't, no, never, hardly, scarcely, only*).

EXAMPLE                    Standard Dialect

| Positive | Negative |
|----------|----------|
| I'll have *some* of that. | I won't have *any* (*some*) of that. |

Notice that it's common to change *some* and *every* to *any* when *not* or *n't* is added. You'd be more likely to say "I won't have *any* of that" than to say "I won't have *some* of that."

Some community dialects, in addition to using the negative pronoun, use *n't* after the helping verb or *ain't* in place of the helping verb.

EXAMPLES                    Community Dialect

> *No one ain't* knocking at the door.
> *No one can't* pass this course.
> I *won't* have *none* of that.

Other community dialects also move the *ain't* or *n't* with the helping verb to the beginning of the sentence.

EXAMPLES                    Community Dialect

> *Ain't no one* knocking at the door.
> *Can't no one* pass this course.
> *Ain't no one can* pass this course.

To change these community dialects into the standard dialect you do one or two things: you take out the *ain't* or *n't*; and you put the helping verb after the indefinite pronoun.

### Summary: Indefinite Pronouns in Negative Statements

| Community Dialect | | Standard Dialect |
|---|---|---|
| I don't have none. | I have some. | I *don't* have *any*. |
| Ain't nobody here. | Everybody is here. | *Nobody* is here. |

## Recognition Drill

Underline the negative words in the following sentences. Then mark SD next to the sentences that are written in the standard dialect. The first three have been done for you.

_____ 1. I <u>ain't</u> got <u>none.</u>

_____ 2. <u>Can't</u> <u>nobody</u> go <u>nowhere</u> in this job.

__SD__ 3. We have <u>hardly</u> any friends left.

_____ 4. Ain't nobody going nowhere in this rain storm.

_____ 5. Nobody knew where Jane left her bicycle.

_____ 6. Bob ain't got no use for school.

_____ 7. You don't know nothing.

_____ 8. They ain't seen nobody they knew at the high school reunion.

_____ 9. Don't nobody know nothing around here.

_____ 10. Shirley don't mean nothing to Carl.

_____ 11. We have completed only some of the homework.

_____ 12. I knew hardly anyone at the dance.

_____ 13. Nobody on our block is unfriendly.

_____ 14. I've never seen anyone as beautiful as Doris.

_____ 15. I don't owe you nothing.

_____ 16. She ain't never been nowhere with Jackson.

_____ 17. Ain't nobody telling me what to do with my life.

_____ 18. Nobody cares about Marvin.

_____ 19. Gary understands nothing the doctor says.

_____ 20. Nothing you do will ever matter.

## Pattern Practice

Change the following positive statements into negative statements in the standard dialect. The first two have been done for you.

1. Everything King Midas touched turned to gold.

   Nothing King Midas touched turned to gold.

2. I gave him something special for his birthday.

   I didn't give him anything special for his birthday.

   (or) I gave him nothing special for his birthday.

3. Everybody is always talking about me.

4. Everything I have is yours.

_____

5. Has anybody seen my old friend Theodore?

_____

6. I know somebody who is interested in repairing cars.

_____

7. We can think of something that would please him.

_____

8. There is a place for Mike somewhere in the entertainment field.

_____

9. Bill has found some way to help Evelyn with her mathematics.

_____

10. Earnest has somewhere to go every Saturday night.

_____

11. They have some suggestions to make to the chairman of the corporation.

_____

12. There is always somebody ahead of you when you are in a hurry.

_____

13. Everybody should be able to attend the church picnic.

_____

14. Ed always sets aside some time for relaxation.

_____

15. I have discovered some way to unravel the mystery.

_____

16. We know your shoes must be somewhere in your bedroom.

_____

17. You can take some food to the party.

_____

18. I know something about Richard that you don't know.

_____

19. Everything can be perfect.

_____

20. There is room in the hall for everybody.

_____

## Conversion Drill

Reread the sentences in the Recognition Drill. Convert each sentence that you did not mark SD into the standard dialect.

# INDEFINITE PRONOUNS IN NEGATIVE QUESTIONS  **11**

So far we have studied forms of questions in the standard dialect, and forms of negative statements in the standard dialect. Now we want to look at their combined form: negative questions. The only time community dialects are likely to differ from the standard dialect is when *no* and the indefinite pronouns are used.

In the standard dialect, when you want to make a negative question out of a positive question with an indefinite pronoun, you always insert *not* or *n't* following the helping verb. In addition, you may change *some* or *every* forms to *any* forms. But you do not use *no* or the negative forms of the indefinite pronouns.

Standard Dialect

**Positive**                          **Negative**

Can you have some candy?        Ca*n't* you have *any* candy?
Is everyone at home?            Is*n't* *anyone* at home?


Some community dialects use both *no* or the negative form of the indefinite pronoun and insert *n't* or *ain't*.

EXAMPLES                   Community Dialect

**Positive**                          **Negative**

Can you have some candy?        Ca*n't* you have *no* candy?
Is everyone at home?            Is*n't* *no* one at home?

### Summary: Indefinite Pronouns in Negative Questions

| Community Dialect | Standard Dialect |
|---|---|
| Do you have some? | |
| Don't you have none? | Don't you have *some* (*any*)? |
| Ain't you got none? | Haven't you got *some* (*any*)? |

## Recognition Drill

Underline negative words in the following sentences. Then mark SD next to each negative question that is in the standard dialect. The first three have been done for you.

_____ 1. <u>Ain't</u> you got <u>no</u> friends?

__SD__ 2. <u>Don't</u> you ever visit anybody?

_____ 3. <u>Ain't</u> <u>nobody</u> coming to the party?

_____ 4. Ain't you seen Ruby nowhere?

_____ 5. Don't they seem unlike anybody we've known before?

_____ 6. Haven't we enrolled everybody in the speech class?

_____ 7. Doesn't somebody know the correct time?

_____ 8. Ain't there nothing the insurance company can do about the accident?

_____ 9. Don't you have no steak for supper tonight?

_____ 10. Ain't you never cared for nobody except yourself?

_____ 11. Doesn't everything he does seem wonderful?

_____ 12. Don't spending your money on records and movies leave you with nothing?

_____ 13. Don't you have nothing to say for yourself?

_____ 14. Ain't your little cousin never been away from home before?

_____ 15. Don't nobody understand me?

_____ 16. Haven't you spent some time in France?

_____ 17. Ain't there nothing nobody can do to make you change your mind?

_____ 18. Can't they take some time off from work?

_____ 19. Shouldn't somebody be there in case the doctor comes late?

_____ 20. Doesn't anybody want to come with me?


## Pattern Practice

Change the following positive questions into negative questions in the standard dialect. The first two have been done for you.

1. Can you go to see somebody?

   Can't you go to see anybody?
   _____

2. Are you singing in concerts this year?

   Aren't you singing in any concert this year?
   _____

3. Is there something strange about John's behavior?

   _____

4. Is somebody going to drive Teddy to the hospital?

   _____

5. Is there some way I can meet you downtown?

   _____

6. Is there somewhere quiet where we can meet to discuss the matter?

   _____

7. Has the doctor got some time this afternoon to treat the emergency patient?

_____

8. Have you seen some of the latest fashions from Paris?

_____

9. Don't all lawyers know something about criminal law?

_____

10. Do you have some time tomorrow to look at my new Ford station wagon?

_____

11. Have you got some idea when the train from New Orleans will arrive?

_____

12. Do you expect us to believe that some people are more honest than others?

_____

13. Do they know somebody who might be interested in buying a pet alligator, four weeks

old?

_____

14. Can we work out our differences somehow?

_____

15. Do we agree with Doris and Donald in some way?

_____

16. Can we travel somewhere where there is less excitement than New York?

_____

17. May I see you again some time?

_____

18. Would you like to do some repairs in the kitchen?

_____

19. Would you be willing to take some extra food and wine to the party?

_____

20. Can Virginia appreciate some of the problems our family is having?

_____

## Pattern Practice

Change the following positive statements into negative questions in the standard dialect. The first two have been done for you.

1. He gave her some candy for her birthday.

   Didn't he give her some candy for her birthday?

2. Uncle Jim gave everyone a big hug.

   Didn't Uncle Jim give everyone a big hug?

3. I can give you everything but love, baby.

   _____

4. There is something in the way you move that makes me love you.

   _____

5. Somewhere there is a place for us.

   _____

6. Somewhere over the rainbow I will find happiness.

   _____

7. I'll get along without you somehow.

   _____

8. Somebody on the board of directors likes Susan.

   _____

9. Joe looks like somebody I know.

   _____

10. Some people in the class are cold and unfriendly.

_____

11. You want something special for your birthday.

_____

12. They know something about Norma that I don't know.

_____

13. Rose knows somebody in the president's office.

_____

14. We have found some way to meet the deadline.

_____

15. I lost my hat somewhere.

_____

16. Everybody on the block has a new car.

_____

17. William Shakespeare has written some of the most beautiful poetry in the world.

_____

18. She has some time to spend with her sister.

_____

19. David and Lisa own some very fine furniture.

_____

20. Esther always has some excuse to avoid meeting new people.

_____

## Conversion Drill

Reread the sentences in the Recognition Drill. Convert each sentence that you did not mark SD into the standard dialect.

# PART V:
# SENTENCE PATTERNS

# PHRASES, CLAUSES, AND SENTENCES

**1**

In this section we will be discussing what many traditional grammar books call comma faults, sentence fragments, and run-on sentences. The main problem for students in these areas has to do with conventional ways of writing down the spoken language—particularly in regard to punctuation. Since comma faults, sentence fragments, and run-on sentences have more to do with punctuation than with sentence structure, there are no differences between community dialects and the standard dialect. For both it is a matter of knowing the conventional methods of punctuation.

Because punctuation conventions require knowing something about sentence structure, however, we will first look at what the different structures are in English sentences—not because you don't already know how to use them (everyone does who speaks English) but because knowing more about them will help you to understand conventional punctuation.

In the first three parts of this book we discussed relatively small units like words and word endings. In Part IV (Questions and Negatives) we studied the largest unit—the sentence. In this section we will see how the smallest and largest units are related. First we will look at the smallest unit that contains more than one word—that is, the phrase. Then we will look at a larger unit, the clause. Finally, we will see how phrases and clauses are combined into sentences. Here is a brief description of each of those units.

A **phrase** is a group of words that are related to each other in one of several ways. We will describe those ways in the next chapter, but here are just a few examples (each phrase is enclosed in brackets):

I walked [*down the street*].
He walked [*very quickly*].
[*My mother's Siamese cat*] always sleeps [*on the coffee table*].

A **clause** is a group of words with both a subject and a complete verb. We will describe what we mean by "complete verb" in Chapter 3 when we discuss clauses. For the time being, however, here are some examples of clauses (each clause is enclosed in brackets):

[*Because I flunked my chemistry class*] [*I have to take it over again*].
[*John went to the store*] and [*he bought himself a new Honda*].

A **sentence** is a group of words that has at least one independent clause. We will discuss what we mean by "independent clause" in Chapter 3, but in the meantime here are some examples of sentences:

*John married Mary.*
*John and Mary are merry because they got married.*

# PHRASES

**2**

A phrase is a group of words that are related to each other in one of several ways. Below are some examples of types of phrases.

1. A prepositional phrase begins with a preposition, and includes a noun and words related to that noun (like adjectives). Prepositions include the following words:

| | | | |
|---|---|---|---|
| *about* | *below* | *in* | *since* |
| *above* | *beneath* | *inside* | *through* |
| *across* | *beside* | *into* | *throughout* |
| *after* | *between* | *like* | *to* |
| *against* | *beyond* | *near* | *toward* |
| *along* | *by* | *of* | *under* |
| *among* | *down* | *off* | *underneath* |
| *around* | *during* | *on* | *until* |
| *at* | *except* | *outside* | *up* |
| *before* | *for* | *over* | *with* |
| *behind* | *from* | *past* | *without* |

In the following examples prepositions are in italics, and the entire phrase is enclosed in brackets.

EXAMPLES

I walked [*down* the street].
The North fought [*against* the South] [*in* the Civil War].
The car ran [*into* the telephone pole].

2. An infinitive phrase begins with an infinitive and includes any words that describe or complete the infinitive. (Remember that we discussed the infinitive in Chapter 23 of the Verb section.) It usually fills the position of a noun in the sentence. In the following examples infinitives are in italics and the entire phrase is enclosed in brackets.

EXAMPLES

He wanted [*to be* fair].
   (used as noun-object)
[*To be*] or [*not to be*]—that is the question.
   (both used as noun-subject)

3. An *ing* phrase begins with a noun or adjective made from an *ing* verb (see Part II, Chapter 7 and Part III, Chapter 2) and includes words that describe or complete it. In the following examples, *ing* words are in italics and the entire phrase is enclosed in brackets.

## EXAMPLES

[*Skating*] was John's favorite hobby.
   (used as noun-subject)
[*Running* down the street,] he tripped and fell.
   (used as adjective)

4. Finally, some phrases begin with an adjective made from the compound past form of the verb (see Part II, Chapter 2) and include words that describe or complete it. In the following examples, compound past adjectives are in italics, and the entire phrase is enclosed in brackets.

## EXAMPLES

[The *finished* manuscript] was sent to the publishers.
   (used as noun-subject)
[*Finished* with the dishes,] my mother sat down to rest.
   (used as adjective)

## Identification Drill

Underline the prepositions and put brackets around the prepositional phrases in the following sentences. See the list above for help in identifying prepositions. The first two have been done for you.

1. I know all [ <u>about</u> Ertha] and she knows all [ <u>about</u> me].

2. [ <u>After</u> breakfast] I like to brush my teeth [ <u>with</u> Colgate Dental Cream].

3. I am against the use of violence.

4. Selonia will meet you at 10 o'clock at the show.

5. Don't put the cart before the horse.

6. My bedroom is above the kitchen.

7. The basement is below the first floor.

8. During the tornado, I went into the basement.

9. The book was written by Dickens.

10. Eleanor's mother chased her pet snake out the window.

11. My father came from Harlan, Kentucky.

12. Did you know that the cow jumped over the moon?

13. I like to stand on the corner and watch the girls.

14. We all contributed money to buy a present for the boss' daughter who is getting married on Saturday.

15. The swallows came back to San Francisco.

16. We saw a beautiful love scene in this show.

17. Do you know anything about Peter's grandmother's dog?

18. Over the river and through the woods to Grandmother's house we go.

19. During Caesar's reign, Rome expanded its empire.

20. Garth had to appear before the judge.


## Identification Drill

Underline the infinitives and put brackets around the infinitive phrases in the following sentences. The first two have been done for you.

1. I would like [ to dance with you].

2. The oyster would like [ to kiss the shrimp].

3. The chocolate chip cookies are good to eat.

4. To know you is to love you.

5. To be with you is to be laugh.

6. We love to ride our bikes in the spring.

7. I am planning to walk to Kalamazoo to see my foot doctor.

8. Tinkerbell is planning to go on a long trip to get away from it all.

9. To be successful in love, one needs to have a lot of experience.

10. I'd like to spend one hour a day with you.

11. The important thing is not to know how to die, but how to live.

12. My ambition is to become a citizen of the United States.

13. Griffin wants to order a strawberry milkshake all the time.

14. His mother encourages him to drink tea.

15. Aveline is always complaining that she has to sharpen the pencils.

16. You have to learn to work with other people if you want to survive in this world.

17. You have to keep on trying.

18. Do you know how to live a happy life?

19. There are many ways to skin a cat.

20. What do you want to do with the rest of your life?


## Identification Drill

Underline the *ing* words and put brackets around the *ing* phrases in the following sentences. The first two have been done for you.

1. [ Floating down the river on a Sunday afternoon] is my idea of heaven.

2. The Dodgers broke the Braves' [ winning streak].

3. Kissing Juliet was Romeo's last action before he died.

4. Locking the doors is not the only way to keep thieves out.

5. Gossiping Gladys saw Singing Sam slink down the street.

6. Admiring Guido's car, Waldo began dreaming about buying one of his own.

7. Jumping into the pool, Bill discovered the water was too cold.

8. Shoeing horses is hard work.

9. The ticking clock woke the sleeping man.

10. Albert bit his lips, holding back his anger before he answered.

11. Barking dogs can't bite scratching cats.

12. Never again would Cosimo know the moments of glowing tenderness.

13. He sat there quietly with his shining little black eyes darting this way and that way.

14. Recalling the days of wine and roses, he found himself laughing again.

15. Hanging curtains hurts my aching back.

16. He pulled the glistening fish from the foaming waves.

17. All of her suffering left her broken in spirit.

18. Your cheating heart will tell on you.

19. Living with you is like picking crab apples.

20. Her only response to my passionate yearning for food was handing me a dog biscuit.

## Identification Drill

Underline adjectives made from the compound past forms of regular (*ed*)
verbs and put brackets around phrases made from them. The first two have
been done for you.

1. The [captured princess] refused to tell the pirates where the treasure was hidden.

2. [Pleased with the child's improvement,] the doctor allowed him to go home.

3. I like beef any way it's cooked—braised, boiled, or baked.

4. The bored patrons left the theater early.

5. The performance forced the excited spectators to cheer and shout.

6. The disappointed guests looked sadly at the burned steak.

7. The alleged kidnapper hid his face from the television camera.

8. The frightened rats ran from the determined terrier.

9. Jim sat heavily on the newly glued chair.

10. Reba sat heavily on the freshly painted chair.

11. An embarrassed silence followed their movements.

12. Upon Harry's return from college, they were impressed by his changed appearance.

13. Maintained by a strong religious faith, the minister bore her suffering quietly.

14. The dress, trimmed with Irish lace and pink ribbons, was lovely.

15. The bracelet engraved with her name was her Christmas gift.

## Identification Drill

Underline adjectives made from the compound past form of irregular verbs and put brackets around phrases made from them. The first two have been done for you.

1. The [newly <u>cut</u> hay] smelled sweet.

2. The car bumped into a [ <u>fallen</u> tree].

3. The tire, swollen by the heat, burst on the highway.

4. All she could see was the bent fender on her new station wagon.

5. Hit by bad luck, the Pistons had a poor year.

6. The laundry, blown dry by the wind, was ready to be taken off the line in an hour.

7. The long lost money was found between the pages of a book.

8. The newly found money was sent to hungry relatives.

9. Overcome with appreciation, the relatives moved in with the family.

10. Now grown too large for comfort, the combined families looked for a bigger house.

## Review Exercise

The following sentences contain phrases of all four types: prepositional, infinitive, *ing*, and compound past (regular *ed* and irregular). Put brackets around all these phrases. The first two have been done for you.

1. Something [in you] gives me so much confidence.

2. I stole a glance [at Maria] [to see how she would take what I had said].

3. The reducing diet was not effective.

4. The sewing group was made up of determined women.

5. Jerome is a spoiled young man with pleasant manners.

6. The police found the stolen bike.

7. When I think of you, the forgotten years of my youth come back to me.

8. A wild longing to own an elephant rages in me.

9. My professor is the most distinguished person I know.

10. I don't blame other people for my problems.

11. A high standard of living is hard to maintain.

12. The satisfied dog curled up and went to sleep.

13. The shaken crowd turned away from the accident.

14. You can learn to dance the tango in one hour.

15. I have an engraving of my mother.

16. Leaving home has been a terribly uprooting experience.

17. It is possible that one day Harry will learn to know himself.

18. I ordered a decorated cake for my mother's birthday.

19. Ted and Carol have become sworn enemies since the New Year's Eve party.

20. The salesman had a controlled approach to selling ladies' shoes.

# CLAUSES

# 3

A clause is a group of words (which may include phrases) that has a subject and a complete verb. A "complete verb" is a main verb in its simple present or past form, or a compound verb with main verb form and its helping verbs. Here are the possible combinations of subject and verb that form a "complete verb" and that are necessary to call a group of words a clause:

| | |
|---|---|
| *He walks.* | (subject + simple present verb) |
| *He walked.* | (subject + simple past verb) |
| *He has walked.* | (subject + recent past verb) |
| *He had walked.* | (subject + distant past verb) |
| *He is walking.* | (subject + present progressive verb) |
| *He was walking.* | (subject + past progressive verb) |
| *He can walk.* | (subject + modal + main verb) |

There is one instance in English where you don't need a subject to make a clause—that is with a command such as "Sit down, please!" The subject (the person who is supposed to sit down) is understood to be *you* but it is not written in the sentence. Commands always use the simple present form of the verb.

If a group of words does not have a subject (except commands) and a complete verb (one of those listed on page 369), it does not qualify as a clause. For example, the following groups of words do not have subjects (and are not commands) and do not have complete verbs:

1. *coming* very late
2. *to go* to school
3. *finished* with his homework

The words *being*, *to go*, and *finished* may look like verbs, but they are not because they all require something else to make them complete. Actually they are adjectives and nouns made from verbs. (See Part II, Chapter 7, and Part III, Chapter 2.) Since they are adjectives and nouns, in order to make them into clauses we need to add a subject and verb:

1. *Coming* late, *John sat* in the back of the room.
    (Here we have an adjective phrase, *coming late*, which describes the subject, *John*. The verb, then, is *sat*.)
2. *John wanted to go* to school.
    (Here we have an infinitive phrase, *to go to school*, which acts as an object noun. The verb is *wanted* and the subject is *John*.)
3. *Finished* with his homework, *John went* to the movies.
    (Here we have a phrase made from the compound past verb form, which acts as an adjective describing *John*. The subject is *John* and the verb is *went*.)

In the above three sentences, we changed phrases into clauses by adding a subject and a main verb. We could also change phrases 1 and 3 into clauses by treating the underlined words as parts of verbs and adding helping verbs to make them complete:

1. John *is* always *coming* late.
    (By adding the helping verb *is*, we change *coming* from an adjective into a verb.)
2. John *had finished* with his homework.
    (By adding the helping verb *had*, we change *finished* from an adjective into a verb.)

## Identification Drill

Put brackets around the clauses in the following sentences. Underline the subject and verb in each clause. The first two have been done for you.

1. [After I say] [that I love you,] [ I kiss you].

2. [When Santa Claus gets your letter,] [I really do believe] [that he will smile].

3. If your television set broke down, how would you spend your nights?

4. I want to sing but I can't.

5. I have a rock collection and it nearly fills my basement.

6. The first time that I visited Wyoming, I cried.

7. Amos is one of the most amazing people in the world, and he is ninety-seven years old and lives all by himself.

8. Although Debbie and Alonzo are friends, they are not the best of friends.

9. On this special diet I have to drink twelve glasses of water and eat cottage cheese and eggs even though I don't want to.

10. Jonathan Tarwell is a great scholar and gentleman.

11. Greek food is spicy; Arabic food is spicier; Indian food is spiciest.

12. I may be mistaken but haven't I met you someplace before?

13. What is a nice girl like you doing in a place like this?

14. Big George rides his bike and little George rides on the back.

15. While I was in Paris, I saw robins for sale in the delicatessen.

16. Because you have a good heart, I know you will loan me fifty dollars.

17. The old gray mare isn't what she used to be.

18. My pay was raised ten dollars a week after I sold so many stereo sets.

19. Although I weigh only eighty-one pounds, I would like to be a star fullback for the NFL.

20. Since Violette's brother is only five feet six inches, he can't play with the Celtics.


## Identification Drill

Decide whether each of the following groups of words is a phrase or a clause; mark either P or C next to each sentence. If it is a clause underline the subject and verb. The first two have been done for you.

   __P__    1. To go to school.

   __C__    2. I want to go to school.

_____ 3. Seeing Rosalind at the beach.

_____ 4. I saw Rosalind last week.

_____ 5. Running home from the game.

_____ 6. I was running home.

_____ 7. The offended citizen.

_____ 8. The missing money.

_____ 9. A completed book.

_____ 10. The grown man.

_____ 11. Maryanne went downtown.

_____ 12. After she saw the comet.

_____ 13. The turn of the screw.

_____ 14. He hammered the nails.

_____ 15. During the rainstorm.

## Pattern Practice

Following is a group of phrases. Change the phrases into clauses first by adding a subject and a main verb and second by adding a subject and a helping verb. The first two have been done for you.

1. singing in the choir

   I like singing in the choir. _____

   Jane was singing in the choir. _____

2. the well-done roast

   The well-done roast was very dry. _____

   The roast was well-done. _____

3. to the moon

   _____

4. to celebrate Christmas together

_____

_____

5. turning off the light

_____

_____

6. the satisfied customer

_____

_____

7. the sunken ship

_____

_____

8. to the zoo

_____

_____

9. to visit me next Sunday

_____

_____

10. moving to Buffalo

_____

_____

11. the irritated parents

_____

_____

12. the frozen orange juice

_____

_____

13. in the sun

_____

_____

14. to bring you health, wealth, and happiness

_____

_____

15. singing in the shower

_____

_____

# SENTENCES AND INDEPENDENT CONJUNCTIONS 4

We have seen that a phrase is a group of closely related words without a subject and a verb. And we have seen that a clause is a group of words that has both a subject (except commands) and a complete verb. Now we want to look at the largest unit of structure—the sentence. We can define a sentence as a structure that has at least one independent clause, but that may have any number of other clauses (independent, dependent, and relative) and phrases as well. Now what is an "independent clause?"

An independent clause is a clause that does not begin with either a dependent conjunction or a relative pronoun. We will discuss relative pronouns in the next chapter. Here is a list of the most common dependent conjunctions:

| | | | | |
|---|---|---|---|---|
| *after* | *before* | *than* | *unless* | *where* |
| *although* | *how* | *through* | *until* | *while* |
| *as* | *if* | *till* | *when* | *why* |
| *because* | *since* | | | |

If clauses are preceded by any of these words, they are dependent clauses and not independent—that is, they depend for their meaning on another clause, an independent clause. In the following examples of dependent clauses, the dependent conjunction is italicized.

## EXAMPLES

> *after* he went to bed
> *while* he was riding the bus
> *how* we could have done it

If you want to make these dependent clauses into sentences, you have to add an independent clause. In the following examples, clauses are enclosed in brackets and dependent conjunctions are in italics.

## EXAMPLES

> [*After* he went to bed,] [his house was robbed.]
> [*While* he was riding the bus,] [he fell asleep.]
> [We wondered] [*how* we could have done it.]

All clauses that do not have one of those dependent conjunctions or a relative pronoun in front of them are independent clauses; that is, they can be used alone as sentences or in combination with other clauses and phrases.

Notice that the following conjunctions are independent—that is, they can be used before an independent clause. Be careful to distinguish these from dependent conjunctions and relative pronouns (see next chapter).

> *and*    *but*    *for*    *nor*    *or*    *so*    *yet*

## Identification Drill

In the following list of clauses, mark I next to those that are independent and D next to those that are dependent. Then add an independent clause to each dependent clause, and a dependent clause to each independent clause. Each exercise will then be a sentence containing a dependent and independent clause. The first two have been done for you.

   D    1. Although she liked to dance.

Although she liked to dance, she didn't know how to twist.

   I    2. He went to New York for a vacation.

He went to New York for a vacation because he liked big cities.

_____ 3. When I finally got in to see the doctor.

_____

_____ 4. After I go to the movie.

_____

_____ 5. Angela was the unsung heroine of our graduation class.

_____

_____ 6. Before I returned to my seat on the bus.

_____

_____ 7. Because I hate fudge ripple ice cream.

_____

_____ 8. Papa invited us all to his engagement party.

_____

_____ 9. While I was on vacation.

_____

_____ 10. Until the poor grow rich and the rich grow poor.

_____

_____ 11. He wore a snow white blouse with some kind of a pendant around his neck.

_____

_____ 12. Since I was ten years of age.

_____

_____ 13. He could have finished the job.

_____

_____ 14. I feel very unimportant compared to you.

_____

_____ 15. Why the limousine came to a stop before us.

_____

## Conversion Drill

Each of the following is an independent clause. On the line below each exercise convert the two clauses into one sentence by joining with *and*, *but*, *or*, or *so*. The first two have been done for you.

1. Eloise and Betty agreed to meet at one o'clock.

   Betty forgot the time.

   Eloise and Betty agreed to meet at one o'clock but Betty forgot the time.

2. You used to yell at me.

   I would yell back.

   You used to yell at me so I would yell back.

3. One of the boys must drive the station wagon.

   We will have to come home on the bus.

   _____

4. Darlene hated hot dogs.

   Robert always ordered steak.

   _____

5. The window blind was down.

   We had to raise it to see what was going on in the street.

   _____

6. Life is a work of art.

   I am an artist of life.

   _____

7. All of the children had been married.

   Rosalie had a divorce.

   _____

8. He has escaped.

   He has evaporated.

   _____

9. The train stopped at the station.

   Six people got on.

   _____

10. The fireworks were exploding all over the sky.

    The people were excited and exclaiming at their beauty.

    _____

# SENTENCES AND RELATIVE PRONOUNS

# 5

In Chapter 4 we said that a sentence had to include at least one independent clause. And we said that an independent clause was one that does not begin with either a dependent conjunction (which would make it a dependent clause) or a relative pronoun (which would make it a relative clause). In this chapter we will look more closely at relative pronouns.

There are only a few relative pronouns. They are listed below:

*who     whom     whose     which     that*

Relative pronouns appear in relative clauses (usually at the beginning of the clause) and refer back to a noun or pronoun in the independent clause.

Below are some examples of sentences with an independent clause and a relative clause. The independent clause is marked **I** and the relative clause is marked **R**.

EXAMPLES

<table>
<tr><td align="center">**I**</td><td align="center">**R**</td></tr>
<tr><td>[Joan is the girl]</td><td>[*who* came to the party.]</td></tr>
<tr><td align="center">**I**</td><td align="center">**R**</td></tr>
<tr><td>[Joan is the girl]</td><td>[*whom* I saw you dancing with.]</td></tr>
<tr><td align="center">**I**</td><td align="center">**R**</td></tr>
<tr><td>[Joan is the girl]</td><td>[*whose* party was a success.]</td></tr>
</table>

Notice that *who* is used as the subject of the relative clause; *whom* is used as the object of the preposition; and *whose* is a possessive pronoun. *Who, whom,* and *whose,* then, correspond to the three personal pronouns (see Part II, Chapter 9): *he, him,* and *his;* or *I, me,* and *my.*

Here are some examples of sentences with the relative pronouns *that* and *which.*

EXAMPLES

<table>
<tr><td align="center">**I**</td><td align="center">**R**</td></tr>
<tr><td>[There is the book]</td><td>[*that* won the prize.]</td></tr>
<tr><td align="center">**I**</td><td align="center">**R**</td></tr>
<tr><td>[There is the book]</td><td>[*that* I told you about.]</td></tr>
<tr><td align="center">**I**</td><td align="center">**R**</td></tr>
<tr><td>[There is the book]</td><td>[*which* won the prize.]</td></tr>
<tr><td align="center">**I**</td><td align="center">**R**</td></tr>
<tr><td>[There is the book]</td><td>[*which* I told you about.]</td></tr>
</table>

Notice that both *which* and *that* can occupy the same position in the sentence as *who;* or they can occupy the same position as *whom.* Either *which* or *that,* in other words, can be the subject of the clause, and either can be the object.

How do you know when to use *which* or *that,* and when to use *who* (*whom*)? Usually *who* (*whom*) is used only to refer to human nouns, and *which* to refer to nonhuman nouns. *That* can refer to either human or nonhuman nouns.

(It is interesting to note that the standard dialect is changing—at one time *whom* was always used as object and *who* only as subject. Recently, however, *who* has come to be used as both subject and object and *whom* is being used less and less frequently.)

Like dependent conjunctions, relative pronouns always occur in a clause that is not independent and therefore cannot stand by itself as a sentence. There are two important things to notice about relative clauses:

1. The relative pronoun may be left out when the subject of the relative clause immediately follows it.

> She is the girl *whom I married.*
> She is the girl *I married.*
> That is the book *which I like best.*
> That is the book *I like best.*

Therefore the following clauses (from the sentences above) are all relative and may not stand alone as sentences:

> *whom I married*
> *I married*
> *which I like best*
> *I like best*

To make them into complete sentences, you must add an independent clause, as in the four sentences below.

> *She is the girl* whom I married.
> *She is the girl* I married.
> *That is the book* which I like best.
> *That is the book* I like best.

2. The relative clause may come at the end of or in the middle of the independent clause.

**EXAMPLES**

> That is the book *which I like best.* (at the end)
> The book *which I like best* is on the table. (in the middle)

## Identification Drill

In the following sentences, put brackets around each clause. Then put an R above relative clauses and an I above independent clauses. Wherever there is a relative clause alone, add an independent clause to it to make a complete sentence. The first two have been done for you.

           R
1. [Which was on the table.]

   I saw the book which was on the table.

       I           R
2. [I wondered [whose book she had].]

3. Whose story was a lie.

4. The dog who lived down the street chased his tail round and round.

_____

5. After the good meal, Papa contentedly lowered himself into the chair that was beside the

fireplace.

_____

6. Which was the finest suit he had ever had.

_____

7. Who was scurrying around before the party.

_____

8. The bakery truck that stopped at our house sold the best bread in the city.

_____

9. Whose book had been published early in the spring.

_____

10. The novel which he wrote is wild and unpredictable.

_____

11. Whose tire was flat.

_____

12. That brought good luck to all of us.

_____

13. Sebastian loved to watch T.V. shows that gave away big prizes.

_____

14. My favorite foods were the ones that always gave me a stomach-ache.

_____

15. Tugging at the gate which had rusty hinges.

_____

## Pattern Practice

In the following sentences fill in the blanks with the appropriate relative pronoun. The first two have been done for you.

1. He had married a beautiful girl <u>who</u> loved him with all her heart.

2. Pampinellea was a name <u>that</u> people couldn't pronounce.

3. I knew the howls were coming from my dog _____ was lonesome.

4. I examined the trees _____ had fallen during the storm.

5. The Red Cross helped all of the people _____ houses had been damaged.

6. The police found the girl _____ had crashed into our car.

7. The family _____ train tickets had been lost were badly upset.

8. The company _____ moved our furniture was very careful.

9. We appreciated our new neighbors _____ were all very helpful.

10. The family _____ house is next to ours was the kindest of all.

11. Olaf trapped the raccoons _____ got into our garbage can.

12. Oranges are a fruit _____ has large amounts of vitamin C.

13. Anna Maria is a talented violinist _____ plays for people's pleasure.

14. She was the one _____ performance was so highly applauded.

15. He kissed her on her eyelids _____ were red from crying.

16. Where is the puppy _____ you want to buy?

17. There is the table _____ needs dusting.

18. There is the stereo _____ I would love to own.

19. Where was the game _____ you bet on?

20. There is the horse _____ I expected to win the race.

# PUNCTUATION IN PHRASES, CLAUSES, AND SENTENCES    6

Now that we have studied the difference between phrases, clauses, and sentences, we are ready to discuss conventional punctuation used in the standard dialect. Remember that punctuation is only an arbitrary and conventional means of recording in written language the pauses we make in spoken language. It is important for students who want to write in the standard dialect to know the conventional means of punctuation in that dialect.

## End Punctuation

There are three common marks of punctuation that are always used at the end of sentences:

1. Ordinary statements begin with a capital letter and end with a period.

EXAMPLE      I gave him a book.

2. Questions begin with a capital letter and end with a question mark.

EXAMPLE      Did I give him a book?

3. Commands begin with a capital letter and end with a period or an exclamation mark.

EXAMPLES

> Shut up!
> Give him a book.

## Semicolons

Sentences that contain two independent clauses may use a semicolon between them. The first independent clause in the sentence begins with a capital letter and ends with a semicolon, while the second independent clause (with or without an independent conjunction) begins with a small letter and ends with a period.

EXAMPLES

> I gave him a book; but he said he didn't like it.
> I gave him a book; he said he didn't like it.

## Commas

A comma may separate two independent clauses if an independent conjunction precedes the second clause.

### EXAMPLE

I gave him a book, but he didn't like it.

With this one exception, commas are used only between phrases and dependent clauses. They are only used with independent clauses if there is an independent conjunction there also.

The most common kinds of unconventional punctuation are those listed in most English grammar books as "sentence fragments," "comma faults" or "comma splices," and "run-on sentences." These are referred to in most grammar books as "errors in sentence structure." We do not believe they have much to do with sentence structure, but rather with punctuation. We will refer to the traditional phrases below only as a convenience for you, as you will probably meet the terms later in your college career.

## Sentence Fragments

What traditional grammars call sentence fragments are the result of using end punctuation (the three types we described above) to mark the end of something that is not a sentence. Students often use periods or other end punctuation to separate phrases, dependent clauses, or relative clauses. (As we saw above, periods and other end punctuation are used only to separate independent clauses.)

### EXAMPLES                    Unconventional Punctuation

1. I wanted to go to the party. Because I knew he would be there.
2. He won a gold medal. Being the fastest player on the high school team.
3. He went out to play. Finished with all his work.
4. His friends told him. To place his trophy on the mantel.
5. He saw the sparrows quarreling over the crumbs. In the cold rainy dawn.
6. I saw the gold trophy. Which he won in the school olympics.

In the above examples, the periods separate an independent clause not from another independent clause, but from (1) a dependent clause, (2) an *ing* phrase, (3) an *ed* phrase, (4) an infinitive phrase, (5) a prepositional phrase, and (6) a relative clause.

To make the punctuation of these sentences conventional, either change the period to a comma (and the capital letter following to a small letter), or just eliminate the period altogether if the sentence isn't too long (and change the capital letter following to a small letter).

1. I wanted to go to the party because I knew he would be there.
2. He won a gold medal, being the fastest player on the high school team.
3. Finished with all his work, he went out to play.
4. His friends told him to place his trophy on the mantel.
5. He saw the sparrows quarreling over the crumbs in the cold, rainy dawn.
6. I saw the gold trophy which he won in the school olympics.

(Remember that a comma, like all punctuation, represents a pause in your speech. That should be a guide to help you decide whether to use a comma or not. A comma usually represents a shorter pause than a period or other end punctuation. A semicolon represents a pause that is longer than a comma but shorter than a period.)

## Comma-Splices (Comma-Faults)

Students often use a comma to separate two independent clauses where there is no independent conjunction before the second clause.

EXAMPLE                    Unconventional Punctuation

I asked him a question, he didn't answer it.

To make the punctuation conventional, you can do one of three things:

1. Add an independent conjunction.

EXAMPLE                    Conventional Punctuation

I asked him a question, *but* he didn't answer it.

2. Use a period instead of a comma and start the next clause with a capital letter.

EXAMPLE                    Conventional Punctuation

I asked him a question. He didn't answer it.

3. Use a semicolon instead of a comma.

EXAMPLE                    Conventional Punctuation

I asked him a question; he didn't answer it.

How do you choose among these three methods? Use your ear as a guide. How big a pause or separation do you want between your ideas? Example 1 has the least separation; example 2 has the most, and example 3 is in between the two.

# Run-On Sentences

In a "run-on sentence," the punctuation between two sentences has been eliminated.

EXAMPLE               Unconventional Punctuation

         I asked him a question he didn't answer it.

Since that sentence contains two independent clauses, they must be separated somehow—either with a conjunction, or with punctuation, or with both. Any of the solutions proposed for "comma-faults" above would, therefore, be appropriate here to make the sentence conventional in punctuation.


# Identification Drill

Bracket the independent clauses in the following list. Beside each clause or group of clauses (or phrases) mark whether the punctuation is conventional (C) or unconventional (U).

Then rewrite each exercise you marked U so that it uses conventional punctuation. The first two have been done for you.

   __U__   1. [At the picnic the Coke went fast.] Because it was the children's favorite.

          At the picnic the Coke went fast, because it was the children's favorite.

   __C__   2. [I think I am a good brother,] giving him advice and loaning him money.

   _____   3. There were wild thoughts in my mind that were driving me insane.

   _____   4. I wanted to escape this life. By traveling for years and years.

   _____   5. I am acquainted with the facts. That govern my life.

   _____   6. Mary Ellen begged her mother. To let her go downtown alone.

   _____   7. Since Mary Ellen was only ten, her mother wouldn't let her go.

_____ 8. Her sister who was older. Promised to take her.

_____

_____ 9. Miss Hutchins loved the springtime. Because the flowers were blooming.

_____

_____ 10. Before the flowers started to bloom. She began her allergy shots.

_____

_____ 11. Dreaming about her new car. Lilly forgot she was in the schoolroom.

_____

_____ 12. The teacher asked Lilly a question she didn't hear her.

_____

_____ 13. The children played ball in the street, they learned how to dodge cars.

_____

_____ 14. That car belongs to the young lady. Whose mother you just met.

_____

_____ 15. May is taking five subjects this term so she can finish her degree early.

_____

_____ 16. This year I am going south next year I am going to Europe.

_____

_____ 17. I can't learn a thing I can't hear the teacher!

_____

_____ 18. A blast of rain beating me on the back. I ran for the bus.

_____

_____ 19. Too many people take happiness for granted, they should look at the suffering of others.

_____

_____ 20. Crouched over the frightened child. The woman comforted him.

_____

_____ 21. The theme of the story is that love overcomes evil I like this theme.

_____

_____ 22. Did you get good grades when you took your final exams?

_____

_____ 23. I felt relieved. After the doctor came.

_____

_____ 24. He made important points in his sermon.

_____

_____ 25. They were concerned about themselves they gave no help to others.

_____

_____ 26. Bostwick loved fast cars, and he hated slow trains.

_____

_____ 27. The cowboys rode into the sunset, they all drove blue pickup trucks.

_____

_____ 28. Give to the poor but don't steal from the rich!

_____

_____ 29. Before the nursery school teacher played with the children, she gave them milk
           and cookies.

_____

_____ 30. Fetch the ball and bring it back!

_____

_____31. The saint took the thorn from the lion's paw the lion licked his hand.

_____

_____32. She polished the brass lamp until it shone like sunshine.

_____

_____33. The dog hid under the bed. During the thunder storm.

_____

_____34. The barber trimmed my beard, he cut my hair too short.

_____

_____35. All good things come to an end what the end is like can not be predicted.

_____

## Review Exercise

Write an essay describing the actions of the people in the above picture. Use complete sentences, and after you have finished, underline all phrases and clauses.

# INDEX

(Note: When an entry is found on more than one consecutive page, only the first page number of the series is listed.)

C 6
D 7
E 8
F 9
G 0
H 1
I 2
  3
J 4